Linux in Plain English

Patrick Volkerding & Kevin Reichard

The MIS:Press Slackware Series

Henry Holt & Co., • New York

12/97.

MIS:Press
A Subsidiary of Henry Holt and Company, Inc.
115 West 18th Street
New York, New York 10011
http://www.mispress.com

Limits of Liability and Disclaimer of Warranty

The Author and Publisher of this book have used their best efforts in preparing the book and the programs contained in it. These efforts include the development, research, and testing of the theories and programs to determine their effectiveness.

The Author and Publisher make no warranty of any kind, expressed or implied, with regard to these programs or the documentation contained in this book. The Author and Publisher shall not be liable in any event for incidental or consequential damages in connection with, or arising out of, the furnishing, performance, or use of these programs.

All products, names and services are trademarks or registered trademarks of their respective companies.

First Edition—1997

Library of Congress Cataloging-in-Publication Data

```
Volkerding, Patrick
    Linux in Plain English / by Patrick Volkerding, Kevin Reichard,
      p.      cm.
      ISBN 1-55828-542-3
    1. Linux ( 2.Operating systems—(computers) I. Reichard, Kevin.
    II. Title.
    QA76.76,063V645      1997
    005.4'469--dc21
                                                        97-11374
                                                            CIP
```

MIS:Press and M&T Books are available at special discounts for bulk purchases for sales promotions, premiums, and fundraising. Special editions or book excerpts can also be created to specification.

For details contact: Special Sales Director
                             MIS:Press and M&T Books
                             Subsidiaries of Henry Holt and Company, Inc.
                             115 West 18th Street
                             New York, New York 10011

10 9 8 7 6 5 4 3 2 1

Associate Publisher: *Paul Farrell*   **Managing Editor:** *Shari Chappell*
Editor: *Laura Lewin*   **Production Editor:** *Maya Riddick*
Copy Edit Manager: *Karen Tongish*   **Copy Editor:** *Winifred Davis*

Contents

Introduction

Welcome to *Linux in Plain English*! Whether you're a novice Linux user or an advanced Linux hack, we think you'll find this book very useful. This book is meant for any Linux user: the curious user seeking an alternative to the Microsoft/Apple personal-computer operating systems, the programmer who wants a version of UNIX for the office or home, the Webmaster who wants a stable Internet server, the end user who wants a stable operating system with all the tools for local and Internet usage, the networking engineer who wants to set up a Linux server, or the student who wants to know more about a state-of-the-art operating system. They'll all be very happy using Linux as their operating system.

A Little Linux History

What is now known as Linux began life as a small student project at the University of Helsinki in Finland. Linux Torvalds wanted a small, UNIX-like operating system, and so he set out to write one. He received help from volunteers all around the globe, who collaborated via bulletin-board, electronic mail, and the Internet to create the Linux operating system.

The crew ended up creating a rather remarkable operating system that works very well, is very stable, and rivals offerings from Microsoft, Apple, and Sun. Linux offers the following features:

- **Multitasking**—Linux natively runs more than one task (program) at a time in a UNIX-like fashion. It also supports preemptive multitasking, where priorities can be set for different processes.

1

- **Multiuser**—Many users can be networked to a single Linux server. Linux is the least expensive, and perhaps best-featured, multiuser operating system on the planet today.
- **User-friendly**—The X Window System interface and a slew of great tools make Linux easy to use.

Today, Linux claims half a million users, and that number keeps growing every day. One reason is cost—Linux itself is free of charge, and only those who package a Linux distribution charge for it (and many don't charge at all). These distributions, such as Red Hat Linux, vary as to their installation processes and accompanying tools. You can get a full-blown, powerful operating system for the price of a book; see the Bibliography for a listing of books in the Slackware Series that ship with Slackware Linux on an accompanying CD-ROM.

Although this book covers all Linux implementations, the real focus is on the Slackware Linux distribution. Some of the commands, such as **httpd** (the Apache Web server) and **pkgtool** (used for updating software packages), aren't found in all Linux distributions. We've noted where there's a Slackware-only command listed.

Acquiring Linux

This book does not feature a CD-ROM with Linux. However, we strongly urge you to check out one of the other titles in the Slackware Series, all of which contain Slackware Linux on an accompanying CD-ROM. You can check out the title list in the bibliography.

The Free Software Foundation

Linux is the product of many devoted volunteers, and many of the same volunteers also gave their time to the Free Software Foundation. The FSF is an idealistic group lead by Richard Stallman, and their belief is that all software should be free or no charge, so they issue a lot of useful software to the world, either directly or under the auspices of the GNU License.

The result is a slew of GNU commands incorporated into Linux; we've noted them with an icon. These GNU commands are typically clones of the most popular UNIX commands, created in such a way that UNIX licensing schemes don't kick in. As such, they're very useful, and they tend to work very well. (However, there's no such thing as "GNU Linux" or "Linux-based variants of the GNU system," no matter what the Free Software Foundation claims. We're not going to get into the politics of FSF and Linux; we'll just point out that Linux is a reality.)

You can reach the Free Software Foundation at:

Free Software Foundation
59 Temple Place, Suite 330
Boston, MA 02111-1307
1-617-542-5942 (voice)
1-617-542-2652 (fax)
gnu@prep.ai.mit.edu
http://www.gnu.org/

Conventions Used in this Book

We took a consistent approach to the commands listed in Chapter 5 of this book. All the commands are set up in the same fashion: a headline, a sample command-line usage, the purpose of the command (in some detail), the command-line options (usually all of them), any commands if the command itself requires further input (e.g., **mail** or **ftp**), an example of actual usage, and related commands. We think this consistency will help you expand your Linux usage and master new commands and concepts.

In addition, the text itself features the following conventions:

- Commands to be entered directly into a Linux system are in a `monospaced` font.
- New concepts are marked with *italic* text.
- X Window System and GNU commands are noted with special icons.

3

Contacting Us

You can drop us a line via electronic mail at *reichard@mr.net*. Because of the amount of electronic mail we receive, we can't guarantee an immediate response. You can also visit a Web site devoted to the Slackware series from MIS:Press at *http://www.mispress.com/linux/index.html*.

1

Linux Structures and Commands

Depending on your background, Linux is either an amazingly complex and, inscrutable operating system (that is, if your background is in the Microsoft Windows or Macintosh worlds) or just another simple, command-line–driven operating system (if your background is in the MS-DOS or UNIX worlds). The truth lies somewhere in between: yes, Linux can be inscrutable at times, and yes, it is built around the command line, even if you're running the X Window System. However, as far as operating systems go, Linux isn't any more complex than MS-DOS or UNIX, and it's actually got some tools that rival those of Windows and the Macintosh.

As you prepare to plumb the depths of the Linux operating system, two rules will make your life easier:

- Linux is really a collection of small, easy-to-use commands. If you can simplify your tasks and break them down into discrete elements, you can do just about anything.

- Even when you're working with XFree86, the Linux version of a graphical interface, you're still basically working with a collection of small, easy-to-use commands.

It would be easy to deduce that anyone wanting to master Linux should first be eager to master its command structure. That's where this book comes in: *Linux in Plain English* is a listing of the Linux command structure. But before you can use these commands, you need to know how Linux deals with commands and how to enter these commands into the system.

The Command Line

We've already mentioned that Linux is a *command-line–driven* operating system. Commands are given to the operating system on the command line. You know that Linux is ready to accept a command when you see the following on your screen:

$

This can appear in a full screen when you're running in *terminal* mode, or it can appear in an **xterm** window when you're running the X Window System, as shown in Figure 1.1.

Figure 1.1 Xterm running in the X Window System.

The dollar sign is called a *prompt,* and it's the mechanism Linux uses to tell you that it's ready to accept a command. At tthe prompt, you can enter a single command or a combination of commands and options, the sum of which is called a *command line.*

A *command* is exactly that. No matter what you enter at the prompt, Linux interprets it as a command, or an order to do something. You can use commands directly to do something, such as moving and copying files. You can also use commands to run other programs, such as **elvis** or **emacs**. Linux has a specific set of commands, so if you type

6

in something that doesn't match one of its commands, it tells you it can't find the command. (You can actually see the list of commands when you look in directories, but we're getting ahead of ourselves here.) There are literally hundreds of commands in the Linux operating system.

Commands have *options*, which serve to better specify the behavior of a command. These options can tell a command to perform an action only under certain circumstances. This can be best seen with a general command and some of its options.

The **ls** command is one of the most basic and most used commands. It's used to list the files in the current directory. By itself, it merely lists the files in a given directory, as shown in Figure 1.2.

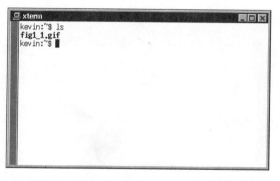

Figure 1.2 Using the ls command by itself.

This tells us that this particular directory contains a single file called **fig1_1.gif**. (The names of the files and directories in this chapter aren't important; all you need to know are the mechanisms for calling these files and directories and how they can be applied to almost any command.) However, the **ls** command by itself refers only to files that are accessible to all users and aren't hidden in some way. Hidden files begin with a dot (.), and so you need to tell the **ls** command to look for all files, including hidden files. This is done with an *option*. When we add the -*a* option to the **ls** command, we get a listing of all files and directories, including hidden files, as shown in Figure 1.3.

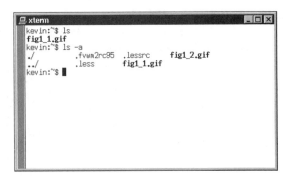

Figure 1.3 Adding the -a option to the ls command.

Taking the example one step further, we can ask the **ls** command to return a long listing for the files or directories in the current directory with the *-l* option, as shown in Figure 1.4.

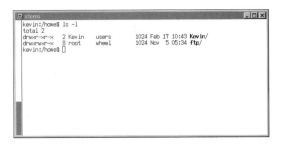

Figure 1.4 Adding the -l option to the ls command.

There are very few Linux commands that don't have options or arguments of some sort. Chapter 5, which lists all the commands, devotes a lot of space to these options.

Files

The **ls** command is used to list the files in the current or a given directory. In some ways, it's an oddity in the Linux world, as it's not used directly on a file, which is the method Linux uses for organizing information. As you browse through the rest of this book, you'll see that the vast majority of commands are used in conjunction with files.

This isn't surprising when you stop to consider that everything in the Linux operating system is a file. You saw the **ls** command used to list files in a directory, and the reason that command is so handy is that everything in Linux is a file. Commands are actually files that are invoked as programs. Devices attached to your PC are actually represented in the Linux operating system by files (usually beginning with **dev**). When you print a file, you're actually sending a file to a file representing the printer.

At a basic level, a file is nothing more than an organized area of a storage device (like a hard disk or a floppy drive), made up of *bits*. Bits are nothing more than digital players in an electronic format, representing either 0 or 1. The Linux operating system takes these bits and formats them in a way that's recognizable to both you and the operating system. Without this organization, the contents of a hard drive would just be random zeroes and ones. This organizational scheme is called the *filesystem*.

That's why the main function of the Linux operating system is to keep track of and manipulate these files. The importance of the **ls** command can't be overstated, since it lets you know which files are in a portion of the filesystem at a given time. That's why the most frequently used commands in Linux relate to manipulating files on basic levels, such as **elvis** for editing files, **del** for deleting files, and **mv** for moving files.

There are four types of files:

- Device files
- Directories
- Links
- Ordinary files

Each is explained, in order of its importance in the Linux operating system:

- *Ordinary files* are the rank and file of Linux files, usually containing data that's acted upon by other programs and the operating system itself. An ordinary file can be an ASCII text file, a data file for a program (such as a formatted file for a page-layout program or a database file for a database manager), a command file (which contains further instructions for a program but is stored in ASCII text, such as a Perl or Tcl script), or an executable program file.

- *Directories* are files that represent information about other files. Files in the Linux operating system are stored hierarchically, with files stored within collections of other files. Directories will be explained later in this chapter.

- *Device files* represent the devices attached to your PC. These devices are stored in the **/dev** directory; for instance, a tape drive is represented by **/dev/st0**.

- *Links* are multiple names in the filesystem that represent the same file. Links aren't that big a deal with Linux, unless you're working on a network. Links are a remnant of the old UNIX days, when hard-disk space was so tight users would share one file, but because of the needs of the network, different names were given to the file.

Directories

As you saw earlier, directories are merely files that are used to store other files. Directories are an absolute must for an operating system like Linux. In Linux, every command is a file, every device is a file, and every program is at least one file (but usually many more). Add up all of these files, and you'll end up with a mess of a filesystem, with thousands of individual files. To make matters worse, Linux is designed to be on a network, which means that every user has access to thousands of other files across the network and possibly on a file server. There would be no workable way to keep track of these files unless they could be stored in some sort of hierarchy. That's where directories come in.

The directory hierarchy in Linux, which you can visualize as a pyramid, is actually pretty simple. There's a *root*

directory, which is at the top of the pyramid, and it's represented by a slash (/). Every directory is a *subdirectory* of the
root directory. In addition, there are subdirectories within
subdirectories.

As a user, you are "in" a directory at all times. This is
called the *current directory*. Your command prompt usually
lists the name of the current directory (beginning with a
slash, which indicates that the directory hierarchy begins
with a root directory).

A standard Linux installation, such as Slackware Linux,
has a fairly predictable set of directories. When your current
directory is the root directory, Linux features a set of subdirectories like those shown in Figure 1.5.

```
xterm                                                         _ □ ✕
kevin:/$ ls
bin/        core        home/        mnt/        sbin/        usr/
boot/       dev/        lib/         proc/       shlib/       var/
cdrom/      etc/        lost+found/  root/       tmp/         vmlinuz
kevin:/$ ▉
```

Figure 1.5 The root directory in a typical Slackware Linux installation.

Some of these directories are found in almost all Linux and
UNIX installations, such as **etc**, **sbin**, **usr**, and **var**. Other
directories are unique to Linux, such as **boot**, **cdrom**, **mnt**,
proc, and **shlib**. Still others are devoted to users, such as
root and **users**. If you installed Linux on your own, you
probably have at least one *home directory* (**root**, used when
you're logged in as the root user) and probably two (like a
named directory under **users**).

Linux features a number of commands for creating your
own directories, which are covered throughout the course of
this book.

11

Standard Input/Output and Redirection

The third piece in the Linux puzzle concerns linking commands and files in the form of *standard input and output* (I/O). Don't be dismayed by this techie term: standard I/O really concerns how command lines are structured and where the results of a command should be sent.

Linux is like every other operating system in that it needs to know where input is going to come from and where output should be sent. Other operating systems, such as Windows and the Macintosh, make assumptions when it comes to input and output. And in some circumstances so does Linux. But in most other circumstances, you need to put some thought into where your work comes from and where it goes. The basic principles behind standard I/O can be best explained with an example.

The **cat** command is an amazingly versatile command. It can be used to display the contents of files, add to files, and more. It can be used as a rudimentary text editor when run on a command line by itself:

```
$ cat
```

The cursor will go to the next line, and then you can enter text. Because you have not specified where the text should go, Linux and the **cat** command assume that the input should go to the screen. After the input goes to the screen, it's lost forever, as there's no mechanism for saving the text to disk. Most Linux commands assume that standard input means input from the keyboard, and standard output means display on the terminal. Under these circumstances, **cat** can be used for improving your typing skills, but otherwise it's of little use.

However, **cat**'s usefulness increases when youcombine it with filenames in a command line. Combining **cat** and a filename displays an existing file on the screen, as shown in Figure 1.6.

Figure 1.6 Combining cat with a file.

Instead of using standard input from the keyboard, **cat** uses standard input from a file. The contents of the file haven't been altered; they've merely been displayed on the screen.

You can use **cat** to store keystrokes to a file with the use of *redirection* symbols. These symbols, which are part of the core operating system, are used to alter standard I/O. You could combine **cat**—or any other Linux command, for that matter—with a redirection symbol to redirect its output to a file. In the following example, the output from **cat**, which is normally sent to the screen, is instead redirected to a file named **kevin.report**:

```
$ cat > kevin.report
```

The output is sent one keystroke at a time to the file **kevin.report**. Typing **Ctrl-D** stops the redirection and ends the **cat** command.

Redirection can be used both for input and output. The **cat** command can be told to copy a file to a new filename in the following manner:

```
$ cat kevin.report > pat.report
```

Here, the input is **kevin.report**, and the output is **pat.report**. Nothing about **kevin.report** is changed.

There is a separate redirection symbol for appending text to an existing file. Here, the contents of **kevin.report** are appended to an existing file named **pat.report**:

```
$ cat kevin.report >> pat.report
```

If you were to omit a filename as the input, **cat** would assume that keystrokes should be used for appending. The following command line lets you append keystrokes directly to the end of the file named **kevin.report**:

```
$ cat >> kevin.report
```

There are actually four redirection symbols:

- > is used to send the output of a command to a file or another command. For example, **cat > file** is used to send the output of the **cat** command to **file**.

- < is used to send the input of a file or command to a command. For example, **cat < file** means that **cat** should use **file** as input.

- >> is used to append input to an existing file. For example, **cat >> file** tells Linux to append the keystrokes to an existing file named **file**.

- I is the pipe symbol. It's used when you want to run a command and then send its output to another command. For instance, **cat I grep** runs the **cat** command and sends the output to the **grep** command, which is then run. (We'll cover pipes later in this chapter.)

When you look at these symbols, it may seem that there are a few different ways to do the same thing. Indeed, < and > are interchangeable, depending on how the command line is structured. However, both symbols are needed. Command lines that look similar can actually be dealt with quite differently by the operating system. For instance, this command line:

```
$ cat pat.file
```

is functionally the same as:

```
$ cat < pat.file
```

The two command lines are actually different, however. In the first, **pat.file** is an *argument* for the **cat** command. In the Linux world, arguments are command-line modifiers that are variables; in this instance, the argument happened to be a file. In the second example, **pat.file** is input to the **cat** command.

There is no limit to the complexity of command lines when it comes to redirection symbols. It's not uncommon to see two redirection symbols used as follows, especially in a shell script:

```
$ cat < file1 > file2
```

This tells **cat** to use input from **file1** and send the output to **file2**.

Pipes

A pipe, as noted by |, is merely one additional redirection tool. It has the advantage of working directly with commands, telling one command to use as input the output of another command. Here's how it is used:

```
$ command1 | command2
```

The combination of commands and a pipe symbol is called a *pipeline*. Pipes are often used when preparing files for printing.

X Window System Options

Throughout Chapter 5 there are X Window System commands. These commands share a common set of command-line options. Rather than listing these options with every command, we're listing them here.

OPTION	PURPOSE
-background *red green blue*	Sets the background color to *red green blue*.
-background *color*	Uses *color* for the window background.
-bg *color*	Uses *color* for the window background.
-display *host:disp_num*	Connects to a display, as specified with a *disp_num*-numbered *X server* (which is almost always 0) on a given *host*.
-fg *color*	Uses *color* for the window foreground.
-fn *fontname*	Uses a specified *fontname*.

-font *fontname*	Uses a specified font.
-foreground_color *red green blue*	Sets the foreground color to *red green blue*.
-foreground *color*	Uses *color* for the window foreground.
-geometry *WidthxHeight+x+y*	Sets the window size (**Widthx Height**) and position (*x+y*).
-geometry *WidthxHeight*	Sets the window size.
-geometry *+x+y*	Sets the position of a window's upper-left corner.
-height *rows*	Sets the height of base window in *rows*.
-position *x y*	Sets the location of the upper-left corner of window, in *x y* pixels.
-reverse	Reverses the foreground and background colors.
-rv	Reverses the foreground and background colors.
-size *width height*	Sets the window size, in *width x height* pixels.
-Wb *red green blue*	Sets the background to *red green blue*.
-Wf *red green blue*	Sets the foreground color to *red green blue*.
-WG *WidthxHeight+x+y*	Sets window size (**Widthx Height**) and position (*x+y*).
-WG *WidthxHeight*	Sets the window size.
-WG *+x+y*	Sets the position of window's upper-left corner, in *x y* pixels.
-Wh *rows*	Sets the height of the base window in *rows*.
-Wi	Starts window as an icon, rather than as a full window.
-width *columns*	Sets the width of the base window in *columns*.
-Wp *x y*	Sets the location of the upper-left corner of window in *x y* pixels.
-Wr *host:disp_num*	Connects to a display, as specified with a *disp_num*-numbered X server (which is almost always 0) on a given *host*.
-Ws *width height*	Sets the base window size in *width x height* pixels.
-Wt *fontname*	Uses specified *fontname*.
-Ww *columns*	Sets the width of the base window in *columns*.

2

Linux in Plain English

Human beings don't think in computerese, which is why we need a reference work like this one. Commands tend to be rather obscure, and their purpose isn't always apparent. To further your Linux efforts, we've compiled this listing of commands and organized them by keyword and function. You can look up an italicized keyword in the left column— say, *print*—and see which Linux commands help perform that task. Then go to Chapter 5 for a complete explanation of the command.

control server *access*	xhost
append files	cat
know your machine *architecture*	arch
create *archive*	cpio, tar
work with *archives*	ar
convert *ASCII* to bitmap	atobm
convert bitmap to *ASCII*	bmtoa
print *at* specific time	atq
run command *at* specific time	at
list *atoms*	xlsatoms
manage *authorization* information	xauth
set *background* attributes	xsetroot
set *background* image	xpmroot
print a *banner*	banner
display file *basename*	basename
run *batch* commands	batch
display *beginning* of file	head
display *end* of file	tail
convert ASCII to *bitmap*	atobm
convert *bitmap* to ASCII	bmtoa
view and edit *bitmaps*	bitmap
compile *C* programs	gcc
compile *C++* programs	gcc, g++
perform *calculations*	bc, pname, xcalc
view a *calendar*	cal
clear your screen	clear
list running *clients*	xlsclients
display contents of *clipboard*	xclipboard
display a *clock*	oclock, xclock
show *color database*	showrgb
display *colormap*	xcmap
set *colormap* properties	xstdcmap
cut *column*	cut
create *columns*	column
combine files	cat, join

run *command* at specific time	**at**
build *command lines*	**xargs**
compare files	**cmp, diff, diff3, sdiff, zcmp, zdiff**
compare compressed files	**zcmp, zdiff**
compare sorted files	**comm**
compare text files	**diff, diff3, sdiff**
compare three text files	**diff3**
compile C programs	**gcc**
compile C++ programs	**gcc, g++**
compile Fortran programs	**g77**
compress executable file	**gzexe**
compress file	**gzip, znew**
connect to another computer	**minicom, seyon**
copy files	**cp, cat**
count words	**wc**
return the *current* date	**date**
change the *date* on your system	**date**
decode file	**uudecode**
delete files	**rm**
delete directories	**rmdir**
change *directory*	**cd**
make *directory*	**mkdir**
print current *directory*	**pwd**
list *disk* free space	**df**
lock *display*	**xlock**
view *display* information	**xdpyinfo**
query *DNS* server	**dnsquery**
show *domain name*	**dnshostname**
echo input	**echo**
edit text file	**elvis, emacs, vi, vim, xedit**
create *electronic mail*	**elm, mail, metasend, pine**
encode *electronic mail*	**mimencode, mmencode**
format *electronic mail*	**formail**
notify of incoming *electronic mail*	**biff, xbiff, wnewmail**

**Linux in
Plain English**

If you want to...	Use the Linux command...
create multimedia *electronic mail*	**metasend**
print *electronic mail*	**printmail**
read *electronic mail*	**elm, mail, pine, readmsg**
reply via *electronic mail*	**Rnmail**
retrieve *electronic mail* via POP	**popclient**
send batches of *electronic mail*	**fastmail**
split MIME *electronic mail*	**splitmail**
launch *electronic-mail* server	**imapd, sendmail**
encode file	**uuencode**
return *environment* variables	**printenv**
set *environment* variables	**env**
view *event* information	**xev**
make *FIFO*	**mkfifo**
check *files*	**cksum**
find files	**find**
change *finger* information	**chfn**
return *finger* information	**finger**
launch *font* server	**xfs**
view *font server* information	**fsinfo**
list *fonts*	**fslsfonts, showfont, xfd, Xfontsel, xlsfonts**
format file	**fmt, groff**
format floppy disk	**fdformat**
compile *Fortran* programs	**g77**
generate *fractals*	**xfractint**
launch *FTP* server	**ftpd**
edit *graphics*	**xv**
change *group*	**chgrp, newgrp**
view online *help*	**apropos, info, man, whatis, Xman**
return *host* information	**host**
set *hostname*	**hostname**
view *keyboard* information	**dumpkeys, kdb_mode**
modify *keymaps*	**xmodmap**
save *keystrokes to* file	**script**

view *keyword* information	whatis
edit *images*	xv
launch *IMAP* mail server	imapd
launch *Internet* server	inetd
join sorted files	join
link files	ln
list files	dir, ls
lock display	xlock
login remotely	rlogin
login system	login
view *login name*	logname
create electronic *mail*	elm, mail, metasend, pine
encode electronic *mail*	mimencode, mmencode
format electronic *mail*	formail
notify of incoming electronic *mail*	biff, xbiff, wnewmail
create multimedia electronic *mail*	metasend
print electronic *mail*	printmail
read electronic *mail*	elm, mail, pine, readmsg
reply via electronic *mail*	Rnmail
retrieve electronic *mail* via POP	popclient
send batches of electronic *mail*	fastmail
split MIME electronic *mail*	splitmail
launch *mail* server	imapd, sendmail
list free *memory*	free
merge files	paste
MIME-encode electronic mail	mimencode, mmencode
split *MIME* electronic mail	splitmail
change *mode*	chmod
mount disk	mount
mount floppy disk	fdmount
mount tape drive	mt
move files	mv
create *multimedia* electronic mail	metasend
list *network* users	rusers
check Usenet *news*	checknews

Linux in Plain English

21

post Usenet *news*	**Pnews, postnews**
read Usenet *news*	**trn**
list Usenet *newsgroups*	**getlist**
run commands *nicely*	**nice**
set *options*	**xset**
change *owner*	**chown**
display X *pixmap*	**sxpm**
partition drive	**fdisk**
change *password*	**passwd**
change *permissions*	**chmod**
retrieve electronic mail via *POP*	**popclient**
view *PostScript* file	**ghostview**
print at specific time	**atq**
print electronic mail	**printmail**
print file	**lpr**
prepare file for *printing*	**pr**
delete *print job*	**lprm**
view *process* status	**ps, w**
end *process*	**kill, killall, xkill**
reprioritize *process*	**snice**
return a *process ID*	**pidof**
list the *processes* eating the most CPU time	**top**
display X *properties*	**xprop**
refresh your screen	**xrefresh**
remove files	**rm**
remove directories	**rmdir**
set X *resource database*	**xrdb**
list X *resources*	**appres, listres, viewres**
reverse file lines	**rev**
set *root* attributes	**xsetroot**
set *root* image	**xpmroot**
change *root directory*	**chroot**
schedule tasks	**cron**
clear your *screen*	**clear**

magnify *screen*	**xmag**
refresh your *screen*	**xrefresh**
create *screen capture*	**xwd, xv**
display *screen capture*	**xwud, xv**
search files	**egrep, fgrep, grep**
search compressed files	**zegrep, zfgrep, zgrep**
launch *session manager*	**xsm**
control *server* access	**xhost**
view X *server* performance	**x11perf**
compare X *server* performance	**x11perfcomp**
change your *shell*	**chsh**
create *shell archives*	**shar**
unpack a *shell archive*	**unshar**
run two *shells* in two windows	**splitvt**
trace signal	**strace**
sort files	**sort**
check *spelling*	**ispell**
split file	**csplit, split**
launch a *spreadsheet*	**pname, xspread**
trace *system call*	**strace**
display *system usage*	**uptime, w**
display *system load*	**tload, xload**
display *system statistics*	**systat**
create *tape archive*	**cpio, tar**
mount *tape drive*	**mt**
run *Tcl* command shell	**wish**
telecommunicate with another computer	**minicom, seyon**
launch *terminal* emulator	**rxvt, xterm**
change *terminal* settings	**stty**
view *texinfo* information	**info**
find *text* in binary file	**strings**
edit *text* file	**elvis, emacs, vi, vim, xedit**
trace system call	**strace**
transfer files	**ftp, tftp**

Linux in
Plain English

send data to *two* files	**tee**
determine file *type*	**file**
unmount filesystems	**umount**
unzip file	**gunzip, gzip, zcat**
unzip zipped file	**unzip**
check *Usenet news*	**checknews**
post *Usenet news*	**Pnews, postnews**
read *Usenet news*	**trn**
list *Usenet newsgroups*	**getlist**
list *user* information	**who, rwho**
substitute *user*	**su**
list logged-in *users*	**users**
list network *users*	**rusers**
return environment *variables*	**printenv**
set environment *variables*	**env**
configure *video card*	**SuperProbe**
view files	**cat, less, more**
view compressed files	**zmore**
search *whatis* database	**apropos**
set page *width*	**fold**
display *window* information	**xwininfo**
count *words*	**wc**
browse *World Wide Web*	**lynx**
launch *World Wide Web server*	**httpd**
launch *X Window System*	**startx**
generate *XF86Config* file	**Xf86config**
receive via *xmodem*	**rx**
send via *xmodem*	**sx**
receive via *ymodem*	**rb**
send via *ymodem*	**sb**
receive via *zmodem*	**rz**
send via *zmodem*	**sz**

3

Linux/DOS
Cross Reference

There are more similarities between DOS and Linux than
you might expect—both DOS and Linux have their roots in
UNIX, and for the most part, commands and filesystems
behave the same way in all three operating systems. If your
background is in DOS, you certainly can make the leap to
Linux. This chapter lists some popular DOS commands and
their Linux counterparts.

DOS COMMAND	LINUX COMMAND
APPEND	*None*
ASSIGN	*None*
ATTRIB	chmod
BACKUP	cpio, tar
BREAK	*None*
CALL	exec
CD	cd
CHCP	*None*
CHDIR	cd
CHKDSK	e2fsck
CHOICE	*None*
CLS	clear, reset
COMMAND	bash, csh, sh
COMP	cmp, diff, diff3, sdiff
COPY	cp, cat
CTTY	stty
DATE	date
DBLSPACE	*None*
DEFRAG	*None*
DEL	rm
DELTREE	rmdir
DIR	dir, ls
DISKCOMP	*None*
DISKCOPY	*None*
DOSKEY	history (Korn and bash shells)
DOSSHELL	*None*
ECHO	echo
EDIT	vi
EXIT	*None*
EXPAND	gunzip, uncompress, unpack
FASTHELP	apropos, man, xman, whatis
FASTOPEN	*None*
FC	cmp, diff, diff3, sdiff
FDISK	fdisk

DOS COMMAND	LINUX COMMAND
FIND	**find**
FOR	**for** (shell command)
FORMAT	*None*
GOTO	**goto** (C shell)
GRAFTABL	*None*
GRAPHICS	*None*
HELP	**apropos, man, whatis**
IF	**if** (shell command)
INTERLNK	*None*
INTERSVR	*None*
JOIN	*None*
LABEL	*None*
LOADFIX	*None*
LOADHIGH	*None* (thankfully)
MEM	**free**
MIRROR	*None*
MKDIR	**mkdir**
MODE	**stty, tty**
MORE	**less, more, xmore**
MOVE	**mv**
MSAV	*None*
MSBACKUP	**cpio, tar**
MSD	*None*
NLSFUNC	*None*
PATH	**env**
PAUSE	**sleep**
POWER	*None*
PRINT	**lpr**
PROMPT	**PS1**
RECOVER	*None*
REM	**#**
RENAME	**cat**
REPLACE	*None*
RESTORE	**cpio, tar**

DOS COMMAND	LINUX COMMAND
RMDIR	**rmdir**
SET	**env**
SETVER	*None*
SHARE	*None*
SHIFT	*None*
SMARTDRV	*None*
SORT	**sort**
SUBST	*None*
SYS	*None*
TIME	**date**
TREE	*None*
TYPE	**cat, less, more**
UNDELETE	*None*
UNFORMAT	*None*
VER	**uname**
VERIFY	*None*
VOL	*None*
VSAFE	*None*
XCOPY	**cp**
XTREE	**mkdir**

4

Linux Commands A to Z

Here is an alphabetical listing of the commands described in Chapter 5. This doesn't constitute the entire Linux command set—check out the online manual and info pages for that—but it does list the commands you'll probably use most of the time.

ansi2knr	Programming Commands
answer	Internet/Electronic-Mail Commands
appres	General-Purpose Commands
apropos	General-Purpose Commands
ar	Programming Commands
arch	General-Purpose Commands
as	Programming Commands
at	System-Administration Commands
atq	System-Administration Commands
atrm	System-Administration Commands
atobm	General-Purpose Commands
audiocompose	Internet/Electronic-Mail Commands
audiosend	Internet/Electronic-Mail Commands
banner	General-Purpose Commands
basename	File-Management Commands
bash	General-Purpose Commands
batch	System-Administration Commands
bc	General-Purpose Commands
bdftopcf	General-Purpose Commands
biff	Internet/Electronic-Mail Commands
bison	Programming Commands
bitmap	General-Purpose Commands
bmtoa	General-Purpose Commands
bpe	Text-Processing Commands
cal	General-Purpose Commands
cat	Text-Processing Commands
cc	Programming Commands
cd	File-Management Commands
checknews	Internet/Electronic-Mail Commands
chgrp	File-Management Commands
chmod	File-Management Commands
chown	File-Management Commands
chroot	File-Management Commands
chsh	General-Purpose Commands

cksum	General-Purpose Commands
clear	General-Purpose Commands
cmp	Text-Processing Commands
colcrt	General-Purpose Commands
colrm	Text-Processing Commands
column	Text-Processing Commands
comm	Text-Processing Commands
cp	File-Management Commands
cpio	System-Administration Commands
chfn	Internet/Electronic-Mail Commands
cpp	Programming Commands
cron	System-Administration Commands
csh	General-Purpose Commands
csplit	Text-Processing Commands
ctlinnd	System-Administration Commands
ctags	Programming Commands
cut	Text-Processing Commands
date	General-Purpose Commands
diff	Text-Processing Commands
diff3	Text-Processing Commands
dir	File-Management Commands
diskd	System-Administration Commands
diskseek	System-Administration Commands
df	System-Administration Commands
dnshostname	Networking Commands
dnsquery	Networking Commands
du	System-Administration Commands
dumpkeys	General-Purpose Commands
echo	General-Purpose Commands
egrep	Text-Processing Commands
elm	Internet/Electronic-Mail Commands
elvis	Text-Processing Commands
emacs	Text-Processing Commands
env	General-Purpose Commands

Linux Commands
A to Z

Command	Section
etags	Programming Commands
expand	Text-Processing Commands
fastmail	Internet/Electronic-Mail Commands
faucet	Networking Commands
fdformat	System-Administration Commands
fdisk	System-Administration Commands
fdmount	System-Administration Commands
fdrawcmd	System-Administration Commands
fgrep	Text-Processing Commands
file	File-Management Commands
find	File-Management Commands
finger	Internet/Electronic-Mail Commands
flex	Programming Commands
fmt	Text-Processing Commands
fold	Text-Processing Commands
formail	Internet/Electronic-Mail Commands
free	System-Administration Commands
frm	Internet/Electronic-Mail Commands
fsinfo	General-Purpose Commands
fslsfonts	General-Purpose Commands
fstobdf	General-Purpose Commands
ftp	Internet/Electronic-Mail Commands
ftpcount	Internet/Electronic-Mail Commands
ftpd	System-Administration Commands
ftpwho	System-Administration Commands
funzip	File-Management Commands
fuser	Networking Commands
g77	Programming Commands
gawk	Programming Commands
gcc	Programming Commands
getfilename	File-Management Commands
getkeycodes	General-Purpose Commands
getlist	Internet/Electronic-Mail Commands
getpeername	Networking Commands

Command	Section
ghostview	Text-Processing Commands
gprof	Programming Commands
grep	Text-Processing Commands
grodvi	Text-Processing Commands
groff	Text-Processing Commands
grolj4	Text-Processing Commands
grops	Text-Processing Commands
grotty	Text-Processing Commands
gunzip	File-Management Commands
gzexe	File-Management Commands
gzip	File-Management Commands
head	Text-Processing Commands
hose	Networking Commands
host	Networking Commands
hostname	Networking Commands
httpd	System-Administration Commands
id	General-Purpose Commands
imake	Programming Commands
imapd	System-Administration Commands
inetd	System-Administration Commands
inews	System-Administration Commands
info	General-Purpose Commands
injnews	System-Administration Commands
innd	System-Administration Commands
ispell	Text-Processing Commands
join	Text-Processing Commands
kdb_mode	General-Purpose Commands
kill	General-Purpose Commands
killall	General-Purpose Commands
less	Text-Processing Commands
lilo	System-Administration Commands
listres	General-Purpose Commands
ln	File-Management Commands
locate	File-Management Commands

locatedb	File-Management Commands
lockfile	File-Management Commands
login	General-Purpose Commands
logname	General-Purpose Commands
look	Text-Processing Commands
lpq	Text-Processing Commands
lpr	Text-Processing Commands
lprm	Text-Processing Commands
ls	File-Management Commands
lynx	Internet/Electronic-Mail Commands
mail	Internet/Electronic-Mail Commands
make	Programming Commands
makedepend	Programming Commands
makefloppies	System-Administration Commands
makestrs	Programming Commands
makewhatis	General-Purpose Commands
man	General-Purpose Commands
manpath	General-Purpose Commands
mattrib	Mtools
mbadblocks	Mtools
mc	File-Management Commands
mcd	Mtools
mcookie	General-Purpose Commands
mcopy	Mtools
md5sum	System-Administration Commands
mdel	Mtools
mdir	Mtools
messages	Internet/Electronic-Mail Commands
metamail	Internet/Electronic-Mail Commands
metasend	Internet/Electronic-Mail Commands
mformat	Mtools
mimencode	Internet/Electronic-Mail Commands
minicom	General-Purpose Commands
mkdir	File-Management Commands

Linux Commands
A to Z

Command	Section
ping	Networking Commands
pkgtool	System-Administration Commands
pname	General-Purpose Commands
Pnews	Internet/Electronic-Mail Commands
popclient	Internet/Electronic-Mail Commands
postnews	Internet/Electronic-Mail Commands
pr	Text-Processing Commands
printenv	General-Purpose Commands
printf	Text-Processing Commands
printmail	Internet/Electronic-Mail Commands
procmail	Internet/Electronic-Mail Commands
ps	General-Purpose Commands
psbb	Text-Processing Commands
pwd	File-Management Commands
quota	System-Administration Commands
rb	General-Purpose Commands
rcp	Networking Commands
rdjpgcom	General-Purpose Commands
readmsg	Internet/Electronic-Mail Commands
readprofile	System-Administration Commands
reconfig	General-Purpose Commands
ref	Programming Commands
refer	Text-Processing Commands
relaynews	System-Administration Commands
renice	General-Purpose Commands
reset	General-Purpose Commands
resize	General-Purpose Commands
rev	Text-Processing Commands
rexecd	System-Administration Commands
richtext	Internet/Electronic-Mail Commands
rlogin	Networking Commands
rm	File-Management Commands
rmail	Internet/Electronic-Mail Commands
rmdir	File-Management Commands

COMMAND	SECTION
rmmod	System-Administration Commands
Rnmail	Internet/Electronic-Mail Commands
rpcgen	Programming Commands
rsh	Networking Commands
rstartd	System-Administration Commands
rstart	Networking Commands
runscript	General-Purpose Commands
ruptime	General-Purpose Commands
users	Networking Commands
rwall	Networking Commands
rwho	Networking Commands
rx	General-Purpose Commands
rxvt	General-Purpose Commands
rz	General-Purpose Commands
sb	General-Purpose Commands
script	General-Purpose Commands
sdiff	Text-Processing Commands
sed	Text-Processing Commands
selection	Text-Processing Commands
sendmail	System-Administration Commands
sessreg	System-Administration Commands
setfdprm	System-Administration Commands
setterm	System-Administration Commands
seyon	General-Purpose Commands
shar	General-Purpose Commands
shelltool	General-Purpose Commands
showaudio	Internet/Electronic-Mail Commands
showexternal	Internet/Electronic-Mail Commands
showfont	General-Purpose Commands
shownonascii	Internet/Electronic-Mail Commands
showpartial	Internet/Electronic-Mail Commands
showpicture	Internet/Electronic-Mail Commands
showrgb	General-Purpose Commands
shrinkfile	File-Management Commands

Linux Commands
A to Z

size	File-Management Commands
skill	General-Purpose Commands
sleep	General-Purpose Commands
sliplogin	Networking Commands
smproxy	General-Purpose Commands
snice	General-Purpose Commands
sockdown	Networking Commands
soelim	Text-Processing Commands
sort	Text-Processing Commands
split	Text-Processing Commands
splitmail	Internet/Electronic-Mail Commands
splitvt	General-Purpose Commands
sq	File-Management Commands
startx	General-Purpose Commands
strace	General-Purpose Commands
strings	General-Purpose Commands
strings-gnu	General-Purpose Commands
strip	Programming Commands
stty	General-Purpose Commands
su	General-Purpose Commands
sum	File-Management Commands
sunst	General-Purpose Commands
superformat	System-Administration Commands
SuperProbe	System-Administration Commands
sx	General-Purpose Commands
sxpm	General-Purpose Commands
systat	General-Purpose Commands
sz	General-Purpose Commands
tac	Text-Processing Commands
tail	Text-Processing Commands
talk	Networking Commands
tee	General-Purpose Commands
telnet	Networking Commands
telnetd	System-Administration Commands

test	File-Management Commands
tftp	Internet/Electronic-Mail Commands
tload	General-Purpose Commands
top	General-Purpose Commands
tr	Text-Processing Commands
trn	Internet/Electronic-Mail Commands
troff	Text-Processing Commands
true	General-Purpose Commands
ul	General-Purpose Commands
umount	System-Administration Commands
unexpand	Text-Processing Commands
uniq	Text-Processing Commands
unshar	General-Purpose Commands
unsq	File-Management Commands
unzip	File-Management Commands
unzipsfx	File-Management Commands
updatedb	File-Management Commands
uptime	General-Purpose Commands
users	General-Purpose Commands
uucp	Networking Commands
uudecode	Internet/Electronic-Mail Commands
uuencode	Internet/Electronic-Mail Commands
uustat	Internet/Electronic-Mail Commands
uux	Internet/Electronic-Mail Commands
vi	Text-Processing Commands
viewres	General-Purpose Commands
vim	Text-Processing Commands
vrfy	Internet/Electronic-Mail Commands
w	General-Purpose Commands
wc	Text-Processing Commands
whatis	General-Purpose Commands
who	General-Purpose Commands
whoami	General-Purpose Commands
wish	General-Purpose Commands

Command	Section
wnewmail	Internet/Electronic-Mail Commands
write	Networking Commands
x11perf	General-Purpose Commands
x11perfcomp	General-Purpose Commands
xargs	General-Purpose Commands
xauth	General-Purpose Commands
xbiff	Internet/Electronic-Mail Commands
xcalc	General-Purpose Commands
xclipboard	General-Purpose Commands
xclock	General-Purpose Commands
xcmap	General-Purpose Commands
xcmsdb	General-Purpose Commands
xconsole	General-Purpose Commands
xcpustate	General-Purpose Commands
xcutsel	General-Purpose Commands
xdfcopy	System-Administration Commands
xdm	General-Purpose Commands
xdpyinfo	General-Purpose Commands
xedit	Text-Processing Commands
xev	General-Purpose Commands
xeyes	General-Purpose Commands
xf86config	General-Purpose Commands
xfd	General-Purpose Commands
xfilemanager	File-Management Commands
xfm	File-Management Commands
xfontsel	General-Purpose Commands
xfractint	General-Purpose Commands
xfs	General-Purpose Commands
xgc	General-Purpose Commands
xgettext	Programming Commands
xhost	General-Purpose Commands
xieperf	General-Purpose Commands
xinit	General-Purpose Commands
xkill	General-Purpose Commands

COMMAND	SECTION
xload	General-Purpose Commands
xlock	General-Purpose Commands
xlogo	General-Purpose Commands
xlsatoms	General-Purpose Commands
xlsclients	General-Purpose Commands
xlsfonts	General-Purpose Commands
xmag	General-Purpose Commands
xman	General-Purpose Commands
xmessage	General-Purpose Commands
xmh	Internet/Electronic-Mail Commands
xmkmf	Programming Commands
xmodmap	General-Purpose Commands
xon	General-Purpose Commands
xpaint	General-Purpose Commands
xpmroot	General-Purpose Commands
xrdb	General-Purpose Commands
xrefresh	General-Purpose Commands
xset	General-Purpose Commands
xsetroot	General-Purpose Commands
xsm	General-Purpose Commands
xsmclient	General-Purpose Commands
xspread	General-Purpose Commands
xstdcmap	General-Purpose Commands
xterm	General-Purpose Commands
xv	General-Purpose Commands
xvidtune	General-Purpose Commands
xvpictoppm	General-Purpose Commands
xwd	General-Purpose Commands
xwininfo	General-Purpose Commands
xwud	General-Purpose Commands
xxgdb	Programming Commands
yacc	Programming Commands
yes	General-Purpose Commands
ytalk	Networking Commands

Linux Commands
A to Z

COMMAND	SECTION
zcat	File-Management Commands
zcmp	Text-Processing Commands
zdiff	Text-Processing Commands
zegrep	Text-Processing Commands
zfgrep	Text-Processing Commands
zforce	File-Management Commands
zgrep	Text-Processing Commands
zmore	Text-Processing Commands
znew	File-Management Commands
zoo	File-Management Commands

5

Linux Commands, Organized by Group

This section covers the major Linux commands, sorted by group and function. The eight categories are:

- General-Purpose Commands
- File-Management Commands
- Text-Processing Commands
- Internet Commands
- Programming Commands
- Networking Commands
- System-Administration Commands
- Mtools

The format of each of these commands is the same. The name of the command is given, following by an example command line, an explanation of the command, the command-line options available, examples, and related commands. Variables are listed in *italics*. Also, we note when a command is a GNU command or an X Window System command.

GENERAL-PURPOSE COMMANDS

These commands are used for your everyday computing chores.

X Window System Command

X WINDOW

appres *class toolkitoptions*

PURPOSE

The **appres** command lists the resources specified by an application. You can specify a general application, or you can specify a particular widget.

The output can be quite voluminous, so you may want to pipe the output to another file.

EXAMPLE

```
$ appres XTerm
*mainMenu*interrupt*Label:      Send INT Signal
*mailMenu*logging*Label:        Log to File
*mainMenu*quit*Label:    Quit

...
```

RELATED COMMANDS

listres

xrdb

apropos *keyword*

PURPOSE

The **apropos** command searches the **whatis** database for information concerning a specified keyword and returns the information in the default EDITOR. The **whatis** database contains short text summaries of commands.

EXAMPLE

```
$ apropos xterm
resize (1x)          - set TERMCAP and terminal settings
     to current xterm window size
xterm (1x)           - terminal emulator for X
```

RELATED COMMANDS

man

whatis

xman

Linux Commands,
Organized by Group

arch

PURPOSE

Lists the machine architecture of the PC running Linux. This can be i386, i486, or i586 (for Pentium-based PCs).

EXAMPLE

```
$ arch
i586
```

RELATED COMMANDS

uname

atobm *option(s) filename*

PURPOSE

The **atobm** command converts ASCII strings to a bitmap file. See
the **bitmap** command for more explanation about X Window
System bitmap files.

OPTIONS

-chars cc   Sets the characters to use to specify the 0s and 1s
                       that make up the bitmap file. The default is to use
                       dashes (-) for 0s and sharp signs (#) for the 1s.

-name *variable*   Sets the variable name used when writing the con-
                       verted bitmap filename. The default is to use the
                       basename of the filename command-line argument.

-yhot *number*   Sets the "hot spot" Y-coordinate.

RELATED COMMANDS

bitmap

bmtoa

banner *option message*

PURPOSE

The **banner** command prints a banner of up to 10 characters using asterisks. The total width of the banner is 132 characters, and the banner is printed sideways.

EXAMPLE

$ banner kevin

OPTION

-w *num*   Sets the width of the banner of *num* characters.

GNU Command

bash *option(s)*

PURPOSE

The **bash** command launches the Bourne Again Shell, a clone of the popular UNIX shell. See Chapter 6 for more on **bash**.

bc *option(s) files*

GNU Command

PURPOSE

The **bc** command acts as an online calculator, as well as a tool for unlimited-precision arithmetic. It can be used to enter numerals directly. It can be embedded into shell scripts, using a syntax similar to the C programming language. It can also be used to convert numerals to different bases.

After entering the **bc** command on a command line, arithmetic functions can be entered directly. When you're through using the **bc** command, type **EOF**, **quit**, or **Ctrl-C**.

OPTIONS

-l   Adds functions from the math library.

-s   Overrides extensions, achieving POSIX conformity.

-p   Prints a warning when using extensions to POSIX **bc**.

EXAMPLE

```
$ bc
scale=5
sqrt((55*6)/5)
8.12402
quit
```

COMMON INSTRUCTIONS

+	Addition.
-	Subtraction.
/	Division.
*	Multiplication.
%	Remainder.
^	Exponentiation.
sqrt(*n*)	Square root.

Continued

VALUE STORAGE

scale=*n*   Sets scale using *n* decimal spaces; the default is 0. This is
               best used with base 10. The default also means that the
               output is in integers. The current value can be seen by
               entering only **scale** (and no value) by itself. For digits
               between 10 and 15, use the letters A–F.

ibase=*n*   Sets the input base (the default is 10). The current value
               can be seen by entering only **ibase** (and no value) by itself.
               For digits between 10 and 15, use the letters A-F.

obase=*x*   Sets the output base (the default is 10). The current value
               can be seen by entering only **obase** (and no value) by itself.
               For digits between 10 and 15, use the letters A–F.

last   Returns the last value. For digits between 10 and 15, use
               the letters A–F.

KEYWORDS

for (*exp***) [***statements***]**   Performs the *statements* if *exp* is true.

if (*exp***) [***statements***]**   Performs the *statement* if the *exp* is true. Can
(else [*statements***])**   also be used with the **else** extension; in this
                                       case, the alternate *statements* will be performed.

while (*exp***) [***statements***]**   Repeats the *statement* if *exp* is true.

break   Ends a **for** or **while** statement.

continue   Jumps to the next iteration in a **for** state-
                                       ment. This is a GNU extension.

define *a*(*b*)   Defines the function *a* with the argument *b*.

GNU EXTENSIONS

halt   Halts the **bc** command.

limits   Returns the local limits on the **bc** command.

print *list*   An odd command used to print a series of special charac-
               ters. The *list* is a list of comma-delimited expressions and
               strings, printed in order.

Continued

Strings can include special characters, including the following:

a	bell
b	backspace
f	form feed
n	newline
r	return
q	double quote
t	tab
\	backslash

OTHER OPERATORS AND KEYWORDS

assignment	=+ =- =* =/ =^ =
relational	< <= > >= == !=
unary	- ++ —

MATH-LIBRARY FUNCTIONS

s	Sine.
c	Cosine.
a	Arctangent.
e	Exponential; base e.
l	Natural logarithm.
j(n,x)	Bessel function.

OTHER SYMBOLS

/* */	Comment lines.
{ }	Brackets statements.
[ ]	Array index.

| **bdftopcf** | **Bitmap Font Conversion** |

X Window System Command

X WINDOW

bdftopcf *option(s) fontfile.bdf*

PURPOSE

The **bdftopcf** command converts fonts from the X Bitmap Distribution Format (BDF) to the Portable Compiled Format (PCF), which is more easily used by the X font server. PCF fonts can be read by any machine.

OPTIONS

-i	Inhibits computation of ink metrics. Bypassing computation can speed processing.
-l	Sets the font bit order to least significant bit (LSB) first.
-L	Sets the font byte order to least significant bit (LSB) first.
-m	Sets the font bit order to most significant bit (MSB) first.
-M	Sets the font byte order to most significant bit (MSB) first.
-o *outputfile*	Specifies the name of the output file.
-p*n*	Padding for the font glyph is set to *n*. Each glyph has each scanline padded to 1, 2, 4, or 8 bytes.
-t	Convert fonts to "terminal fonts" when possible. This option allows fonts to rendered more quickly by the font server.
-u*n*	Sets the font scanline unit to *n*. This option is necessary when the font bit order is different than the font byte order; *n* can be 1, 2, or 4 bytes.

EXAMPLE

```
$ bdftopcf -t -o fontfile.pcf fontfile.dbf
```

Linux Commands, Organized by Group

X Window System Command

bitmap *option(s) filename basename*

PURPOSE

The **bitmap** program is used to create and edit bitmaps. *Bitmaps* are image files laid out in a grid and used in the X Window System for a variety of purposes, from icons and cursors to Web-page graphic elements. They are stored as actual C code, which can be inserted directly into programs.

This program can specify a "hot spot" for use with a cursor, which tells the window manager where the cursor is specifically pointing, such as a tip of an arrow or the middle of a crosshair.

The basename is used with the C code input file.

To see how the image will actually appear, press **Alt-I**.

There are a number of commands available when this program is actually running, such as inverting the present image and marking a section of the bitmap. These are available through buttons on the left side of the window.

OPTIONS

-size *WIDTHxHEIGHT* Specifies the size of the bitmap grid.

-sw *dimension* Specifies the width of squares in pixels.

-sh *dimension* Specifies the height of squares in pixels.

-gt *dimension* Sets the grid tolerance; if the size of the dimensions falls below the dimension, the grid will be turned off.

-grid Turns off the grid lines.

+grid Turns on the grid lines.

-axes Turns off the major axes.

+axes Turns on the major axes.

-dashed Turns off the dashing for the frame and grid lines.

+dashed Turns on the dashing for the frame and grid lines.

Continued

-stippled	Turns off the stippling of highlighted squares.
+stippled	Turns on the stippling of highlighted squares.
-proportional	Turns off proportional mode, where the square width is equal to square height.
+proportional	Turns on proportional mode, where the square width is equal to square height.
-dashes *filename*	Sets the bitmap *filename* to be used as a stipple for dashing.
-stipple *filename*	Sets the bitmap *filename* to be used as a stipple for highlighting.
-hl color	Sets the *color* used for highlighting.
-fr color	Sets the *color* used for the frame and grid lines.

RELATED COMMANDS

atobm

bmtoa

Linux Commands,
Organized by Group

X Window System Command

bmtoa *option filename*

PURPOSE

The **bmtoa** command converts X Window System bitmap files to ASCII strings. See the **bitmap** command for more information on X Window System bitmap files.

EXAMPLE

```
$ bmtoa bitmap_file
```

OPTION

-chars cc   Sets the characters to use to specify the 0s and 1s that make up the bitmap file. The default is to use dashes (-) for 0s and sharp signs (#) for the 1s.

RELATED COMMANDS

atobm

bitmap

cal *option(s) month year*

PURPOSE

The **cal** command displays a calendar for a three-month period (with the current month bracketed by the previous month and the next month), for a specific month and year when the *month* and *year* are specified, or a calendar for 12 months of a specific year when only *year* is specified. The *year* can be between 1 and 9999, while the *month* can be between 1 and 12.

The **cal** command is based on the British/American convention. To see the Gregorian calendar, use a command line of *cal 1752*.

EXAMPLES

```
cal
cal 7 1997
cal 1997
cal 1752
```

OPTIONS

month	Specifies a month.
year	Specifies a year.
-j	Returns Julian dates, where days are numbered between 1 and 365 (except for leap years).

RELATED COMMANDS

date

Linux Commands, Organized by Group

chsh *option(s) shell*

PURPOSE

The **chsh** command changes your login shell. You can specify a shell, or you can choose a shell from a list of available shells.

OPTIONS

-**L**   Lists the available shells, as listed in **/etc/shells**, without making a change.

-**s**   Specifies a new shell.

EXAMPLES

```
$ chsh zsh
```

cksum *file(s)*

PURPOSE

The **cksum** command performs a cyclic redundancy check (CRC) on the specified *file(s)* to make sure that the files are not corrupted.

EXAMPLE

```
$ cksum CHANGES.TXT
4005661398      2344   CHANGES.TXT
```

clear

PURPOSE

The **clear** command clears the screen if you're working in terminal mode.

EXAMPLE

```
clear
```

colcrt *option(s) file*

PURPOSE

The **colcrt** command corrects the formatting of escape characters and reverse linefeeds generated by the **tbl** or **nroff** commands. This command applies if you're working with Linux in terminal mode. It's not usually used on its own, but rather as part of a longer command line.

OPTIONS

-　　　　　　　　Turns off underlining.

-2　　　　　　　Turns on double spacing.

csh

PURPOSE

The **csh** launches the C shell, one of the many Linux command-line shells. See Chapter 6 for more on shells.

date *option +format*

date *option string* **(for privileged users)**

PURPOSE

The **date** command displays the current date and time. The many formats allow you to control the format. A privileged user, such as the root user, can use the command to set the system date.

OPTIONS

+format   Displays the date in a specific *format;* format options
                  are listed in the next section.

-s   Sets the date. The option is available only to privileged users.

-u   Returns the time in universal time, also known as
                  Greenwich Mean Time
                  (GMT).

FORMATS

%a   Abbreviates the day of the week (Sun, Mon, etc.).

%A   Spells out the day of the week (Sunday, Monday, etc.).

%b   Abbreviates the month (Jan, Feb, etc.). The same as **%h**.

%B   Spells out the month (January, February, etc.).

%c   Returns the time for a specific country.

%d   Returns the day in two digits (01–31).

%D   Returns the date in *mm/dd/yy* format.

%e   Returns the day as a numeral (1–31).

%h   Abbreviates the month (Jan, Feb, etc.). The same as **%b**.

%H   Returns the hour in military time (00–23).

%I   Returns the hour in nonmilitary time (00–12).

%j   Returns the date in Julian format (1–365).

%k   Returns the hour in military time, without leading zeroes (1-23).

%l   Returns the hour in nonmilitary time, without leading
                  zeroes (1–12).

%m   Returns the month as two numerals (01 for January, 02
                  for February, etc.).

Continued

%M	Returns the number of minutes (0–59).
%n	Inserts a newline.
%p	Changes time of day to a.m. and p.m. (as opposed to the default AM and PM.
%r	Returns *hh:mm:ss:a/pm* in 12-hour format.
%s	Returns the number since "The Epoch," 1970-01-01 00:00:00 UTC.
%S	Returns the number of seconds (0–59).
%t	Inserts a tab.
%T	Specifies time returns in the *hh:mm:ss* format.
%U	Returns the day of the month (01–31).
%w	Returns the day of the week as a numeral (Sunday is 0).
%W	Returns the week as a number (0–51), with the week beginning on a Monday.
%x	Returns a country-specific time format.
%X	Returns a country-specific date format.
%y	Returns the year in two digits (97).
%Y	Returns the year in four digits (1997).
%Z	Returns a time-zone name.

DATE-SETTING OPTIONS

A privileged user can also use the **date** command to set a system date. The date can be numeric or nonnumeric format. A numeric string must be in the format *Mmddhhmmyy*.

EXAMPLE

```
$ date 0101153097
```

This sets the date to January 1 (*0101*), 1997 (*97*), at 3:30 p.m. (*1530*).

dumpkeys *option(s)*

PURPOSE

The **dumpkeys** command returns information about the current keyboard driver.

OPTIONS

-c*charset*	Specifies a *charset* to interpret the returned values; *charset* must be **iso-8859-1** (ASCII English; the default), **iso-8859-2, iso-8859-3, iso-8859-4,** or **iso-8859-8.**
--compose-only	Returns information about key combinations.
-f	Prints the entire output for each key in canonical format.
--funcs-only	Returns information about function keys.
-i	Prints limited information about each key: acceptable keycode
	keywords, the number of actions that can be bound to a key, the ranges of the action codes, and the number of function keys supported by the Linux kernel.
--keys-only	Returns information about key bindings, not string definitions.
-l	Prints information about each key: acceptable keycode keywords, the number of actions that can be bound to a key, the ranges of the action codes, the number of function keys supported by the Linux kernel, and the supported action symbols and their numeric values.
-n	Returns information in hexadecimal format.

echo *option string*

PURPOSE

The **echo** command echoes text or a value to standard output, normally the screen. It actually exists in three versions: as a Linux command (**/bin/echo**), as a C shell command, and as a Bourne shell command. The three are used interchangeably. The only real difference is that the C shell version is much more limited not supporting control characters and the **-n** option, as they are here.

OPTION

-n   Avoids printing of a newline at the end of the text.

CONTROL CHARACTER

\a	Alert (bell).
\b	Backspace.
\c	No newline.
\f	Form feed.
\n	Newline.
\r	Carriage return.
\t	Horizontal tab.
\v	Vertical tab.
\\	Backslash.
nnn	ASCII code of any character.

EXAMPLE

```
$ echo "Good afternoon!"
```

This prints the string *Good afternoon!* to the screen.

```
$ echo "We are testing the printer" | lp
```

This sends the string *We are testing the printer* to the printer.

env *option [variable=value] command*

PURPOSE

The **env** command changes environment variables or displays the current environment variables with their values. Your Linux system has a set of variables that can be applied to various situation; for instance, instead of every command and program having its own text editor, most of them just summon the EDITOR environment variable and call a system editor. Other variables control the default shell, your terminal type, your command path, and your home directory.

OPTIONS

-	Ignores the current environment entirely.
-i	Ignores the current environment entirely.
u *variable*	Unsets the specified *var*.

X Window System Command

fsinfo -server *servername*

PURPOSE

The **fsinfo** command returns information about a running X
Window System font server.

RELATED COMMANDS

fslsfonts

xfs

Continued

 X Window System Command

fslsfonts *option(s) pattern*

PURPOSE

The **fslsfonts** command lists the fonts served by a running X font server. You can list all the fonts (which can be quite voluminous), or you can match fonts with a *pattern*, which supports wildcards. (If you use the * and ? wildcards, you must quote them.)

OPTIONS

-1	Formats output in a single column.
-C	Formats output in multiple columns.
-l	Lists font attributes.
-ll	Lists font properties.
-lll	Works the same as the **-lll** option with **xlsfonts**.
-m	Lists the minimum and maximum bounds of each font.
-server *host:port*	Specifies the X font server.
-w *width*	Sets the width for output; the default is 79 characters.
-n *columns*	Sets the number of columns for the output.
-u	Leaves output unsorted.

RELATED COMMANDS

xfs

showfont

xlsfonts

fstobdf *option(s)*

PURPOSE

The **fstobdf** reads an X font from a font server and generates a BDF font.

OPTIONS

-fn *fontname*	Specifies the font from the X font server.
-server *servername*	Specifies the X font server.

RELATED COMMANDS

xfs

bdftopcf

fslsfonts

getkeycodes

PURPOSE

The **getkeycodes** command returns the scancode-to-keycode mapping table from the kernel.

id *option(s) username*

PURPOSE

The **id** command returns information about yourself or another specified *username*. This information includes user and group IDs, as well as effective user and group IDs when applicable.

OPTIONS

-g	Returns only group information.
-G	Returns supplementary group information.
-n	Returns names (not numbers) when used with the **-g**, **-G**, or **-u** options.
-r	Returns real user ID and group ID, not effective IDs.
-u	Returns user ID only.

GNU Command

info *option topic*

PURPOSE

The **info** command returns hypertext information about a given
topic, which can be a command or a subject. This information is
stored in GNU **texinfo** format in an outline fashion; once you have
launched **info** with a topic, you can move up and down the outline, looking at related topics. If you launch **info** without a topic,
you'll see the opening **info** screen (stored in **/usr/local/info/dir**),
explaining how **info** works and how you can maneuver through
the system.

OPTIONS

-d *directory*	Uses *directory* instead of the standard **info** directory (**/usr/local/info/dir**).
--dribble *file*	Stores keystrokes in *file*, which can then be used by the **--restore** option to go back to a specific place in an **info** session.
-f *file*	Uses *file* instead of the standard **info** file.
--help	Displays help information about the **info** command.
-n *node*	Specifies *node* to begin.
-o *file*	Sends information to *file* instead of standard output.
--restore *file*	Runs *file* (created with the **--dribble** option).
--subnodes	Displays subtopics.
--version	Displays **info** version.

RELATED COMMANDS

man

xman

kdb_mode   Keyboard Mode

kdb_mode *option(s)*

PURPOSE

The **kdb_mode** command returns the current keyboard mode or changes it.

OPTIONS

-a	Sets mode to XLATE (ASCII).
-k	Sets mode to MEDIUM-RAW.
-s	Sets mode to RAW.
-u	Sets mode to Unicode.

kill *option(s) PID*

PURPOSE

The **kill** command ends a process ID (PID). Only owners of the PID or a privileged user (i.e., root user) can kill a process.

This command is also built into the **bash** and C shells, although it works somewhat differently there.

OPTIONS

-l	Lists process IDs.
-signal	Specifies a *signal* returned by **ps -f** or **kill -l**.

RELATED COMMANDS

killall

ps

killall   Kill All Processes

killall *option(s) name*

PURPOSE

The **killall** command kills all processes by name, no matter how many processes are using a command. To kill a process running an executable file, use / somewhere in the command name.

OPTIONS

-i	Confirms that processes should indeed be killed.
-l	Lists process IDs.
-v	Runs in verbose mode; outcomes and IDs are listed.
-signal	Specifies a *signal* returned by **ps -f** or **killall -l**.

RELATED COMMANDS

kill

ps

X Window System Command

X WINDOW

listres *option(s) widget*

PURPOSE

The **listres** command returns a list of a widget's resource database. The class in which each resource is first defined, the instance and class name, and the type of each resource is listed. If no specific widgets or the **-all** option is given, a two-column list of widget names and their class hierarchies is printed.

OPTIONS

-all	Returns information for all known widgets and objects.
-nosuper	Ignores resources inherited from a superclass.
-variable	Identifies widgets by the names of the class-record variables, not the class name.
-top *name*	Specifies the *name* of the widget to be treated as the top of the hierarchy.
-format *printf-string*	Specifies the *printf*-style format string to print out the name, instance, class, and type of each resource.

login *username option*

PURPOSE

The **login** command is used to log in a Linux system. If you don't specify a *username* on the command line, the **login** command will prompt for one.

The command performs some administrative acts, such as setting the UID and the GID of the tty, as well as notifying the user if any mail is waiting. A root user can set up the **login** command to perform some basic authentication (see the manual pages for more information). In addition, the **login** command can be used to specify where a root user can log in; the list of **ttys** is at **/etc/securetty** and is checked by **login**. Additional security restrictions can be stored in **/etc/usertty**.

OPTIONS

-f	Skips a second login authentication; doesn't work properly under Linux.
-h *host*	Passes the name of a remote *host* to **login**; used by servers and set by the superuser.
-p	Preserves the previous environment used by **getty**.

logname   Prints Login Name

GNU Command

logname *option(s)*

PURPOSE

The **logname** command returns the login name of the calling process, as found in the file **/etc/utmp**. If no logname is found, an error message is generated.

OPTIONS

--help   Prints a short help message, then exits.

--version   Prints a version number, then exits.

makewhatis   Make Whatis

makewhatis *option(s) manpath*

PURPOSE

The **makewhatis** command builds and updates the **whatis** database used by the **whatis** and **apropos** databases. **Perl** must be installed for this to work.

OPTIONS

-u	Updates the database with only newer manual pages only. The default is to completely rebuild the database.
-w	Returns the **manpath**.

RELATED COMMANDS

apropos

man

xman

man *option(s) section title*

PURPOSE

The **man** command formats and displays pages from the online manual pages. These pages are the official documentation of the Linux and UNIX operating systems and come in a strict format. These are useful when seeking out obscure options and obscure commands.

Normally, you must match a specific command with the **man** command. However, you can begin searching in sections and narrow your search that way.

The **man** command will ask you if you want to save formatted pages. Saving them will save time if you revisit the **man** pages.

OPTIONS

-a	Displays all manual pages matching *title*, not just the first.
-c	Reformats a **man** page, even if a formatted page exists.
-C *config_file*	Specifies the **man.config** file to use; default is **/usr/lib/man.config**.
-d	Displays debugging information and not the actual **man** page.
-D	Displays debugging information and the **man** page.
-f	Calls a summary a la the **whatis** command.
-h	Prints a one-line summary of the **man** command.
-k	Same as the **apropos** command.
-m *system*	Searches for **man** pages at *system*.
-M *path*	Specifies the *path* to use when searching for **man** pages. By default, the environment variable MANPATH is used. If this is not set, the list is looked for at **/usr/lib/man.config**.
-p *string*	Specifies preprocessors to run before **nroff** or **troff**. Not very applicable to Linux.
-P *pager*	Specifies the pager to use; the default is **/usr/bin/less -is**.
-S *section_list*	Specifies the *section_list* to search.

Linux Commands, Organized by Group

Continued

-t	Uses **/usr/bin/groff -Tps -mandoc** to format the **man** page.
-w	Displays the locations of the **man** pages, not the actual pages.
-W	Displays the locations of the **man** pages, not the actual pages, with one filename per line.

RELATED COMMANDS

apropos

manpath

whatis

xman

man *option(s)*

PURPOSE

The **manpath** command sets or returns the path for the **man** command. It first checks the $MANPATH variable, then **/etc/manpath.conf**, and finally the user environment variables and the current working directory.

OPTIONS

-c	Uses **catpath** to find formatted pages.
-d	Prints debugging information.
-g	Creates MANPATH from global references in **/etc/manpath.conf**.
-m *system*	Searches *system* for **man** pages.
-q	Suppresses error messages.

RELATED COMMANDS

apropos

man

whatis

xman

X Window System Command

mcookie

PURPOSE

The **mcookie** command creates magic cookies (specifically, a 128-bit random hexadecimal number) for the **xauth** X authority system. It's usually used directly with the **xauth** command.

RELATED COMMANDS

xauth

minicom *option(s)*

PURPOSE

The **minicom** command launches a serial-communications package that somewhat resembles Telix. It features a dialing directory
with auto-redial, support for UUCP-style lock files on serial
devices, a separate script language interpreter, capture to file, multiple users with individual configurations, and more.

When you run **minicom**, there are a number of available options
and commands. Check the online manual pages for more information; also, go ahead and investigate **minicom** after you launch it.

There is an X Window System version, **xminicom**, available. It
works the same as **minicom**, except in a X window.

OPTIONS

-a	Sets attribute usage.
-c	Sets color usage.
-d	Directly dials a directory input on startup.
-l	Specifies a literal translation of characters with the high bit set.
-m	Overrides the command key with the **Alt** (**Meta**) key.
-M	Overrides the command key with the **Alt** (**Meta**) key, assuming that the **Alt** key is the 8th bit of the character high (sends 128 + character code).
-t	Sets a terminal type, overwriting the environment TERM variable.
-o	Skips initialization.
-s	Launches **minicom** in setup mode, with configura- tion menus displayed. (Only for root users.)
-z	Displays the terminal status line.

RELATED COMMAND

seyon

GNU Command

nice option *command argument(s)*

PURPOSE

The **nice** command allows you to set priorities for commands; if there's a heavy system load, the command won't run or use up too many system resources. The niceness can be set between 15 (the lowest priority) to -20 (the highest priority), but a privileged user is the only one that can set a negative priority.

If there are no arguments, the **nice** command prints the current scheduling priority.

 This description is of the GNU command, not the **nice** shell command.

OPTION

-*adjustment*   Adds *adjustment* instead of 10 to the command's priority.

GNU Command

nohup *command arguments*

PURPOSE

The **nohup** command ensures that a command specified on the same command line is run without interruption, even if you log off the system.

X Window System Command

oclock *option(s)*

PURPOSE

The **oclock** command launches a round analog clock.

OPTIONS

-fg *color*	Sets the color for the hands and the jewel of the clock.
-bg *color*b	Sets the background color.
-jewel *color*	Sets the color for the jewel.
-minute *color*	Sets the color for the minute hand.
-hour *color*	Sets the color for the hour hand.
-bd *color*	Sets the color for the window border.
-bw *width*	Sets the width for the window border.
-transparent	Pares the clock down to the jewel, the hands, and the border.

RELATED COMMAND

xclock

passwd *name password*

PURPOSE

The **passwd** changes your password. You can run **passwd** by itself and be prompted for the old password and then the new password.

A new password must be at least six characters long with both upper- and lowercase letters.

A privileged user can change the password for another user by specifying a username and a new password on the command line.

Linux Commands, Organized by Group

pathchk Check Path

 GNU Command

pathchk *option filename*

PURPOSE

The **pathchk** command checks whether *filename* is valid (that is, whether directories in the pathname are searchable) or portable (meeting length requirements).

OPTION

-p   Checks for POSIX portability.

pidof *option(s) program*

PURPOSE

The **pidof** command lists the process ID of a running program. You usually don't use it by itself, but rather in run-level change scripts. It's actually a link to the **killall5** command.

OPTIONS

-s	Returns only one PID.
-o *pids*	Omits *pids*.

RELATED COMMANDS

halt

init

reboot

shutdown

Linux Commands,
Organized by Group

pname *option(s) filename*

PURPOSE

The **pname** spreadsheet calculator works like a financial spread-sheet: you enter your data into rows and columns of cells, which can contain values, label strings, or expressions (formulas). Calculations are made in the same manner as a spreadsheet.

OPTIONS

-c	Starts **pname** with recalculation being done in column order.
-m	Starts **pname** with automatic recalculation disabled.
-n	Starts **pname** in quick numeric entry mode.
-r	Starts **pname** with recalculation done in row order.
-R	Starts **pname** with automatic newline action set to increment the row.
-x	Causes the **Get** and **Put** commands to encrypt and decrypt data files.
-C	Starts **pname** with automatic newline action set to increment the column.

COMMANDS

There is an extensive set of commands that can be used with **pname**. Check the online-manual pages for a complete listing.

GNU Command

printenv *variable*

PURPOSE

The **printenv** command prints your environment variables. If you specify a variable, this command returns information about that variable; if you don't specify a variable, the **printenv** command prints information about all variables.

Linux Commands, Organized by Group

95

ps *option(s)*

PURPOSE

The **ps** command returns information about a process. There's a long, complicated set of options available with this command; check the online-manual pages for more information.

rb *option(s)*

PURPOSE

The **rb** command is used to receive files using the Ymodem transfer protocol.

OPTIONS

a	Strips carriage returns and all characters beginning with the first **Ctrl-Z**.
b	Binary file-transfer override.
D	Output file data to **/dev/null**; for testing.
q	Works in quiet mode.
t *time*	Changes timeout to *time* tenths of seconds.
v	Works in verbose mode, causing a list of filenames to be appended to **/tmp/rzlog**.
y	Clobbers any existing files with the same name.

Linux Commands, Organized by Group

rdjpgcom *option jpeg_file*

PURPOSE

The **rdjpgcom** command reads a ***jpeg_file*** file and prints the text comments within. The JPEG format allows for "comment" (COM) blocks, ordinarily used for annotations and titles. The maximum size is 64K but there's no limit to how many blocks can be in a file.

OPTION

-verbose   Prints the JPEG image dimensions as well as the comments.

RELATED COMMANDS

cjpeg

djpeg

wrjpgcom

X Window System Command

reconfig *<Xconfig> XF86Config*

PURPOSE

The **reconfig** command converts an old **Xconfig** file (used in versions of XFree86 before 3.1) to a new **XF86Config** file. You'll need to edit the new **XF86Config** file.

renice *priority who option(s)*

PURPOSE

The **renice** command alters the scheduling priority of one or more running processes.

OPTIONS

-g	Forces *who* parameters to be interpreted as process group IDs.
-p	Resets *who* interpretation to be (the default) process IDs.
-u	Forces *who* parameters to be interpreted as user names.

reset

PURPOSE

The **reset** command resets the terminal. It calls on a number of commands to do so.

RELATED COMMANDS

reset

stty

tput

X Window System Command

resize *option(s)*

PURPOSE

The **resize** command sets the TERM and TERMCAP settings to the current **xterm** size. For this to happen, the command must be part of the command line or redirected to a file.

OPTIONS

-u	Generates Bourne shell commands, even if the Bourne shell is not the current shell.
-c	Generates C shell commands, even if the C shell is not the current shell.
-s [*rows columns*]	Uses Sun console escape sequences instead of the **xterm** escape codes. If *rows* and *columns* are specified, the **xterm** window will be asked to resize itself.

runscript *scriptname*

PURPOSE

The **runscript** command is a script interpreter for the **minicom** terminal software. It's usually used to automate logging into a remote UNIX server or a bulletin-board system.

The following commands are recognized within scripts: expect, send, goto, gosub, return, exit, print, set, inc, dec, if, timeout, verbose, sleep, break, and call. The actual scripting language is close to BASIC, and the **minicom** source code comes with two example scripts: **scriptdemo** and **unixlogin**.

RELATED COMMAND

minicom

ruptime *option(s)*

PURPOSE

The **ruptime** command shows the host status of a local machine. This is formed from packets broadcast by each host on the network once a minute. Machines for which no status report has been received for 11 minutes are shown as being down.

RELATED COMMANDS

rwho

uptime

rx *option(s) filename*

PURPOSE

The **rx** command receives files using the Xmodem transfer protocol.

OPTIONS

a	Strips carriage returns and all characters, beginning with the first **Ctrl-Z**.
b	Binary file-transfer override.
c	Request 16-bit CRC.
D	Output file data to **/dev/null**; for testing.
e	Forces sender to escape all control characters; normally XON, XOFF, DLE, **CR-@-CR**, and **Ctrl-X** are escaped.
q	Works in quiet mode.
t *time*	Changes timeout to *time* tenths of seconds.
v	Works in verbose mode, causing a list of filenames to be appended to **/tmp/rzlog**.

X Window System Command

X WINDOW

rxvt *option(s)*

PURPOSE

The **rxvt** command is a VT100 terminal emulator for the X Window System. It's actually a scaled-down version of the popular **xterm** terminal emulator, lacking some **xterm** features (Tektronix 4014 emulation, session logging, and toolkit-style configurability) that you might not miss. The advantage is that **rxvt** uses much less swap space than **xterm**. If you're operating in a tight-memory environment, you might want to consider switching from **xterm** to **rxvt**.

See the **xterm** command for more on resources, since **rxvt** accepts most of the same resources as **xterm**.

OPTIONS

-7	Runs in 7-bit mode, stripping the 8th bit from all characters typed on the keyboard.
-8	Runs in 8-bit clean mode, allowing the 8th bit of characters typed at the keyboard to be passed to the application.
-bg *color*	Sets the background color to *color*.
-bigfont *keysym*	Sets **Alt-***keysym* as the toggle for increasing the font size, instead of the default **Alt->**.
-C	Captures system console messages.
-display *display-name*	Opens **rxvt** on the specified *display-name*.
-e *command* [*options*]	Runs a *command* and its command-line *options* immediately after launching **rxvt**. If this option is used, it must be the last on the command line.
-fat	Uses a fat scrollbar instead of the default thin scrollbar.
-fg *color*	Sets the foreground color to *color*.
-font *fontname*	Sets the text font to *fontname*.

Continued

-geometry *geometry*	Opens the window with the specified X *geometry*.
-ic	Starts iconified.
-ls	Adds **-** to *argv[0]* of the window's shell, causing it to be a login shell.
-ls-	Takes away **-** to *argv[0]* of the window's shell, causing it to be a login shell. It also tells **rxvt** to stay iconified if it received a bell character.
-ma	Opens **rxvt** from an icon if it receives a bell character.
-meta *string*	Alters **alt+***key* setting. By default, **rxvt** sends an escape prefix when it receives an **alt** keypress. You can specify *escape*, *8thbit*, or *ignore* for *string*.
-n *text*	Sets the name in the window icon or the icon manager to *text*. It also sets the window's title in the titlebar to *text* unless the **-T** option is also set.
-pagedown *keysym*	Sets **Alt-***keysym* as the toggle for scrolling down a page, instead of the default **Alt-Next_Page**.
-pageup *keysym*	Sets **Alt-***keysym* as the toggle for scrolling up a page, instead of the default **Alt-Prev_Page**.
-secure *keysym*	Sets **Alt-***keysym* as the toggle for increasing the font size, instead of the default **Alt-s**.
-sl *number*	Saves *number* of lines of scrolled text, instead of the default 64.
-smallfont *keysym*	Sets **Alt-***keysym* as the toggle for decreasing the font size, instead of the default **Alt-<**.
-T *text*	Sets the string in the titlebar to *text*.
-thin	Uses a thin scrollbar no matter what.

Linux Commands, Organized by Group

rs *option(s)*

PURPOSE

The **rz** command is used to receive batch files using the Zmodem protocol. Pathnames are supplied by the sending program, and directories are made if necessary (and possible). Normally, the **rz** command is automatically issued by the calling Zmodem program, but some defective Zmodem implementations may require starting **rz** the old-fashioned way.

OPTIONS

a	Strips carriage returns and all characters beginning with the first **Ctrl-Z**.
b	Binary file-transfer override.
D	Output file data to **/dev/null**; for testing.
e	Forces sender to escape all control characters; normally, XON, XOFF, DLE, **CR-@-CR**, and **Ctrl-X** are escaped.
p	Skip file if destination file exists.
q	Works in quiet mode.
t *time*	Changes timeout to *time* tenths of seconds.
v	Works in verbose mode, causing a list of filenames to be appended to **/tmp/rzlog**.
y	Clobbers any existing files with the same name.

sb *option(s) filename*

PURPOSE

The **sb** command sends a file to another system using the
Ymodem protocol. There's a long list of options to this command;
see the online-manual page for more information.

script *option filename*

PURPOSE

The **script** command saves every character from a terminal session to a specified text *filename*. If no *filename* is specified, the characters are saved to **typescript**.

OPTION

-a *filename*   Appends keystrokes to existing *filename*.

X Window System Command

X WINDOW

seyon *option(s)*

PURPOSE

The **seyon** command is an X Window based telecommunications package for connection to remote clients and bulletin-board systems. All the options and command are present in the interface, although there are a few additional options that can be set when **seyon** is launched on the command line.

This command supports a wide range of resources, as well as a scripting language. See the online-manual pages for more information.

OPTIONS

`--`	Passes the rest of the command line to the terminal emulator.
-dial	Overrides the *dialAutoStart* resource.
-emulator *terminal-emulator*	Specifies a terminal emulator for **seyon**; if none is specified, then **xterm** is used.
-entries *entries-list*	Overrides the *defaultPhoneEntries* resource with *entries-list*.
-modems *device-list*	Overrides the existing **modems** resource.
-nodefargs	Does not pass along terminal-emulation options.
-noemulator	Tells **seyon** not to launch its own terminal emulator.
-script *script*	Executes *script* after **seyon** is launched.

Linux Commands, Organized by Group

111

shar *option(s) filename*

PURPOSE

The **shar** command creates shell archives (also known as shar files) that are in text format and can be mailed to another user, who can unpack and execute them with **bin/sh**.

OPTIONS

-a	Automatically generates headers.
-b	Uses **-X** as a parameter when compressing. (This is an option to be avoided, for many reasons.)
-B	Treats all files as binary files. (This is an option to be avoided, for many reasons.)
-c	Starts the shar file with a cut line.
-d *XXX*	Uses *XXX* as a file delimiter, instead of the default SHAR_EOF.
-f	Restores by filename only, instead of restoring an entire path.
-F	Forces the prefix character to be prepended to every line even if it is not required.
-g	Uses **-X** as a parameter to **gzip** when compressing. (This is an option to be avoided, for many reasons.)
-l *XX*	Limits shar file to *XX* kilobytes, but does not split files.
-L *XX*	Limits shar file to *XX* kilobytes, but splits files.
-m	Avoids generating **touch** commands to restore the file-modification dates when unpacking files from the archive.
-M	Determines if a file is text or binary and archives appropriately, which means that binary files are uuencoded. (This is an option to be avoided, for many reasons.)
-n *name*	Specifies the name of archive to be included in the header of the shar files.
-o *XXX*	Saves the archives to files ***XXX*.01** thru ***XXX*.nn** instead of standard output.

112

Continued

-p	Allows positional parameter options.
-P file.	Uses temporary files instead of pipes in the shar
-s *who@where*	Overrides automatically determined submitter name.
-S	Reads the list of files to be packed from standard input, not the filename.
-T	Treats all files as text.
-V	Produces vanilla shar files, which need only **sed** and **echo** in the unsharing environment.
-v	Works in quiet mode, disabling the inclusion of comments to be output when the archive is unpacked.
-w	Does not check with **wc -c** when an archive is unpacked.
-x	Overwrite existing files without checking.
-X	Checks before overwriting existing files.
-z	Uses **gzip** and **uuencode** to compress all files prior to packing. (This is an option to be avoided, for many reasons.)
-Z	Uses **compress** and **uuencode** to compress all files prior to packing. (This is an option to be avoided, for many reasons.)

RELATED COMMAND

unshar

shelltool *option(s)*

PURPOSE

The **shelltool** command runs a shell or a program in a terminal window. Despite what the **shelltool** documentation says, you don't need OpenWindows installed in your Linux environment to run this command, although there's actually little reason to run it unless you're using OpenWindows applications.

OPTIONS

-B *boldstyle*	Set the style for displaying bold text.
-C	Redirects system console output to **shelltool**.
-I *command*	Passes *command* to the shell.

X Window System Command

showfont *option(s)*

PURPOSE

The **showfont** command shows a font that's managed by the X font server. You need to have the X font server running for this command to work. The information returned includes font information, font properties, character metrics, and character bitmaps. You can use wildcards to match a wide range of fontnames.

OPTIONS

-bitmap_pad*n*	Sets the bitmap-padding unit of the font (*n* is 0, 1, or 2, where 0 is *ImageRectMin*, 1 is *ImageRectMaxWidth*, and 2 is *ImageRectMax*).
-extents_only	Displays only the character extents, not the bitmaps.
-end *char*	Determines the end of the range of the characters to display (*char* is a number).
-fn *name*	Specifies the font to display.
-lsb	Specifies the bit order of the font as LSBFirst (least significant bit first).
-LSB	Specifies the byte order of the font as LSBFirst (least significant byte first).
-msb	Specifies the bit order of the font as MSBFirst (most significant bit first).
-MSB	Specifies the byte order of the font as MSBFirst (most significant byte first).
-pad *n*	Sets the scanpad unit of the font (*n* is 8, 16, 32, or 64).
-server *host:port*	Specifies the X font server to contact.
-start *char*	Determines the start of the range of the characters to display (*char* is a number).
-unit *n*	Sets the scanline unit of the font (*n* is 8, 16, 32, or 64).
-noprops	Does not return font properties.

Linux Commands, Organized by Group

115

Continued

RELATED COMMANDS

fs

fslsfonts

xlsfonts

X Window System Command

showrgb *database*

PURPOSE

The **showrgb** command reads a *database* in the dbm database format and converts it back to source form, printing it to the screen.

skill *option(s) PID*

PURPOSE

The **skill** command signals or reprioritizes a specified process. It sends the *terminate* signal to a set of processes, or else it can give a signal (preceded with -) instead. To see a list of available signals, use the **skill -l** command line.

OPTIONS

-f	Runs in fast mode, where the machine-dependent code responsible for reading processes is allowed to make decisions to improve speed at the expense of error reporting.
-i	Runs in interactive mode, where the user is prompted with each process that is a candidate for action.
-v	Runs in verbose mode, where successful actions are displayed.
-w	Warns when processes are unreachable.
-n	Only displays process IDs.

RELATED COMMANDS

kill

nice

ps

renice

signal

snice

GNU Command

sleep *number*

PURPOSE

The **sleep** command pauses the system for a specified amount of time: *number*s seconds, *number*m minutes, *number*h hours, and *number*d days.

snice *priority PID*

PURPOSE

The **snice** command alters the scheduling priority of selected processes. By default, the new priority is +4, but an argument of the form *+n* (or *-n*) can be used to specify different values. An invalid priority is rounded down (or up) to the first acceptable value.

OPTIONS

-f	Runs in fast mode, where the machine-dependent code responsible for reading processes is allowed to make decisions to improve speed at the expense of error reporting.
-i	Runs in interactive mode, where the user is prompted with each process that is a candidate for action.
-v	Runs in verbose mode, where successful actions are displayed.
-w	Warns when processes are unreachable.
-n	Only displays process IDs.

RELATED COMMANDS

kill

nice

ps

renice

signal

skill

120

X Window System Command

smproxy *option(s)*

PURPOSE

The **smproxy** command allows X applications that do not support X11R6 session management to participate in an X11R6 session.

OPTIONS

-clientId *id*   Sets the session ID used in the previous session.

-restore *saveFile*   Sets the file used to save the state in the previous session.

splitvt *option(s) shell*

PURPOSE

The **splitvt** command runs two shells in two windows. The shell is your default shell (usually **xterm**).

To move between windows, use **Ctrl-W**.

OPTIONS

-login	Runs the programs under each window as though they were login shells.
-lower *command*	Runs *command* in the lower window.
-nologin	Doesn't allow the programs under each window to run as though they were login shells.
-norc	Doesn't load ~/**.splitvtrc**.
-rcfile *file*	Loads *file* as the startup file instead of ~/**.splitvtrc**.
-s *numlines*	Sets *numlines* (number of lines) for the top window.
-t *title*	Sets the *title* for the **xterm** titlebar.
-upper *command*	Runs *command* in the upper window.

X Window System Command

startx

PURPOSE

The **startx** command launches an X Window System session from a Linux command line. It's really a front end to the **xinit** command.

When you launch **startx**, it looks for a file called **xinitrc** in your home directory. This file contains information about your X Window setup, as well as what clients you want to run in conjunction with your X environment. Most of these clients should run in the background, except for the last client in the list, which should run in the foreground (this is usually a window manager).

Not many settings are associated with this command; you'll want to check **xinit** for more information.

RELATED COMMAND

xinit

strace *option(s) command*

PURPOSE

The **strace** command is used to trace system calls and signals. You use it to run a specified *command*; **strace** then tracks what system calls and signals are used by a process. The resulting information is printed to the screen or to a file (with the **-o** option). It's a useful command because you don't need the source code to see where a command is having problems.

OPTIONS

-a*column*	Aligns in a specific number of columns.
-c	Counts time, calls, and errors for each system call and reports a summary.
-d	Shows some debugging output of **strace** itself.
-eabbrev=*set*	Abbreviates the output from large structures.
-eraw=*set*	Prints undecoded (hexadecimal) arguments for the specifed set of system calls.
-eread=*set*	Prints all hexadecimal and ASCII information of the specified set.
-esignal=*set*	Traces only the specified subset of signals.
-etrace=*set*	Traces only *set* of system calls.
-everbose=*set*	Dereferences structures for the specified set of system calls.
-f	Traces child processes.
-i	Prints the instruction pointer at the time of the system call.
-o*filename*	Writes the output to *filename*.
-O *overhead*	Set the overhead for tracing system calls to *overhead* microseconds.
-p*pid*	Attaches to the process *pid* and begin tracing.
-q	Suppresses messages.
-r	Prints a relative timestamp upon entry to each system call.
-s *strsize*	Sets the maximum string size to print (the default is 32).

Continued

-Ssortby	Sort the output of the output from the **-c** option by sortby.
-t	Begins each line of the trace with the time of day.
-tt	Begins each line of the trace with the time of day, including microseconds.
-T	Returns the time spent in system calls.
-v	Provides verbose output.
-x	Prints non-ASCII strings in hexadecimal string format.
-xx	Print all strings in hexadecimal string format.

RELATED COMMANDS

ptrace

time

trace

Linux Commands, Organized by Group

strings *option(s) filename(s)*

PURPOSE

The **strings** command searches for printable strings in a file. By default, a string must be at least four characters in length before being displayed. This command is usually used to search for printable text in binary files.

 Most Linux implementations contain two versions of **strings**: the original UNIX version (**strings**) and the GNU version (**strings-gnu**), which is a more advanced version.

OPTIONS

-a	Searches through an entire object file for strings. The default is to search only the text and data segments of an object file.
-f	Prints the name of the file containing the string, as well as the string itself.
-n *num*	Sets the minimum number of characters in a string to *num*, instead of the default four.
-o	Prints the decimal offset of the string within the file, as well as the string itself.

RELATED COMMANDS

hexdump

strings-gnu

GNU Command

strings *option(s) filename(s)*

PURPOSE

The **strings** command searches for printable strings in a file. By default, a string must be at least four characters in length before being displayed. This command is usually used to search for printable text in binary files.

Most Linux implementations contain two versions of **strings**: the original UNIX version (**strings**) and the GNU version (**strings-gnu**), which is a more advanced version.

OPTIONS

-a	Searches through an entire object file for strings. The default is to search only the text and data segments of an object file.
-f	Prints the name of the file containing the string, as well as the string itself.
-n *num*	Sets the minimum number of characters in a string to *num*, instead of the default four.
-o	Prints the decimal offset of the string within the file, as well as the string itself.
-t {*o,x,d*}	Prints the decimal offset of the string within the file, as well as the string itself. The single character argument specifies the radix of the offset–octal, hexadecimal, or decimal.
—target=*bfdname*	Specifies an object code format other than your system's default format.

Continued

GNU Command

GNU COMMAND

stty *setting option(s)*

PURPOSE

The **stty** command returns and changes terminal settings. With no arguments, **stty** returns the current settings: baud rate, line discipline number, and line settings that have been changed from the values set by **stty sane**.

NON-OPTION SETTINGS

The opposite behavior can be toggled by preceding the setting with **-**.

clocal	Disables modem control signals.
cread	Allows input to be received.
crtscts	Enables RTS/CTS handshaking.
cs5 cs6 cs7 cs8	Sets character size to 5, 6, 7, or 8 bits.
cstopb	Uses two stop bits per character (one with -).
hup	Sends a hangup signal when the last process closes the tty.
hupcl	Sends a hangup signal when the last process closes the tty.
parenb	Generates parity bit in output and expect parity bit in input.
parodd	Sets odd parity (even parity when preceded with -).

INPUT SETTINGS

The opposite behavior can be toggled by preceding the setting with **-**.

brkint	Breaks cause an interrupt signal.
icrnl	Translates carriage return to newline.
ignbrk	Ignores breaks.
igncr	Ignores carriage return.
ignpar	Ignores parity errors.

Continued

imaxbel (np)	Enables beeping and not flushing input buffer if a character arrives when the input buffer is full.
inlcr	Translates newline to carriage return.
inpck	Enables input parity checking.
istrip	Strings high (8th) bit of input characters.
iuclc (np)	Translates uppercase characters to lowercase.
ixany (np)	Allows any character to restart output.
ixon	Enables XON/XOFF flow control.
ixoff tandem	Enables sending of stop character when the system input buffer is almost full, and of start character when it becomes almost empty again.
parmrk	Marks parity errors with a 255-0-character sequence).

OUTPUT SETTINGS

The opposite behavior can be toggled by preceding the setting with -.

bs1 bs0 (np)	Sets backspace delay style.
cr3 cr2 cr1 cr0 (np)	Sets carriage-return delay style.
ff1 ff0 (np)	Sets form-feed delay style.
nl1 nl0 (np)	Sets newline delay style.
ocrnl (np)	Translates carriage return to newline.
ofdel (np)	Uses delete characters for fill instead of null characters.
ofill (np)	Uses fill (padding) characters instead of timing for delays.
olcuc (np)	Translates lowercase characters to uppercase.
onlcr (np)	Translates newline to carriage return-newline.
onlret (np)	Uses newline as a carriage return.
onocr (np)	Does not print carriage returns in the first column.
opost	Postprocesses output.
tab3 tab2 tab1 tab0 (np)	Sets horizontal tab delay style.
vt1 vt0 (np)	Sets vertical tab delay style.

Linux Commands, Organized by Group

GNU Command

su *option(s)*

PURPOSE

The **su** command runs a shell with a substitute user and substitute group IDs. Basically, it allows you to login the system as a new user on a temporary basis, with a real and effective user ID, group ID, and supplemental groups. The shell is taken from password entry, or **/bin/sh** if none is specified there. If the user has a password, **su** prompts for it unless the user has a real user ID 0 (the super-user).

The current directory remains the same. If one or more arguments are given, they are passed as additional arguments to the shell.

OPTIONS

-	Makes the shell a login shell.
-c *command*	Passes command to the shell instead of starting an interactive shell.
-f	Passes the **-f** option to the shell. Use this with the C shell and not the Bourne Again SHell.
-m	Leaves the HOME, USER, LOGNAME, or SHELL alone.
-s *SHELL*	Runs *SHELL* instead of the user's shell.

subst *victims substitutions*

PURPOSE

The **subst** substitutes definitions into *filename(s)*. It's used mainly for customizing software to local conditions. Each *victim* file is altered according to the contents of the *substitutions* file.

The *substitutions* file contains one line per substitution. A line consists of two fields separated by one or more tabs. The first field is the *name* of the substitution, the second is the *value*. Neither should contain the character **#**, and use of text-editor metacharacters like **&** and \ is also unwise; the name in particular should be restricted to alphanumeric. A line starting with # is a comment and is ignored.

In the *victims*, each line on which a substitution is to be made (a *target* line) must be preceded by a *prototype* line. Substitutions are done using the **sed** editor.

Linux Commands, Organized by Group

sx *option(s) filename*

PURPOSE

The **sx** command sends a file to another system using the Xmodem protocol. There's a long list of options to this command; see the online-manual page for more information.

X Window System Command

X WINDOW

sxpm *option(s) filename*

PURPOSE

The **sxpm** displays an X pixmap (graphics) file and can convert files formatted with the XPM 1 or XPM 2 format to the newer XPM 3 format.

OPTIONS

-closecolors	Uses "close colors" before reverting to other visuals.
-color	Displays the colors specified for a color visual.
-cp *colorname pixelvalue*	Overrides *colorname* color to *pixelvalue*.
-d *display*	Specifies the display to connect to.
-g *geom*	Sets the window geometry (the default is the pixmap size).
-grey	Displays the colors specified for a greyscale visual.
-grey4	Displays the colors specified for a 4-color greyscale visual.
-hints	Sets *ResizeInc* hints for the window.
-icon *filename*	Creates an icon from pixmap created from the file *filename*.
-mono	Displays a monochrome visual.
-nod	Does not display the pixmap in a window; use this option when converting between formats.
-nom	Ignores a clipmask.
-o *filename*	Write to *filename*.
-pcmap	Uses a private colormap.
-plaid	Shows a plaid pixmap stored as data.
-sc *symbol colorname*	Overrides *symbol* color to *colorname*.
-sp *symbol pixelvalue*	Overrides *symbol* color to *pixelvalue*.
-rgb *filename*	Searches the RGB database in *filename* and writes them out instead of the default RGB values.
-v	Prints extensions in verbose mode.

Linux Commands, Organized by Group

systat *option(s) hostname*

PURPOSE

The **systat** command checks a specified *hostname* for system information via the hostname's own **systat** service. If the **systat** service isn't available, **daytime** or **netstat** information is queried.

OPTIONS

-n	Query the **netstat** service.
-p *port*	Specify a *port* on the host.
-s	Query the **systat** service (the default setting).
-t	Query the **daytime** service.
--netstat	Query the **netstat** service.
--port *port*	Specify a *port* on the host.
--systat	Query the **systat** service (the default setting).
--time	Query the **daytime** service.

sz *option(s) command*

PURPOSE

The **sz** command sends a file to another system using the Zmodem protocol. There's a long list of options to this command; see the online-manual page for more information.

tee *option filenames*

PURPOSE

The **tee** command sends the output of a command to two separate files. If the files already exist, the **tee** command will overwrite the contents of the files.

OPTION

-a　　　　　　　　　Appends routed information to *filenames*, but does not overwrite existing files.

EXAMPLE

```
$ tee output.kr output.pv
```

tload *option(s)*

PURPOSE

The **tload** command lists the system load in a graph.

OPTIONS

-d *delay*   Sets the delay between graph updates in seconds.
-s *scale*   Specifies a vertical scale.

RELATED COMMANDS

ps

top

top *option(s)*

PURPOSE

The **top** command lists the top processes on the system—that is, those processes that are using the most CPU time.

OPTIONS

d	Specifies the delay between screen updates.
q	Refreshes without any delay.
S	Lists CPU time of dead children as well.
s	Runs in secure mode.
i	Ignores zombie or idle processes.

EXAMPLE

```
$ top
```

RELATED COMMANDS

ps

tload

GNU Command

true

PURPOSE

The **true** command does nothing except return an exit status of 0, which means success. This is useful in shell scripts.

ul option(s) terminals

PURPOSE

The **ul** command changes all underscored text to underlined text. This is an issue for terminal users hooked to a Linux system, not to most Linux users.

OPTIONS

-i   Uses a separate line containing appropriate dashes for underlining.

-t *terminal*   Specifies a new terminal type.

unshar *option(s) filename*

PURPOSE

The **unshar** command unpacks a **shar** file.

OPTIONS

-c	Overwrites existing files.
-d *directory*	Changes the directory to *directory* before unpacking files.

RELATED COMMAND

shar

uptime

PURPOSE

The **uptime** command tells how long the system has been running, how many users are currently logged on, and the system-load averages for the past 1, 5, and 15 minutes.

RELATED COMMANDS

users

w

who

GNU Command

users *filename*

PURPOSE

The **users** command lists information about the users currently logged in the Linux system, based on information found in the **/etc/utmp** file. If you want information from another system file, you must specify it on the command line.

RELATED COMMANDS

who

X Window System Command

viewres *option(s)*

PURPOSE

The **viewres** program displays the widget class hierarchy of the Athena Widget Set.

OPTIONS

-top *name*	Specifies the name of the highest widget in the hierarchy to display.
-variable	Displays the widget variable names in nodes rather than the widget class name.
-vertical	Displays top to bottom rather left to right.

w *option(s) usernames*

PURPOSE

The **w** command returns information about the system: users currently logged in the system, usage statistics, and tasks that the users are performing. This is a combination of the **who**, **ps -a**, and **uptime** commands.

System information is returned in a header that includes the following: the current time, how long the system has been running, how many users are currently logged on, and the system-load averages for the past 1, 5, and 15 minutes.

User information includes the following: login name, tty name, the remote host, login time, idle, JCPU, PCPU, and the command line of their current process.

OPTIONS

-h	Suppresses printing of the header.
-u	Ignores the current user while figuring out the current process and CPU times.
-s	Suppresses printing of the login time, JCPU, or PCPU times.
-f	Prints the **from** (*remote hostname*) field.

RELATED COMMANDS

free

ps

top

uptime

whatis — Command Information

whatis *option(s) keyword*

PURPOSE

The **whatis** command invokes a miniature help system, but the topics are listed by keyword (which covers concepts) and not necessarily by commands. Because the Help information is returned as one line, there's not much depth concerning the keywords.

See the online-manual pages for a list of the available options.

EXAMPLE

```
$ whatis cat
```

RELATED COMMANDS

apropos

man

who *option(s) filename*

PURPOSE

The **who** command displays information about the system or a specific user. By itself, the **who** command lists the names of users currently logged in the system. As the command line **who am i**, the **who** command lists information about you.

See the online-manual pages for a list of the available options.

RELATED COMMANDS

w

whoami

whoami

PURPOSE

This is a one-word shortcut to the **who am I** variation of the **who** command. It's also the same as **id -un**.

EXAMPLE

```
$ whoami
kevin
```

RELATED COMMANDS

who

wish *filename arg*

PURPOSE

The **wish** command is a shell window encompassing the Tcl command language, the Tk toolkit, and a main program that reads commands from standard input or from a file. It creates a main window and then processes Tcl commands. It will continue processing commands until all windows have been deleted or until end-of-file is reached on standard input.

OPTIONS

-colormmap new	Creates a new private colormap instead of using the default colormap.
-sync	Executes X server commands synchronously, so errors are reported immediately.
-visual *visual*	Specifies the visual for the window.

RELATED COMMANDS

Tk

X Window System Command

X WINDOW

x11perf *option*

PURPOSE

The **x11perf** command runs a set of tests on an X server and reports on the speed performance. These tests are specific to the X Window System, using benchmarks to determine the time it takes to create and map windows, map a preexisting set of windows onto the screen, and to move windows around the screen. It also measures graphics performance for frequently used X applications, including mapping bitmaps into pixels, scrolling, and various stipples and tiles. The information is actually not as useful as you might think—you can't make any changes to the server (unless you're an experienced programmer and want to work with the X server source code), and you probably won't be changing your X server based on these numbers.

OPTIONS

-display *host:dpy*	Specifies the display.
-pack	Runs rectangle tests so that rectangles are packed next to each other.
-sync	Runs the tests in synchronous mode. This is a fairly worthless option.
-repeat *n*	Repeats each test *n* times. The default is five times.
-time *s*	Sets the time length of each test. The default is five seconds.
-all	Performs all the tests. Go out for a latte; this is a lengthy test.
-range *test1,[test2]*	Runs all the tests starting from the specified *test1* until the name *test2*, including both the specified tests. The testnames should be one of the options starting from **-dot**.
-labels	Generates just the descriptive labels for each test specified.
-fg *color/pixel*	Sets the foreground color or pixel value.

Continued

-bg *color/pixel*	Sets the background color or pixel value.
-clips *default_num*	Sets the default number of clip windows.
-ddbg *color/pixel*	Sets the color or pixel value to use for drawing the odd segments of a DoubleDashed line or arc. The default is the background color.
-rop *rop0 rop1* ...	Uses the specified raster ops (the default is GXcopy).
-pm *pm0 pm1* ...	Uses the specified planemasks (the default is ~0).
-depth *depth*	Uses a visual with *depth* planes per pixel. (The default is the default visual).
-vclass *vclass*	Uses a visual of *vclass*. It can be StaticGray, GrayScale, StaticColor, PseudoColor, TrueColor, or DirectColor. (The default is the default visual.)
-reps *n*	Sets the repetition count (the default is five seconds).
-subs *s0 s1* ...	Sets the number of subwindows to use in the Window tests. The default sequence is 4, 16, 25, 50, 75, 100, and 200.
-v1.2	Performs Version 1.2 tests using Version 1.2 semantics.
-v1.3	Performs Version 1.3 tests using Version 1.3 semantics.
-su	Sets the *save_under* window attribute to True on all windows. The default is False.
-bs *backing_ store_hint*	Sets the *backing_store* window attribute to the given value on all windows created by x11perf. This can be WhenMapped or Always. The default is NotUseful.

There are also a number of options that specify the exact tests to be performed. See the online-manual pages for specifics.

RELATED COMMANDS

X

xbench

x11perfcomp

X Window System Command

X WINDOW

x11perfcomp *option(s) filenames*

PURPOSE

The **x11perfcomp** merges the information returned by several **x11perf** tests in tabular format.

OPTIONS

-l *label_file*	Specifies a label file to use.
-r	Specifies that output should include relative server performance.
-ro	Specifies that output should include only relative server performance.

RELATED COMMANDS

x

x11perf

GNU Command

xargs *option(s) command*

PURPOSE

The **xargs** command reads arguments from standard input, delimited by blanks (protected with double or single quotes or a backslash) or newlines, and executes the *command* (if none is specified, **/bin/echo** will be run) one or more times with any *initial-arguments* followed by arguments read from standard input. Blank lines on the standard input are ignored. It exists with the following status:

0	successful
123	the command exits with status 1–125
124	the command exits with status 255
125	the command is killed by a signal
126	the command cannot be run
127	the command is not found
1	another error occurred

OPTIONS

-0, --null	Filenames are terminated by null characters instead of whitespace, and the quotes and backslash characters are not special characters.
-e[*eof-str*], --eof[=*eof-str*]	Sets the end-of-file string to *eof-str*.
-i[*replace-str*], --replace[=*replace-str*]	Replaces occurrences of *replace-str* in the initial arguments with names read from standard input.
-l[*max-lines*], --max-lines[=*max-lines*]	Uses *max-lines* nonblank input lines per command line; the default is one.
-n *max-args*, --max-args=*max-args*	Use *max-args* arguments per command line.
-p, --interactive	Prompts the user before each command is run.

Continued

-P *max-procs*, **--max-procs=***max-procs*	Runs up to ***max-procs*** processes at a time; the default is one.
-r, --no-run-if-empty	Commands without nonblanks are not run.
-s *max-chars*, **--max-chars=***max-chars*	Uses *max-chars* characters per command line, including the command and initial arguments and the terminating nulls at the ends of the argument strings.
-x, —exit	Exits if the size (as set by **-s**) is exceeded.

X Window System Command

xauth *option(s) command arg...*

PURPOSE

The **xauth** command displays and edits the authorization information used in connecting to the X server. This program doesn't actually contact the X server or create the authority information itself.

OPTIONS

-b	Breaks authority file locks before proceeding. This option is used to clean up stale locks.
-f *authfile*	Sets the authority file to use. The default is the file listed with the XAUTHORITY environment variable or the **.Xauthority** file in the user's home directory.
-i	Overrides authority file locks.
-q	Works in quiet mode and doesn't print unsolicited status messages.
-v	Works in verbose mode, printing status messages indicating the results of various operations.

There is a long list of commands for manipulating authority files;
see the online-manual pages for details.

Linux Commands,
Organized by Group

X Window System Command

xcalc *option(s)*

PURPOSE

The **xcalc** command launches a scientific calculator. It emulates a TI-30 or an HP-10C.

There are a number of user commands available after this program is launched; see the online-manual pages for details.

OPTIONS

-rpn   Uses Reverse Polish Notation, which emulates an HP-10C; if this is not set, the emulation is TI-30.

-stipple   Uses a stipple of the foreground and background colors for the background of the calculator; useful for monochrome displays.

xclipboard *option(s)*

PURPOSE

The **xclipboard** command displays the contents of the clipboard, which contains text selections typically copied there by other applications. A clipboard is how applications can cut and paste within the application and with other applications; text is copied first to the clipboard and then copied from there.

OPTIONS

-w   Wraps lines that are too long to be displayed in one line in the clipboard.

-nw   Does not wrap lines that are too long to be displayed in one line in the clipboard.

RELATED COMMANDS

X

xcutsel

X Window System Command

xclock *option(s)*

PURPOSE

The **xclock** command launches an analog or digital clock.

OPTIONS

-analog	Displays the time with a standard 12-hour analog clock face, with tick marks and hands.
-d, **-digital**	Displays the time with 24-hour digits.
-chime	Sets a chime for once on the half hour and twice on the hour.
-hd *color*	Sets the color of the hands on an analog clock.
-hl *color*	Sets the color of the edges of the hands on an analog clock.
-update *seconds*	Sets how often the clock should be updated, in *seconds*. When a clock is obscured by another window, it is not updated. If *seconds* is 30 or less, a seconds hand will be displayed on an analog clock. The default is 60 seconds.
-padding *number*	Sets the width (in pixels) of the padding between the window border and the clock text or picture. The default is 10 on a digital clock and 8 on an analog clock.

RELATED COMMAND

oclock

X Window System Command

xcmap *option(s)*

PURPOSE

The **xcmap** command displays the contents of the X color in a grid of squares corresponding to entries in the colormap.

X Window System Command

xcmsdb *option(s)*

PURPOSE

The **xcmsdb** command loads, queries, or removes Device Color Characterization data stored in properties on the root window of the screen as specified in Section 7 of the ICCCM. This information is necessary for proper conversion of color specification between device-independent and device-dependent forms.

OPTIONS

-query   Reads the XDCCC properties from the screen's root window.

-remove   Removes the XDCCC properties from the screen's root window.

-format *32|16|8*   Specifies the property format in bits per entry: 32, 16, or 8.

RELATED COMMAND

xprop

X Window System Command

xconsole *option(s)*

PURPOSE

The **xconsole** command displays messages that are usually sent to **/dev/console**.

OPTIONS

-daemon	Runs the command in the background.
-file *filename*	Specifies another device to monitor.
-notify	Displays applications that send new data to the console, even if the application is iconified. This is the default.
-nonotify	Toggles the **-notify** option.
-verbose	Adds an informative first line to the text buffer.
-exitOnFail	Exits when it is unable to redirect the console output.

X Window System Command

xcpustate *option(s)*

PURPOSE

The **xcpustate** displays various CPU states.

OPTIONS

-count *iterations*	Specifies a limit for the number of times the display should be updated. There is no default limit.
-interval *seconds*	Sets the interval between updates; the default is one second.

RELATED COMMANDS

xload

xperfmon

X Window System Command

xcutsel *option(s)*

PURPOSE

The **xcutsel** command copies the current selection into a cut buffer and makes a selection that contains the current contents of a cut buffer. The command is used as a bridge between applications that don't support selections and those that do, although most newer applications do support selections.

OPTIONS

-selection *name*   Sets the name of the function to use; the default is primary. The only supported abbreviations are *-select*, *-sel*, and *-s*.

-cutbuffer *number*   Sets the number of the cut buffer to use; the default is *0*.

RELATED COMMANDS

xclipboard

xterm

X Window System Command

X WINDOW

xdm *option(s)*

PURPOSE

The X Display Manager oversees X displays, whether they are on the local host or remote servers. It oversees the session, prompting for a login name and password, authenticating the user, and running the actual session (which begins and ends with the session manager). When a session is ended, **xdm** resets the X server and restarts the whole process. It can also coordinate between sessions via XDMCP, offering host menus to other terminals.

The **xdm** is a complex command that can't be covered in any depth here. Check out the online-manual page or a good X Window System reference before tackling this command.

N O T E

OPTIONS

-config *configuration_file*	Specifies the configuration file; the default is **<XRoot>/lib/X11/xdm/xdm-config**.
-debug *debug_level*	Sets the debugging level value, needed by the *DisplayManager.debugLevel* resource. However, this debugging information is worthless unless you want to work with the **xdm** source code.
-error *error_logfile*	Sets the value for the *DisplayManager.errorLogFile* resource.
-nodaemon	Uses *false* as the value for the *DisplayManager.daemonMode* resource.
-resources *resource_file*	Sets the value for the *DisplayManger*resources* resource. It contains configuration parameters for the authentication widget.

Continued

-server *server_entry*	Sets the value for the *DisplayManager.servers* resource.
-session *session_program*	Sets the value for the *DisplayManager*session* resource. This sets the program to run as the session after the user has logged in.
-udpPort *port_number*	Sets the value for the *DisplayManager.requestPort* resource, which controls the port number for XDMCP requests. Because XDMCP uses the registered UDP port 177, this is a setting you shouldn't change.
-xrm *resource_specification*	Sets an arbitrary resource.

RELATED COMMANDS

xauth

xinit

X Window System Command

xdpyinfo *option(s)*

PURPOSE

The **xdpyinfo** command displays information regarding a specific X server. It's most useful when looking for graphics information.

OPTIONS

-ext *extension*   Displays information about a specific *extension*. If no *extension* is named, then information about all the extensions is named.

-queryExtensions   Also displays numeric information (opcode, base event, base error) about protocol extensions.

RELATED COMMANDS

xprop

xrdb

xwininfo

X Window System Command

xev *option(s)*

PURPOSE

The **xev** command opens a window and then prints the event information about anything performed on or above the window (mouse movements, window resizings and movings, keyboard input, etc.).

OPTIONS

-id *windowid*	Monitors existing *windowid*, not a new window.
-name *string*	Specifies that *string* be assigned to the new window.
-rv	Displays the window in reverse video.
-s	Enables save-unders on the new window.

RELATED COMMANDS

xdpyinfo

xwininfo

X Window System Command

X WINDOW

xeyes *option(s)*

PURPOSE

The **xeyes** command creates a window with a set of eyes, which follows the movement of the cursor. An excellent way to waste X resources.

OPTIONS

-fg *foregroundcolor*	Sets the color for the pupils of the eyes.
-bg *backgroundcolor*	Sets the background color.
-outline *outlinecolor*	Sets the color for the eye outlines.
-center *centercolor*	Sets the color for the center of the eyes.

X Window System Command

xf86config

PURPOSE

The **xf86config** command generates an **XF86Config** file, needed before the X Window System can be run.

X Window System Command

xfd *option(s)*

PURPOSE

The **xfd** command displays all the characters in an X font in a window containing the name of the font being displayed, a row of command buttons, several lines of text for displaying character metrics, and a grid containing one glyph per cell.

OPTIONS

-fn *font*	Specifies the font to be displayed.
-center	Centers each glyph in its grid.

X Window System Command

xfontsel *option(s)*

PURPOSE

The **xfontsel** provides a point-and-click interface for displaying X Window System font names as well as samples of the fonts, and retrieving the full X Logical Font Description (XLFD) name for a font. You can choose to see all the fonts–which results in a voluminous output–or you can whittle down the list of files by combining a wildcard with the *-pattern* option.

RELATED COMMAND

xfd

Linux Commands,
Organized by Group

X Window System Command

xfractint *option(s)*

PURPOSE

The **xfractint** command is a fractal generator and a port of the MS-DOS **fractint** program.

OPTIONS

-disk	Saves images to file instead of to the screen.
-fast	Updates images frequently (every five seconds), if you're using a fast display.
-fixcolors *num*	Sets the number of colors, as a power of two.
-onroot	Displays images on the root window. You probably won't want to do this, as rubberband zoom boxes don't work on the root window.
-private	Grabs as many color as possible in a private colormap.
-share	Shares the current colormap.
-simple	Specifies simpler keyboard handling.
-slowdisplay	Updates images infrequently, if you're using a slow display.
@*filename*	Loads parameters from *filename*.

X Window System Command

X WINDOW

xfs *option(s)*

PURPOSE

The **xfs** command launches the X Window System font server. It works exactly as the name implies: It serves rendered fonts to requesting applications. This command is configured by a system administrator, who sets it up to launch every time X is launched.

OPTIONS

-config *configuration_file*	Sets the font-server configuration file.
-port *tcp_port*	Specifies the TCP port number.

Linux Commands, Organized by Group

X Window System Command

xgc *option(s)*

PURPOSE

The **xgc** command launches a demo of X graphics capabilities. See the online-manual pages for a list of the options.

X Window System Command

xhost +/- *hostname*

PURPOSE

The **xhost** programs sets the names of hosts or users authorized to make connections to the X server. This isn't a particularly sophisticated method of access control. A hostname preceded by a plus sign (+) is added to the access list, while a hostname preceded by a minus sign (-) is deleted from the access list. Two plus signs (++) allows everyone access, while two minus signs (—) restricts access to those on the access list. With no options, **xhost** will return the current status.

RELATED COMMAND

xdm

Linux Commands, Organized by Group

X Window System Command

xieperf *options*

PURPOSE

The **xieperf** command evaluates the XIE server extension. A complete set of the tests can be found in the online manual pages.

OPTIONS

-all	Runs all tests. This may take a while.
-cache *n*	Sets a photomap cache of *n* entries.
-depth *depth*	Specifies *depth* planes per pixel.
-DirectColor	Uses a DirectColor visual.
-DIS	Runs tests covering only the protocol requests found in the DIS subset of XIE.
-display *host:dpy*	Sets the display.
-errors	Tests error-event generation.
-events	Tests event generation.
-GrayScale	Uses a GrayScale visual for testing.
-images *path*	Sets the *path* for loading images.
-labels	Generates the labels for all the scripts, but does not run the tests.
-loCal	Skips test calibration.
-mkscript	Generates a script file suitable for use with the script option.
-PseudoColor	Uses a PseudoColor visual for testing.
-range *test1 test2*	Runs tests beginning with *test1* and ending with *test2*, including the two specified tests.
-repeat *n*	Repeats each test *n* times (the default is two times).
-reps *n*	Sets the inner-loop repetitions to *n*.
-sync	Runs the tests in synchronous mode.
-script *file*	Runs the tests specified in a script file named *file*.

Continued

-showlabels	Prints a test label on the screen, indicating the test to be run. This is useful to figure out if any tests are crashing the system.
-showevents	Prints information about event and error tests,
-showtechs	Provides a long lists of techniques used by the XIE server.
-StaticColor	Uses a StaticColor visual.
-StaticGray	Uses a StaticGray visual.
-tests	Shows available tests.
-time *s*	Sets the time each test should run, in *s* seconds (the default is five seconds).
-timeout *s*	Sets the time that the test will wait for an event that may never arrive.
-TrueColor	Uses a TrueColor visual.
-WMSafe	Provides more accurate results by informing **xieperf** that it is running in a window-manager environment.

RELATED COMMANDS

x11perf

x11perfcomp

X Window System Command

X WINDOW

xinit *client option(s)*

PURPOSE

The **xinit** command launches the X Window System (as called from **startx**) and can also launch a first client in situations where a system cannot start X directly from **/etc/init**.

In most situations, however, you won't be launching an application from the command line. In these situations, there's a sequence of steps that **xinit** uses when starting X:

- It first looks for a file called **.xinitrc**, which runs as a shell script to start client programs.

- If this file does not exist, **xinit** uses *xterm -geometry +1+1 -n login -display :0* as a command line.

- If no server program exists on the command line, **xinit** looks for **.xserverrc** in the user's home directory.

- If this file does not exist, **xinit** uses *X :0* as a default server.

When you set up an **.xserverrc** script, you must be sure to launch the read X server.

There's a science to writing an **.xinitrc** if you choose not to use the mechanized tools for configuring X Window System. You must be sure that the applications launched in this file are run in the background, except for the last program (usually a window manager), which should run in the foreground in order to ensure that the script doesn't fail.

X Window System Command

xkill *option(s)*

PURPOSE

The **xkill** command forces an X server to sever connections to clients. You can specify a program by a resource identifier. If you do not do this, **xkill** will display a little skull-and-crossbones cursor, and the window underneath this cursor of death will be killed when you click on it.

This is not the best way to go about closing programs, so use this command with caution.

OPTIONS

-all	Kills all clients with top-level windows on the screen. Use this only as a last resource.
-button *number*	Specifies the mouse button to use with the cursor of death. The default is the left mouse button. You can use *all* instead of a number to specify that any button be used with the cursor of death.
-display *displayname*	Specifies the server to contact.
-id *resource*	Specifies the client to be killed.
-frame	Tells **xkill** that you want to kill direct children of the root.

RELATED COMMAND

xwininfo

Linux Commands, Organized by Group

X Window System Command

xload *option(s)*

PURPOSE

The **xload** command periodically polls for the system-load average and relays the information in a histogram.

OPTIONS

-hl *color*	Sets the color of the scale lines in the histogram.
-jumpscroll *pixels*	Sets the number of *pixels* to offset when the graph reaches the right edge of the window. The default is half the width of the current window.
-label *string*	Specifies the *string* to put as the label above the load average.
-lights *n*	Displays the load average with keyboard LEDs. When the load level reaches *n*, **xload** lights the first *n* keyboard LEDs, but displays nothing on the screen.
-nolabel	Displays no label above the load graph.
-scale *integer*	Sets the minimum number of tick marks in the display histogram.
-update *seconds*	Returns new information every *seconds*. The default is 10, and the minimum is 1.

X Window System Command

xlock *option(s)*

PURPOSE

The **xlock** command locks an X display until a password is entered. When this happens, all new server connections are refused, the screen saver is disabled, the mouse cursor is turned off, and the screen is blanked.

OPTIONS

-cycles *num*	Sets the number of cycles until a pattern times out.
-display *dsp*	Sets the display to lock.
-font *fontname*	Sets the *fontname* to be used on the login prompt screen.
-forceLogout *minutes*	Sets *minutes* before auto-logout.
-info *textstring*	Displays informational text on the login screen; the default is *Enter password to unlock; select icon to lock.*
-invalid *textstring*	Sets *textstring* to display when a password is deemed invalid; the default is *Invalid login.*
-lockdelay *seconds*	Sets the number of *seconds* before a screen needs a password to be unlocked.
-logoutButtonHelp *textstring*	Sets *textstring* as the message shown outside the logout button it is displayed.
-logoutButtonLabel *textstring*	Sets *textstring* as a messages shown inside the logout button when the logout button is displayed; the default is *Logout.*
-logoutFailedString *textstring*	Sets the *textstring* to be displayed when a logout fails. The default is *Logout attempt FAILED.\n Current user could not be automatically logged out.*
-message *textstring*	Specifies a message, not a fortune.
-messagefile *filename*	Specifies a file where the contents are the message.
-messagesfile *formatted-filename*	Specifies a file containing a fortune message. The first entry is the number of fortunes, the next line contains the first fortune.

181

Continued

-mfont *mode-fontname*	Specifies the font to be used with the marquee and nose modes.
-mode *modename*	Sets a display mode.
-mono	Displays in monochrome.
-name *resource*	Uses *resource* instead of the Xlock resource when configuring **xlock**. There are 45 of them; check out the online manual pages for a complete list. (Hint: we like the **nose** mode.)
-nice *nicelevel*	Sets the nice level.
-password *textstring*	Shows *textstring* in front of the password prompt; the default is *Password:*.
-program *programname*	Specifies a program to be used to generate a fortune message.
-resources	Displays the default resource file.
-saturation *value*	Sets the saturation of the color ramp.
-timeout *seconds*	Sets the number of *seconds* before the password screen times out.
-username *textstring*	Shows *textstring* in front of the username prompt; the default is *Name:*.
-validate *textstring*	Sets *textstring* to display when validating a password; the default is *Validating login*.
-/+allowroot	Allows the root user to login the system.
-/+echokeys	Displays ? for each key entered. The default is to display nothing.
-/+enablesaver	Keeps the screen saver running.
-/+grabmouse	Grabs the mouse and keyboard (the default).
-/+inroot	Runs **xlock** in a root window. This doesn't actually lock the system.
-/+install	Allows **xlock** to use it own colormap. This will not work with the **fvwm** window manager.
-/+inwindow	Runs **xlock** in a window.
+/-nolock	Works as a screen saver.
-/+remote	Allows you to lock remote X terminals. You should not be locking someone else's X terminal.
-/+timeelapsed	Tells you how long a machine has been locked.
-/+usefirst	Uses the first key pressed as the first key of the password. The default is to ignore the first key, since it's used to get the attention of the system.

X Window System Command

xlogo *option*

PURPOSE

The **xlogo** command displays the X logo. This is useful at trade shows, when gawkers want to know what operating system is running.

OPTION

-shape   Displays the logo window as a shape instead of a rectangle.

X Window System Command

X WINDOW

xlsatoms *option(s)*

PURPOSE

The **xlsatoms** command lists interned atoms from the server. All atoms starting from 1 (the lowest atom value defined by the protocol) are listed.

OPTIONS

-format *string*	Specifies the **printf**-style string used to list each atom. The default is *%ld\t%s*.
-name *string*	Specifies a single atom to list.
-range [*low*]-[*high*]	Specifies the range of atom values to check.

X Window System Command

xlsclients *option(s)*

PURPOSE

The **xlsclients** command lists the client applications running on a
display.

OPTIONS

-a   Lists clients on all screens, not just those on the
              default screen.

-l   Returns information in the long format, giving the
              window name, icon name, and class hints in addi-
              tion to the machine name and command string
              shown in the default format.

-m *maxcmdlen* Specifies the maximum number of characters in a
                command to print out. The default is 10,000.

RELATED COMMANDS

xprop

xwininfo

Linux Commands,
Organized by Group

X WINDOW

X Window System Command

xlsfonts *option(s)*

PURPOSE

The **xlsfonts** command lists the fonts installed on an X Window System. You can choose to see all the fonts—which results in a voluminous output—or you can whittle down the list of files by combining a wildcard with the *-pattern* option.

OPTIONS

-1	Prints information in a single column.
-C	Returns information in multiple columns.
-fn *pattern*	Specifies the font *pattern* to search for.
-l	Lists font attributes on one line, along with its name.
-ll	Lists font properties in addition to **-l** output.
-lll	Lists character metrics in addition to **-ll** output.
-m	Lists minimum and maximum bounds of each font.
-n *columns*	Sets the number of columns.
-o	Performs **OpenFont** (and **QueryFont**, if appropriate) instead of **ListFonts**.
-u	Leaves output unsorted.
-w *width*	Sets the width in characters of the returned information; the default is 79.

RELATED COMMANDS

xfd

X Window System Command

xmag *option(s)*

PURPOSE

The **xmag** command displays a portion of the screen. You can either specify a region on the command line or use a square with a pointer that you can drag over an area to be enlarged. After deciding on an area, a new window will appear, with the area magnified. Typing **Q** or **Ctrl-C** will end the program.

OPTIONS

-source *geom*   Sets the size and location of the area to be magnified.

-mag *integer*   Sets the level of magnification; 5 is the default.

X Window System Command

xman *option(s)*

PURPOSE

The **xman** command displays online manual pages. It's really an X Window System version of the **man** command, albeit with a prettier interface. See the entry for **man** for more information about Linux online help.

OPTIONS

-bothshown   Shows both a manual page and the manual
                        directory.

-helpfile *filename*   Specifies a helpfile other than the default.

-notopbox   Starts without an opening menu.

-pagesize *WxH+X+Y*   Sets the size and location of all the manual
                        pages.

RELATED COMMANDS

apropos

man

whatis

X Window System Command

X WINDOW

xmessage *option(s)*

PURPOSE

The **xmessage** command displays a message or query in a window. It's basically an X-based **/bin/echo**.

OPTIONS

-buttons *button*	Creates one button for each comma-separated *button* argument.
-default *label*	Defines the button with a matching *label* to be the default.
-file *filename*	Displays *filename*.
-print	Prints the label of the button pressed to standard output.

RELATED COMMANDS

cat

echo

Linux Commands,
Organized by Group

X Window System Command

xmodmap *option(s) filename*

PURPOSE

The **xmodmap** command modifies keymaps under the X Window System. These are used to convert event keystrokes into keysyms.

OPTIONS

-e *expression*	Executes *expression*.
-n	Lists potential changes without actually making the changes.
-pk	Displays the current keymap table on standard output.
-pke	Displays the current keymap table on standard output in the form of expressions that can be fed back to **xmodmap**.
-pm	Displays the current modifier map on standard output.
-pp	Displays the current pointer map on standard output.

RELATED COMMAND

xev

X Window System Command

xon option(s) command

PURPOSE

The **xon** command runs an X program on a remote machine. The default is **xterm -ls**.

OPTIONS

-access	Runs **xhost** locally to add the remote host to the host access list in the X server. **Xhost** needs permission to modify the access list if this is to work.
-debug	Works in debugging mode, leaving stdin, stdout, and stderr intact.
-name *window-name*	Specifies an application name and window title for the default **xterm** command.
-nols	Doesn't pass along the **-ls** option to **xterm**.
-screen *screen-no*	Sets the screen number of the DISPLAY variable passed to the remote command.
-user *user-name*	Passes along a username other than your own to the remote machine.

X WINDOW

X Window System Command

xpaint *option(s) filename*

PURPOSE

The **xpaint** command launches a paint program. It allows for the editing of multiple images simultaneously and supports various formats, including PPM, XBM, TIFF, and more.

OPTIONS

-size	Sets the default width and height for new images.
-12	Uses a 12-bit PseudoColor visual.
-24	Uses a 24-bit TrueColor visual.

X Window System Command

xpmroot *filename*

PURPOSE

The **xpmroot** sets the root window of the current X display to an XPM pixmap, as specified by *filename* on the command line.

X Window System Command

xprop *option(s)*

PURPOSE

The **xprop** command displays window and font properties in an X server. You can choose a window or a font on the command line, or you can click on a window to display its properties.

OPTIONS

-f name *format [dformat]*	Specifies the *format* and *dformat* for *name*.
-font *font*	Returns the properties of font *font*.
-frame	Returns information about the window-manager frame instead.
-fs file	Uses *file* as the source of more formats for properties.
-grammar	Prints out a detailed grammar for all command-line options.
-id *id*	Selects window *id* on the command line as the window to be examined.
-name *name*	Specifies that a window named *window* is the window to be examined.
-len *n*	Returns *n* bytes of any property (or less).
-notype	Ignores the type of each property.
-remove *property-name*	Removes the name of a property from a window.
-root	Uses the root window as the window of the client to be examined.
-spy	Examines window properties indefinitely, looking for property change events.

RELATED COMMANDS

xwininfo

X Window System Command

X WINDOW

xrdb *option(s) filename*

PURPOSE

The **xrdb** command returns or sets the RESOURCE_MANAGER property on the root window of screen 0, or the SCREEN_RESOURCES property on the root window of any or all screens, or everything combined. You normally run this program from your X startup file.

The sort of information covered here includes color settings, font management, and more. The RESOURCE_MANAGER property is used for resources that apply to all screens of the display. The SCREEN_RESOURCES property on each screen specifies additional (or overriding) resources to be used for that screen.

OPTIONS

-all   Performs operations on the RESOURCE_MANAG-
                    ER as well as SCREEN_RESOURCES on every
                    screen of the display.

-backup *string*   Appends *string* to backup files.

-cpp *filename*   Specifies the pathname of the C pre-processor pro-
                    gram to be used.

-edit *filename*   Places the contents of the specified properties into
                    filename.

-global   Performs operations only on the
                    RESOURCE_MANAGER property.

-load   Loads input as the new value of the specified prop-
                    erties, replacing the old contents.

-merge   Merges input with the current contents of the speci-
                    fied properties, instead of replacing them.

-n   Changes to the specified properties (when used with
                    -load, **-override**, and **-merge**) or to the resource file
                    (when used with **-edit**) should be shown on the stan-
                    dard output, but should not be performed.

Continued

-nocpp	Does not run the input file through a preprocessor before loading it into properties.
-override	Adds input to, instead of replacing, the current contents of the specified properties, as new entries override previous entries.
-query	Prints the current contents of the specified properties to standard output.
-quiet	Suppresses information about duplicate entries.
-remove	Removes specified properties from the server.
-retain	Does not reset the server if **xrdb** is the first client. The usefulness of this option is highly debatable, as there's very little chance that **xrdb** will ever be the first client of any X server.
-screen	Performs operations only on the SCREEN_RESOURCES property of the default screen of the display.
-screens	Performs operations only on the SCREEN_RESOURCES property of the default screen of the display. For **-load**, **-override**, and **-merge**, the input file is processed for each screen.
-symbols	Symbols defined for the preprocessor are printed to standard output.
-D_name_[=_value_]	Defines symbols to use with the following conditions:
-I_directory_	Specifies a directory to look to for include files.
-U_name_	Removes any definitions of this symbol.

X Window System Command

X WINDOW

xrefresh *option(s)*

PURPOSE

The **xrefresh** command repaints all or part of your screen. It maps a window on top of the desired area of the screen and then immediately unmaps it, causing refresh events to be sent to all applications.

OPTIONS

-black	Shuts down the monitor for a second before repainting the screen.
-none	Repaints all windows without any gimmicks. This is the default, as well it should be.
-root	Uses the root window background.
-solid *color*	Uses a solid background of the specified color.
-white	Uses a white background, which causes the screen to appear to flash brightly before repainting.

X Window System Command

X WINDOW

xset *option(s)*

PURPOSE

The **xset** command is used to set various aspects of X Window System. These settings will be reset to default values when you log out.

OPTIONS

b	Sets bell volume, pitch, and duration. You can set this with three numerical parameters, a preceding dash (-), or an on/off flag. If no parameters are given, the system defaults are restored.
bc	Controls bug-compatibility mode. Ancient X Window System clients (those created before Release 4) sent illegal requests to the server, and old servers would ignore the illegal request.
c	Specifies the key click. You can set this with an optional value, a preceding dash (-), or an on/off flag. If no parameters are given, the system defaults will be used. If the dash or off flag is used, keyclick will be disabled. A value between 0 and 100 indicate volume as a percentage of the maximum.
fp=*path*	Sets the font path.
fp *default*	Resets the font path to the default.
fp *rehash*	Resets the font path to its current value, telling the server to reread the font databases in the current font path.
-fp *entries*	Removes *entries* from the font path. Entries must be a comma-separated list.
+fp *entries*	Prepends *entries* to the font path. Entries must be a comma-separated list.
fp+	Appends *entries* to the font path. Entries must be a comma-separated list.

198

Continued

led
Sets the keyboard LEDs. It accepts an optional integer, a preceding dash (-) or an on/off flag. With no parameters, all LEDs are turned on. With a preceding dash or the *off* flag, all LEDs are turned off. A value between 1 and 32 indicates that LEDs will be turned on or off depending on the existence of a preceding dash.

m
Controls the mouse parameters, one of *acceleration* or *threshold*. *Acceleration* is an integer or a simple fraction, while *threshold* is an integer. The mouse will go *acceleration* times as fast when it travels more than *threshold* pixels in a short time. If no parameters or the *default* flag is used, the system defaults will be used.

p
Sets pixel color values. The parameters are the colormap entry numbers in decimal and a color specification. The root background colors may be changed on some servers by altering the entries for *BlackPixel* and *WhitePixel*. A server may choose to allocate those colors privately, in which case an error will be generated.

r
Sets the autorepeat rate. A preceding dash or the off flag disables autorepeat. With no parameters or the on flag, autorepeat will be enabled.

s
Sets the screen-saver parameters. Flags can be blank/noblank, expose/noexpose, on/off, and activate/reset.

q
Returns the current settings.

RELATED COMMANDS

xmodmap

xrdb

xsetroot

Linux Commands,
Organized by Group

X Window System Command

xsetroot *option(s)*

PURPOSE

The **xsetroot** command controls the settings for the background (root) window on an X display. You really shouldn't be passing along these parameters a lot; typically, you'll experiment with the command line and then send the results in your X startup file.

With no options, the system restores to its default state. Only one of the background color/tiling changing options (**-solid**, **-gray**, **-grey**, **-bitmap**, and **-mod**) may be specified at a time.

OPTIONS

-bg *color*	Sets *color* as the background color.
-bitmap *filename*	Sets the bitmap in *filename* to the window pattern.
-cursor *cursorfile maskfile*	Specifies a new cursorfile.
-cursorname *cursorname*	Specifies a new cursor from the standard cursor set.
-def	Resets unspecified attributes to the default values.
-fg *color*	Specifies *color* as the foreground color.
-gray	Makes the background gray.
-grey	Makes the background gray.
-mod x_y	Implements a plaid-like grid pattern on your screen. The *x* and *y* values are integers ranging from 1 to 16.
-rv	Reverses the foreground and background colors.
-solid *color*	Sets *color* as the background of the root window.
-name *string*	Sets *string* as the name of the root window.

RELATED COMMANDS

xrdb

xset

X Window System Command

xsm *option(s)*

PURPOSE

The **xsm** command launches the X Session Manager. A session is a group of applications in various states. You can set up various sessions for various purposes. After you exit the session, the application states are saved as part of the session.

When you run the command, a session menu is loaded, allowing you to choose between sessions.

OPTION

-session *sessionName*   Loads *sessionName* without the session menu appearing.

RELATED COMMANDS

smproxy

rstart

X Window System Command

xsmclient

PURPOSE

The **xsmclient** tests the X session manager.

RELATED COMMAND

xsm

X Window System Command

xspread *option(s) filename*

PURPOSE

The **xspread** command is a very sophisticated spreadsheet running under the X Window System. You'll want to check the online documentation (specifically, the Xspread Reference Manual in the file **xspread.tex**) to get an overview of its many capabilities.

OPTIONS

-c	Recalculates in column order. The default is row order.
-m	Works with manual recalculation; only values beginning with @ are recalculated. Otherwise, all cells are recalculated when a value changes (the default).
-n	Works in standard data-entry mode, where a user must specify if the data-entry item is numeric or a label.
-r	Recalculates in row order (the default).
-x	Encrypts files.

RELATED COMMANDS

bc

sc

Linux Commands, Organized by Group

X Window System Command

X WINDOW

xstdcmap *option(s)*

PURPOSE

The **xstdcmap** command defines standard colormap properties. You usually don't use this command from the command line, but rather as part of your X startup script.

OPTIONS

-all	Defines all six standard colormap properties.
-best	Indicates that RGB_BEST_MAP should be defined.
-blue	Indicates that RGB_BLUE_MAP should be defined.
-default	Indicates that RGB_DEFAULT_MAP should be defined.
-delete *map*	Deletes a specified standard colormap property, one of **default**, **best**, **red**, **green**, **blue**, **gray**, or **all**.
-gray	Indicates that RGB_GRAY_MAP should be defined.
-green	Indicates that RGB_GREEN_MAP should be defined.
-red	Indicates that RGB_RED_MAP should be defined.

X Window System Command

xterm *option(s)*

PURPOSE

The **xterm** command launches a terminal-emulation window under X. It essentially gives you access to a Linux command line via a window, and as such is probably the most-used X command in Linux.

OPTIONS

There are many options to **xterm**, including one that controls columns in obscure terminal emulations. Here, we'll cover the major options; check the online-manual pages for a more detailed listing of options.

-ah	Always highlights the text cursor.
+ah	Highlights the text cursor if it's over the window with focus.
-aw	Turns on auto-wraparound.
-b *number*	Sets the size of the inner border (the distance between the outer edge of characters and the window border) in pixels. The default is 2.
-cr *colorb*	Sets the color for the text cursor.
-e *program args*	Runs *program* in the **xterm** window. This option must appear last in the command line.
-fb *font*	Sets the font for the bold text.
-j	Sets jump scrolling, where multiple lines can be scrolled at a time.
-ls	Sets the shell started in the **xterm** window as a login shell.
-mc *milliseconds*	Sets the maximum time between multiclick selections.
-ms *color*	Sets the color for the pointer cursor.

Linux Commands, Organized by Group

Continued

-rw	Turns on reverse wraparound.
-s	Sets scrolling asynchronously, so that the screen does not need to be kept up to date while scrolling.
-sb	Saves scrolled lines and displays a scrollbar.
-sl *number*	Sets the *number* of lines to save that have been scrolled off the top of the screen. The default is 64.
-tm *string*	Sets terminal setting keywords and the characters bound to those functions. Keywords are: intr, quit, erase, kill, eof, eol, swtch, start, stop, brk, susp, dsusp, rprnt, flush, weras, and lnext.
-tn *name*	Sets the terminal type in the TERM environment variable.
-vb	Flashes the window—that is, a visual bell—instead of ringing a system bell.

RELATED COMMANDS

tty

X Window System Command

xv *option(s) filename*

PURPOSE

The **xv** image editor displays images in GIF, JPEG, TIFF, PBM, PGM, PPM, X11 bitmap, Utah Raster Toolkit RLE, PDS/VICAR, Sun Rasterfile, BMP, PCX, IRIS RGB, XPM, Targa, XWD, PostScript, and PM formats. It can also be used to generate screen captures in any of these formats.

To use this command you'll want to check out the documentation, which runs to over 100 pages. It's in PostScript format and can be found at **/usr/doc/xv/xvdocs.ps.**

RELATED COMMAND

xvpictoppm

X Window System Command

X WINDOW

xvidtune *option(s)*

PURPOSE

The **xvidtune** command allows you to fine-tune your video performance via the XFree86 X server video-mode extension. With options, **xvidtune** provides a command-line interface to either switch the video mode or get/set monitor power-saver timeouts. With no options, **vidtune** presents various buttons and sliders that can interactively adjust existing video modes. The resulting output can be inserted into an **XF86Config** file.

OPTIONS

-next	Switches to the next video mode.
-prev	Switches to the previous video mode.
-unlock	Turns on mode-switching key combinations.
-saver *suspendtime* [*offtime*]	Sets the *suspend* and *off* screen saver inactivity timeouts. The values are in seconds.
-query	Dispays monitor parameters and extended screensaver timeouts.

RELATED COMMAND

XF86Config

X Window System Command

xvpictoppm

PURPOSE

The **xvpictoppm** command converts thumbnail files created by **xv** to standard Portable PixMap format files.

RELATED COMMAND

xv

X Window System Command

X WINDOW

xwd *option(s)*

PURPOSE

The **xwd** command creates a screen capture of a screen or a portion
of a screen to file. From there it can be printed or converted to
another file format. After running this command, the cursor
changes to a small crosshair icon; place the cursor over the window to be captured and press the left mouse button. Placing the
cursor over the screen background or the root window will capture
the entire screen. System sounds indicate the beginning and end of
the screen capture.

The **xv** command also creates screen captures in a much easier
fashion.

N O T E

OPTIONS

-add *value*   Adds *value* to every pixel.

-frame   Specifically includes the window-manager frame
                    with the screen capture.

-icmmap   Uses the first installed colormap of the entire
                    screen to be used to obtain RGB values, not the col-
                    ormap of the chosen window.

-id *id*   Specifies a window by specific *id* instead of with
                    the pointer.

-name *name*   Specifies that a window with the WM_NAME prop-
                    erty should be captured.

-nobdrrs   Doesn't capture the window border as part of a
                    screen capture.

-out *file*   Specifies a file to store the captured image in.

-root   Automatically captures the root window for the
                    screen capture.

-screen   Automatically captures the root window for the

Continued

screen capture.

-xy   Specifies *xy*-format capturing.

RELATED COMMANDS

xpr

xwud

X Window System Command

X WINDOW

xwininfo *option(s)*

PURPOSE

The **xwininfo** command displays system information about specific windows. You can select a target window with a mouse, specify the window by ID on the command line, or name a window on the command line.

OPTIONS

-all	Requests all information.
-bits	Returns information about the selected window's raw bits and how the selected window is to be stored, including the selected window's bit gravity, window gravity, backing-store hint, backing-planes value, backing pixel, and whether or not the window has save-under set.
-children	Returns information about the root, parent, and children of the selected window.
-english	Returns metric information about the selected window—individual height, width, and x and y positions are displayed in inches and the number of pixels.
-events	Displays the selected window's event masks.
-frame	Includes window-manager frames when manually selecting windows.
-id *id*	Specifies that window information be returned for the window by its *id*.
-int	Displays window IDs as integer values, not the default hexadecimal values.
-metric	Returns metric information about the selected window—individual height, width, and x and y positions are displayed in millimeters and the number of pixels.

Continued

-name *name*	Specifies that window information be returned for the window by its *name*.
-root	Returns information for the root window.
-shape	Displays the selected window's border shape extents.
-size	Displays the selected window's sizing hints, including normal-size hints and zoom-size hints, the user-supplied location, the program-supplied location, the user-supplied size, the program-supplied size, the minimum size, the maximum size, the resize increments, and the minimum and maximum aspect ratios if any.
-stats	Returns a lot of information about the specified window, including the location of the window, its width and height, its depth, border width, class, colormap ID (if any), map state, backing-store hint, and location of the corners.
-tree	Returns information about the root, parent, and children of the selected window, and displays all children recursively.
-wm	Returns information about the selected window's window-manager hints, including whether or not the application accepts input, the window's icon window number and name, where the window's icon should go, and what the window's initial state should be.

RELATED COMMANDS

xprop

X Window System Command

xwud *option(s)*

PURPOSE

The **xwud** displays a window saved by the **xwd** command.

OPTIONS

-in *file*	Specifies the *file* to display.
-new	Creates a new colormap for displaying the image.
-noclick	Doesn't allow any buttonpresses in the window to terminate the program.
-plane *number*	Specifies a single bit plane of the image to display.
-raw	Uses existing color values to display the image.
-rv	Reverses the video.
-std *maptype*	Displays the image using a specified Standard Colormap.
-vis *vis-type-or-id*	Specifies a visual or visual class.

RELATED COMMANDS

xwd

GNU Command

yes *string*

PURPOSE

The **yes** command prints the command-line arguments, separated by spaces and followed by a newline, forever, until it is killed.

215

FILE-MANAGEMENT COMMANDS

These commands are used to manage your files and directories—move them, copy them, delete them, compress them, and more.

Linux Commands,
Organized by Group

GNU Command

basename *filename.suffix*

PURPOSE

The **basename** command (if specified on the command line) strips leading directories and the suffix.

EXAMPLE

```
$ basename changes.txt
changes
```

cd *directory*

PURPOSE

The **cd** command changes the current directory. Although this is actually a shell command, it's normally treated as a standard Linux command.

EXAMPLES

```
$ cd
```

This changes the current directory to your home directory.

```
$ cd /usr/kevin
```

This changes your current directory to the directory named **/usr/kevin**.

```
$ cd kevin
```

This changes your directory to the subdirectory named **kevin**.

```
$ cd ~
```

This changes the current directory to your home directory.

```
$ cd /
```

This changes the current directory to the root directory.

RELATED COMMANDS

pwd   Prints the name of the current directory.

chgrp *option(s) newgroup file(s)/directory*

PURPOSE

The **chgrp** command changes the group assignments associated with a file or directory. Group IDs or group names can be assigned to a file or a directory (the information is stored in **/etc/groups**). You must own a file or be the root user in order to change the groups.

OPTIONS

-c	Prints information about the changes made.
-f	Ignores information about files that can't be changed.
-v	Returns all information about the changes in verbose form.
-R	Recursive mode, which means that subdirectories are also changed.

EXAMPLES

```
$ chgrp management kevin.memo
```

This changes the group for **kevin.memo** to the **restricted** group.

```
$ chgrp -R management /home/kevin/memos
```

This changes the group for the directory **/home/kevin/memos**, its contents, and all subdirectories within to the **restricted** group.

RELATED COMMANDS

chown

chmod

chmod *option(s) mode file(s)*

PURPOSE

The **chmod** command changes the permissions associated with a file or directory. Permissions are set for the owner of a file, a group owner of the file, and the world at large. Permissions are stored in one of two ways: numeric or symbolic form. The symbolic form is used to set values relative to the current permissions, while the numeric method is used to set absolute permissions. These values are in modes, which can be an octal number (when using the numeric form) or a symbol (when using the symbolic method). You can combine modes if you separate them with a comma.

You must own a file or be the root user in order to change the permissions.

The current permissions for a file can be displayed with the **ls** command, which is covered elsewhere in this section. The **ls** command lists the permissions in the following manner:

    rwxr--w--

Permissions are set in trios: owner, group, and world. Any of the three can read (**r**), write (**w**), and execute (**x**). If permission is denied to one of the three, the letter is replaced with a hyphen (**-**). The root user has full permissions for every file.

Permissions are one of the more important things to watch when using the Linux operating system. Many beginners get tripped up because they want to run or access a file, only to find out that they don't have permission to do so.

EXAMPLES USING SYMBOLIC FORM

    $ chmod g+x pat.memo

This command line adds the permission to execute a file (**x**) to the group (**g**). In symbolic form, permissions are added or subtracted to existing permissions.

    $ chmod go-w pat.memo

Continued

This command line removes the write permissions from the group and the world.

```
$ chmod g+x,go-w pat.memo
```

This command line adds the permission to execute a file to the group, while removing the write permissions from the group and the world.

SYMBOLS

The following symbols are used to set the mode:

u	User (the current owner of the file).
g	Group.
o	Other (world).
all	All (the default).
+	Adds a permission to the current permissions.
-	Deletes a permission from the current permissions.
=	Assigns a permission while deleting the other permissions from unspecified fields.
r	Read.
w	Write.
e	Execute.
s	Sets user ID
t	Sets sticky bit, which is used for additional security both on a Linux system and the Internet.
l	Sets mandatory lock.

EXAMPLE USING NUMERIC FORM

```
$ chmod 764 pat.memo
```

This command line combines **chmod** with a mode of 744, applied to the file **pat.memo**. This means that the owner can read, write, and execute the file (that's what the **7** designates), the group can read the file and write to it, but not execute it, and the world can read the file but not execute it or write to it.

Continued

How do we arrive at **764**? Because we add up the numerical value of modes, which we'll cover in the next sections. A mode number can range between **000** and 777; **000** means that no one has any access to a file, while 777 means that everyone has full access to a file. Here's the exact math used to arrive at **764**:

400	Owner has read permission.
200	Owner has write permission.
100	Owner has execute permission.
040	Group has read permission.
020	Group has write permission.
004	World has read permission.
764	(Total)

Using the **ls** command on the file in question, you'd see that it has the following permissions:

```
rwxrw-r--
```

MODES

The mode is a combination of the following:

400	Owner has read permission.
200	Owner has write permission.
100	Owner has execute permission.
040	Group has read permission.
020	Group has write permission.
010	Group has execute permission.
004	World has read permission.
002	World has write permission.
001	World has execute permission.

Linux Commands, Organized by Group

Continued

OPTIONS

-c   Prints information about the changes made.

-f   Ignores information about files that can't be changed.

-v   Verbose mode, where changes and failed changes are listed.

-R   Recursive mode, which means that subdirectories are also changed.

FOUR-DIGIT MODES

Occasionally there will be four-digit modes. In these cases, the extra digit is actually at the beginning of the mode and adds the following permissions:

4   Sets user ID upon execution.

2   Sets group ID upon execution.

1   Sets the sticky bit.

RELATED COMMANDS

chgrp

chown

chown *option(s) newowner file(s)*

PURPOSE

The **chown** command changes the ownership of a file or directory. The new owner is either a username (one of which stored in **/etc/passwd**) or a user ID number. You must be the owner of this file or a privileged user (i.e., root user) to change the ownership.

OPTIONS

-c	Prints information about the changes made.
-f	Ignores information about files that can't be changed.
-v	Verbose mode, where changes and failed changes are listed.
-R	Recursive mode, which means that subdirectories are also changed.

EXAMPLE

```
$ chown kevin report
```

This changes the ownership of **report** to the user *kevin*.

RELATED COMMANDS

chmod

chgrp

225

chroot *path*

PURPOSE

The **chroot** directory changes the root directory of a Linux system to that specified in *path*. Only the root user may change the root directory.

cp *option(s) file1 file2*

cp *option(s) file1 directory*

cp *option(s) directory1 directory2*

PURPOSE

The **cp** command copies files—the contents of one file into another file, the contents of a file into a new directory, or from one directory to another. The existing file isn't changed.

OPTIONS

-a	Retains archival attributes.
-b	Creates a backup instead of overwriting an existing file.
-d	Maintains symbolic links between files.
-f	Forces copying.
-i	Turns on interactive mode, where you are prompted before existing files are overwritten.
-l	Creates hard links between files copied to directories, instead of actually copying the files.
-p	Preserves existing permissions, including the ownership and time stamp.
-r	Copies entire directory and any subdirectories.
-R	Copies entire directory and any subdirectories.
-s	Creates symbolic links between files copied to directories, instead of actually copying the files.
-S	Sets a suffix to all new files; the default is ~ and stored in the SIMPLE_BACKUP_SUFFIX environment variable. Don't change this variable, since other applications (notably **emacs**) also use it.
-u	Doesn't copy to new files that are newer than the existing file.
-v	Turns on verbose mode, where all transactions are printed to screen.
-V	Uses the version-control numbering set with the VERSION_CONTROL environment variable.
-x	Ignores subdirectories on remote filesystems when copying.

Linux Commands, Organized by Group

Continued

EXAMPLES

```
$ cp pat.letter pat.old
```

This copies the file **pat.letter** into a new file called **pat.old**.

```
$ cp kevin.letter /home/Kevin/kevin.letter
```

This copies the file **kevin.letter**, contained in the current directory, to the file **kevin.letter**, stored in the **/home/Kevin** directory.

```
$ cp -r /home/Kevin /home/Kevin/letters
```

This copies the entire contents of **/home/Kevin** into the directory **/home/Kevin/letters**.

dir *option(s) directory*

PURPOSE

The **dir** command lists the content of a directory. It's basically the same as the **ls** command, but it's included because MS-DOS uses **dir** and not **ls** to list directories.

OPTIONS

-A	Does not list. and...
-a	Lists hidden files beginning with...
-B	Ignores backup files, which begin with a tilde (~)
-b	Prints octal escapes for nongraphic characters.
-C	Lists enteries by columns.
-c	Sorts by change time; displays the change time when combined with **-1.**
-D	Generates output suited to the **emacs** *dired* mode.
-d	Lists directory enteries instead of contents.
-e	Lists both the date and the full time.
-F	Appends a character for typing each entry.
-f	Does not sort, enabling **-aU** and disabling **-lsto.**
-G	Inhibits display of group information.
-g	Ignored by **dir**; included for compatibility reasons.
-I*pattern*	Ignores entries matching PATTERN.
-I	Prints the index number of each file.
-k	Uses 1024 blocks, not 512.
-L	Lists enteries pointed to by symbolic links.
-l	Uses a long listing format.
-m	Fills the width with a comma-separated list of entries.
-N	Does not quote entry names.
-n	Lists numeric UIDs and GIDs instead of names.
-o	Displays files in color according to type.
-p	Appends a character for typing each entry.
-Q	Encloses entry names in double quotes.

229

Continued

-q	Prints a question mark (?) instead of nongraphic characters.
-R	Lists subdirectories recursively.
-r	Lists in reverse order while sorting.
-S	Sorts by file size.
-s	Prints the block size of each file.
-T*cols*	Sets tab stops at each *cols* instead of 8.
-t	Sorts by modification time; displays the modification time when used with -1.
-U	List enteries in directory order, without any sorting performed.
-u	Sorts by last access time; displays this time when used with **-1.**
-w*cols*	Assumes a screen width of *cols* instead of current value.
-X	Sorts alphabetically by extension.
-x	Lists enteries by lines instead of by columns.
-1	Lists one file per line.

file *option(s) filename*

PURPOSE

The **file** command returns the file type of a given file. Sometimes the magic file (**/etc/magic**) must be consulted. Don't put a lot of stock into the information returned—the information returned by this command is not always correct, and it works best when detecting text-based or text-oriented file types, like ASCII files, shell scripts, PostScript files, and commands.

OPTIONS

-c	Checks the magic file automatically.
-f *list*	Runs the **file** command on the files in **list**.
-L	Follows symbolic links.
-m *file*	Checks *file* for file types instead of the magic file.
-z	Checks compressed files.

Linux Commands, Organized by Group

231

GNU Command

find *pathname(s) condition(s)*

PURPOSE

The **find** command finds a file. It can be just that simple, or it can be as complex as you'd like. You can enter any number of conditions—wildcards relating to the filename, when the file was created or last accessed, what links are present, and so on. It descends the directory tree beginning with the root directory or another directory that you name.

You can use the **find** command to learn if someone really knows Linux. If they use the **find** command and always place **-print** at the end of a command line, that means that know UNIX, not Linux. In standard UNIX, the **find** command requires **-print** at the end of the command line, to tell the command to print output to the screen. However, the Linux version of **find** doesn't require **-print**, since the assumption is that you always want to print to the screen. So any book or magazine article that includes **-print** as part of the example command lines shows that the author doesn't really know Linux.

OPTIONS

-amin *min*	Finds files that were accessed:	
	+*m*	more than *m* minutes ago.
	m	exactly *m* minutes ago.
	-*m*	less than *m* minutes ago.
-anewer *file*	Finds files that were accessed after they were modified.	
-atime *days*	Finds files that were accessed:	
	+*d*	more than *d* days ago.
	d	exactly *d* days ago.
	-*d*	less than *d* days ago.
-cmin *min*	Finds files that were changed:	
	+*m*	more than *m* minutes ago.
	m	exactly *m* minutes ago.
	-*m*	less than *m* minutes ago.

Continued

-cnewer *file*	Finds files that were changed after they were modified.
-ctime *days*	Finds files that were changed:
	+d more than *d* days ago.
	d exactly *d* days ago.
	-d less than *d* days ago.
-daystart	Assumes that times are calculated from the beginning of the day, not from now.
-empty	Continues the search even if a file is empty.
-exec *command* {}\;	Runs the Linux *command* after a file is found.
-false	Returns a false value if a match is made.
-follow	Follows symbolic links and the associated directories.
-fstype *type*	Finds files stored on specific filesystem *type*: ufs, 4.2, 4.3, nfs, tmp, mfs, S51K, and S52K.
-gid *num*	Finds files belonging to a specific group *num*.
-group *group*	Finds files belonging to a specific *group*, which can be an ID or a name.
-ilname *file*	Searches for symbolic links pointing to *file*, which can include metacharacters and wildcards. The case doesn't matter.
-iname *file*	Finds a file named *file*. The case doesn't matter.
-inum *num*	Finds files with a specific inode number of *num*.
-ipath *name*	Finds files that match *name*, which is an absolute pathname. The case doesn't matter.
-links *num*	Finds files with *num* number of links.
-lname *file*	Searches for symbolic links pointing to *file*, which can include metacharacters and wildcards. The case must match.
-maxdepth *num*	Stops search after descending *num* levels of directories.
-mindepth *num*	Begins search at *num* levels of directories and lower.
-mmin *min*	Finds files that were modified:
	+m more than *m* minutes ago.
	m exactly *m* minutes ago.
	-m less than *m* minutes ago.

Linux Commands, Organized by Group

Continued

-mtime *days*	Finds files that were modified:
	+d more than *d* days ago.
	d exactly *d* days ago.
	-d less than *d* days ago.
-name *file*	Finds a file named *file*. The case must match.
-newer *file*	Finds files that have been modified more recently than *file*.
-nogroup	Finds files whose group owner isn't listed in **/etc/group**.
-nouser	Finds files whose owner isn't listed in **/etc/passwd**.
-ok *command* {}\;	Runs the Linux *command* after a file is found, verifying that you do indeed want to run the command.
-path *name*	Finds files that match *name*, which is an absolute pathname. The case matters.
-perm *nnn*	Finds files that have permissions matching specified file permissions (such as **rwx**).
-size *num*[c]	Finds a file containing *num* blocks or *num* character if **c** is added.
-type *t*	Returns names of file whose type is *t*, which can be **b** (block special file), **c** (character special file), **d** (directory), **f** (plain file), **l** (symbolic link), **p** (pipe), or **s** (socket).
-user *user*	Finds files belonging to specified *user*.

EXAMPLES

```
$ find / -ctime -2
```

This finds all the files on the entire filesystem that have been changed less than two days ago.

```
$ find $HOME
```

This lists all the files and directories in your home directory.

funzip *password input_file*

PURPOSE

The **funzip** command is a filter for extracting from a ZIP archive in a pipe.

RELATED COMMANDS

gzip

unzip

zip

getfilename   Get Filename

getfilename *format-name filename*

PURPOSE

The **getfilename** command asks a user to name a file in a given format. It's not useful on its own but becomes useful when combined with a mailcap-oriented program, such as **mailto**.

RELATED COMMANDS

mailto

metamail

GNU Command

gunzip *option(s) file(s)*

PURPOSE

The **gunzip** command is used to unzip files compressed with the
gzip command or the UNIX **compress** and **pack** commands.

There is no **compress** command with the Linux operating system, unlike other forms of UNIX. To uncompress a file compressed using the UNIX **compress** command, you should use
gunzip.

OPTIONS

-c   Uses standard output without changing the original files.

-N   Keeps the original name and timestamp.

-q   Works in quiet mode, without returning status informa-
            tion.

-t   Tests the new file for data integrity.

-v   Works in verbose mode, with all changes noted to the
            screen, including the name of the new file.

RELATED COMMANDS

gzip

GNU Command

gzexe *option file(s)*

PURPOSE

The **gzexe** command compresses executable files. When you go to run the compressed executable file, it automatically uncompresses and is run. It takes a little longer to run compressed commands, but you can save on precious disk space.

OPTION

-d   Decompresses compressed executable command.

GNU Command

gzip *option(s) file(s)*

PURPOSE

The **gzip** command compresses a file using Lempel-Ziv coding. A compressed *file* is renamed *file.gz* and the original deleted. The access permissions and timestamps associated with the original file are maintained by the new compressed file.

OPTIONS

-c	Uses standard output without changing the original files.
-d	Decompresses files (the same as **gunzip**).
-f	Forces compression in the cases when a compressed file already exists, has multiple links, or is already compressed.
-l	Creates compressed files out of files that are already compressed by **deflate**, **compress**, **gzip**, **lzh**, or **pack**.
-N	Keeps the original name and timestamp.
-q	Works in quiet mode, without returning status information.
-r	Works in recursive mode, where subdirectories are also compressed.
-S *suffix*	Adds specified *suffix* to the new filename, instead of the default *.gz*.
-t	Tests the new file for data integrity.
-v	Works in verbose mode, with all changes noted to the screen, including the name of the new file.

RELATED COMMANDS

gunzip

ln *option(s) originalfile linkfile*

ln *option(s) file(s) directory*

PURPOSE

The **ln** command links two or more files. The purpose is to cut
down on disk space used by files, and on a larger multiuser system
there can be the same files that are used by multiple users in multiple situations. While you may not feel the need to link files on your
single-user Linux system, you may feel the need if you're oversee-
ing a network installation. And Linux itself uses links in a standard
installation; some Linux files are stored in nonstandard locations,
but links make it appear that the standard locations are valid.

There are two types of links: hard links and symbolic links. For
the most part, you'll want to stick with symbolic links, as they're
easier to keep track of with the **ls** command.

You can keep the same name for both files, or else you can have
a new name for the *linkfile*. Always remember that the first name
is the original file and the second name is the new, link file; if you
reverse the order you'll trash your original file.

OPTIONS

-b	Backs up the original file before removing it.
-d	Creates hard links to directories (available only to privileged users).
-f	Forces the link, without asking for permission to overwrite existing files.
-F	Creates hard links to directories (available only to privileged users).
-i	Confirms before overwriting existing files.
-n	Replaces symbolic links before dereferencing them.
-s	Creates a symbolic link.
-S *suffix*	Adds *suffix* to the end of a backed-up file, instead of the standard tilde (~).

Continued

EXAMPLE

`$ ln pat kevin`

This links the file **kevin** to **pat**.

RELATED COMMANDS

chmod

chown

cp

ls

mv

locate *option(s) pattern(s)*

PURPOSE

The **locate** command locates a *pattern* in a database of filenames
and returns the filenames that match. A *pattern* can contain shell-
style metacharacters (∗, **?**, and **[]**), but / and **.** are treated as part of
the filename. If there are no metacharacters, then filenames are
returned in the database that contain the string anywhere. If
metacharacters are included, the **locate** command displays filenames that contain the exact pattern, so use ∗ at the beginning or
end of a pattern with metacharacters.

OPTIONS

-d *path*	Searches the filename database in *path*, a colon-separated list of database filenames.
--help	Prints a list of options and exits.
--version	Returns **locate** version and exits.

RELATED COMMANDS

find

locatedb

lockfile

updatedb

xargs

GNU Command

locatedb *option(s) pattern(s)*

PURPOSE

The **locate** command locates a *pattern* in a database of filenames and returns the filenames that match. A *pattern* can contain shell-style metacharacters (⋆, **?**, and **[]**), but **/** and **.** are treated as part of the filename. If there are no metacharacters, then filenames in the database are returned that contain the string anywhere. If metacharacters are included, the **locate** command displays filenames that contain the exact pattern, so use ⋆ at the beginning or end of a pattern with metacharacters.

RELATED COMMANDS

find

locate

lockfile

updatedb

xargs

lockfile *option filename*

PURPOSE

The **lockfile** command creates one or more semaphore files, which limit access to a file. If **lockfile** can't create the semaphore files in order, it waits for eight seconds and tries again; you can use the **-r** option to specify the number of times it will retry. The resulting files will have an access permission of **0** and need to be removed with **rm -f**.

OPTION

-r *num*   Retries *num* of times before giving up.

RELATED COMMAND

rm

GNU Command

ls *option(s) name(s)*

PURPOSE

The **ls** command lists the contents of a specified directory or extended information about a specified file. If no *name* is given, then it's assumed that you want the contents of the current directory. Files are by default listed in columns, sorted vertically. While this can be a complex command, especially in the option-laden GNU version (with 38 options), chances are good that you'll stick with the **-F** and **-l** options the most, and use the **-u** and **-c** options the least.

OPTIONS

-1	Lists one file per line.
-7	Treats all characters outside the ASCII (ISO 646) set (0x20-0x7E) as nonprintable control characters.
-8	Treats all characters from the 8-bit ISO 8859 character sets (0x20-0x7E, 0xA1-0xFF) as printable, including ASCII. (Default.)
-a	Lists all files in a directory, including hidden files.
-A	Lists all the contents of a directory, except for . and ...
-b	Displays nongraphic characters using alphabetic and octal backslash sequences like those used in C.
-B	Ignores backups (files ending with ~),
-c	Sorts contents according to status change time.
-C	Lists files in columns, sorted vertically.
-d	Lists directories like other files, without their contents.
-e	Lists all times in full.
-f	Displays contents as found in disk, and not sorted in any way.
-F	Lists the file types by character: / for directories, @ for symbolic links, l for FIFOs, = for sockets, and nothing for regular files.

Continued

-G	Omits group ownership when listing files in long format.
-i	Displays an index number of each file.
-I *pattern*	Ignores files that match *pattern*.
-k	Lists file sizes in kilobytes.
-l	Lists files in long format, including the file type, permissions, number of hard links, owner name, group name, size in bytes, and timestamp (the modification time unless other times are selected).
-L	Displays files by symbolic links instead of listing the contents of the links.
-m	Lists files horizontally, separated by commas.
-n	Lists the numeric UID and GID instead of the filenames.
-N	Omits filenames from the listings.
-o	Toggles the display of the files by colors.
-p	Appends a character to each filename indicating the type.
-q	Prints question marks in the place of nongraphic characters in filenames.
-Q	Encloses filenames in double quotes (") and display nongraphic characters like those used in C.
-r	Sorts filenames in reverse order.
-R	Lists contents of directories recursively.
-s	Prints the size of the file (in 1K blocks) to the left of the filename.
-S	Sorts files by file size, not alphabetically, with the largest files first.
-t	Sorts files by timestamp (newest first) instead of alphabetically.
-T*cols*	Sets the tab stops at *cols* columns. The default is 8. Setting *0* disables tabs.
-u	Sorts files by the last time they were accessed, not modified.
-U	Displays contents as found in disk, and not sorted in any way.
-w *cols*	Sets the screen as *cols* characters wide. The default is 80.
-x	Prints listings in columns, sorted horizontally.
-X	Sorts files alphabetically by file extensions.

mc *option(s) directory1 directory2*

PURPOSE

The **mc** command launches the Midnight Commander, a directory browser and file manager for Linux that doesn't require the X Window System. It allows you to move, copy, and delete files and directories, either with mouse actions and pulldown menus or commands entered on a command line as with **vi**.

There is an extensive set of commands associated with the Midnight Commander; see the online-manual pages for more details.

OPTIONS

-b	Works in black and white.
-c	Works in color.
-C *arg*	Uses *arg* color set instead of the default.
-d	Turns off mouse support.
-f	Displays compiled-in search paths for Midnight Commander files.
-l *file*	Saves the **ftpfs** dialog with the server on file.
-P	Prints the last working directory after Midnight Commander exits. (See the manual pages for shell scripts that makes this option very useful.)
-s	Works in slow mode, where line drawings are suppressed and verbose mode is turned off.
-t	Uses TERMCAP for terminal information.
-u	Disables a concurrent shell.
-U	Enables a concurrent shell.
-v *file*	Launches the internal viewer to view *file*.
-x	Works under **xterm**.

Linux Commands, Organized by Group

GNU Command

mkdir *option(s) directories*

PURPOSE

The **mkdir** command is used to create directories. The default mode of new directories is 0777.

OPTIONS

-m *mode*	Sets the mode of the new directories to *mode*.
-p	Creates new parent directories as needed.

mkdirhier *directory*

PURPOSE

The **mkdirhier** creates a directory hierarchy. This command is made redundant by the GNU version of **mkdir** (covered separately), which will create a directory hierarchy.

RELATED COMMAND

mkdir

GNU Command

mkfifo *option(s) filename*

PURPOSE

The **mkfifo** creates a FIFO, or a named pipe. The mode of the new
FIFO is 0666.

OPTIONS

-m *mode*   Sets the mode of new FIFOs to *mode*.

mkfontdir   Make Font Directory

X Window System Command

mkfontdir *directory*

PURPOSE

The **mkfontdir** creates an index of X font files, **fonts.dir**, in the specified *directory*. There's no option to change this filename, and you wouldn't want to—this is the name that the X font server and the X server look to for font information.

RELATED COMMANDS

xfs

xset

mkmanifest *file(s)*

PURPOSE

The **mkmanifest** command create a shell script to restore Linux filenames that have been truncated by the MS-DOS filename restrictions.

RELATED COMMANDS

arc

pcomm

mtools

GNU Command

mknod *option(s) filename filetype major_dev minor_dev*

PURPOSE

The **mknod** command creates special files (FIFO, character special file, or block special file) with the given *filename*. The default mode of these files is 0666. The *filetype* can be one of the following:

p	FIFO
b	Block (buffered) special file
c	Character (unbuffered) special file
u	Character (unbuffered) special file

Major_dev and *minor_dev* refer to major and minor device numbers.

OPTION

-m *mode*   Sets the mode of the new file to *mode*. This is a symbolic value.

mv *option(s) sources target*

PURPOSE

The **mv** command moves files—or, more accurately, gives them a new name and a new location on the file hierarchy. If the *target* names a directory, **mv** moves the sources into files with the same names in that directory. Otherwise, if two files are given as *sources* and *target*, it moves the first file onto the second.

If the new file is unwritable, **mv** will ask you to confirm that you want to overwrite a file.

OPTIONS

-b	Creates backups before removing files.
-f	Removes existing destination files without prompting you.
-i	Prompts you before overwriting destination files.
-S	Sets a new suffix for backups; the system default is ~.
-u	Declines moving a file to a new destination with the same or newer modification time.
-v	Verbose mode; prints the name of each file before moving it.

RELATED COMMANDS

cp

newgrp *GID*

PURPOSE

The **newgrp** command changes your group permissions after you've already logged in the system. If you don't specify a new GID, your login GID is used.

RELATED COMMANDS

login

group

GNU Command

pwd

PURPOSE

The **pwd** command prints the name of the current (working) directory.

GNU Command

GNU COMMAND

rm *option(s) filename*

PURPOSE

The **rm** command removes directories from the Linux filesystem.
You are prompted before the file is actually removed.

Unlike the standard UNIX versions of **rm**, this GNU version
does not remove directories by default.

OPTIONS

-d	Removes linked directories with the **unink** command instead of the **rmdir** command. (Only root users have access to the **-d** option.)
-f	Ignores nonexistent files.
-i	Explicitly sets prompting before removing files.
-r	Removes the contents of directories recursively.
-v	Works in verbose mode, printing the name of each file before removing it.

Linux Commands,
Organized by Group

257

GNU Command

rmdir *option(s) directory*

PURPOSE

The **rmdir** command removes empty directories. Directories with contents will not be deleted.

OPTIONS

-p   Removes parent directories if they're mentioned as part of the command line.

shrinkfile *option(s) filename*

PURPOSE

The **shrinkfile** command shrinks a file on a line boundary, preserving the data at the end of the file. Truncation is performed on line boundaries, where a line is a series of bytes ending with a newline. There is no line length restriction and files may contain any binary data.

OPTIONS

-s num   Changes the maximum size to *num*.

-v   Prints a status line if a file was shrunk.

Linux Commands,
Organized by Group

GNU Command

size *option(s) object-file(s)*

PURPOSE

The **size** command lists the sections sizes and the total size for the *object-file(s)* listed on the command line. One line of output is generated for each file.

OPTIONS

-A	Output resembles System V **size** output.
-B	Output resembles Berkeley **size** format.
-d	Sizes are listed in decimals.
-o	Sizes are listed in octals.
-x	Sizes are listed in hexadecimal.
--target *bfdname*	Specifies object-code format as *bfdname*.

sq *inputfile outputfile*

PURPOSE

The **sq** command squeezes a sorted word list. It's generally used for large text files, such as dictionaries. The squeezing is achieved by eliminating common prefixes and replacing them with a single character, which encodes the number of characters shared with the preceding word.

RELATED COMMAND

unsq

Linux Commands, Organized by Group

GNU Command

sum *option(s) filename(s)*

PURPOSE

The **sum** performs a checksum on a file and counts the blocks. It computes a 16-bit checksum for each named file. It prints the checksum for each file along with the number of blocks in the file. The GNU version of **sum** computes checksums using an algorithm that is compatible with the BSD **sum** and prints file sizes in units of 1K blocks.

OPTIONS

-r   Uses the BSD-compatible algorithm, which is the default.

-s   Uses a System V-compatible algorithm and prints out file-sizes in 512-byte blocks.

GNU Command

test *expression*

PURPOSE

The **test** command returns a status of 0 (true) or 1 (false) depending on the evaluation of the conditional *expression*, which can be unary or binary. There is a long list of expressions available; check the online-manual or **info** pages for more information.

unsq *inputfile outputfile*

PURPOSE

The **unsq** command unsqueezes a sorted word list that's been squeezed by **sq**.

RELATED COMMAND

sq

unzip *option(s)*

PURPOSE

The **unzip** command will unzip a file that's been compressed using the PKZip or WinZip ZIP format found on MS-DOS/Windows systems. See the online-manual pages for more information on the many options.

RELATED COMMAND

unzipsfx

265

unzipsfx *option(s)*

PURPOSE

The **unzipsfx** creates a new archive file with **unzip** prepended to existing ZIP archives, forming self-extracting archives. See the online-manual pages for more information on the many options.

RELATED COMMAND

unzip

updatedb   Update Filename Database

 GNU Command

updatedb *option(s)*

PURPOSE

The **updatedb** command updates a filename database used by the **locate** command. This database contains lists of files that were in particular directory trees when the databases were last updated.

OPTIONS

--localpaths=*path1 path2*	Specifies nonnetwork directories to put in the database.
--netpaths=*path1 path2*	Specifies network directories to put in the database.
--netuser=*user*	Specifies the user to search network directories as.
--old-format	Creates the database in the old format instead of the new one.
--output=*dbfile*	Specifies the database file to build.
--prunepaths=*path1 path2*	Specifies directories not to put in the database.

X Window System Command

X WINDOW

xfilemanager *option(s)*

PURPOSE

The **xfilemanager** command launches an X-based file manager with drag-and-drop capabilities. It can be used to perform all the usual file-manager tasks, such as moving and copying files, launching applications, and managing directories.

OPTIONS

-doubleClickTime *time*	Sets the interval within mouseclicks before they are treated as doubleclicks; the default is 300 milliseconds.
-iconDir *path*	Sets the file-icons directory.
-iconFont *fontname*	Sets the font to be used with the icons.
-multiWindow	Displays directories in separate windows.
-noDragCopyAsk	Doesn't ask for confirmation before copying a file by dragging it.
-noDragDeleteAsk	Doesn't ask for confirmation before deleting a file by dragging it.
-NoDragExecAsk	Doesn't ask for confirmation before executing a file by dragging it.
-noDragMoveAsk	Doesn't ask for confirmation before moving a file by dragging it.
-rootDir *path*	Sets the opening directory. The default is the user's home directory.
-saveWS	Saves workspace settings before exiting.
-selectColor *colorname*	Sets the color used to mark selected files.
-singleWindow	Displays everything in one big window.
-trashcan *directory*	Turns on the trashcan option; deleted files are sent to the trashcan *directory*, rather than deleted from the system.

RELATED COMMANDS

mc

xfm

X Window System Command

xfm *option(s)*

PURPOSE

The **xfilemanager** command launches an X-based file manager with drag-and-drop capabilities. It can be used to perform all the usual file-manager tasks, such as moving and copying files, launching applications, and managing directories. It actually has two different components that work together: an application manager and a file manager.

Before running this command on a new system, use the **xfm.install** script o create new configuration files.

OPTIONS

-appmgr	Launches only the application manager.
-filemgr	Launches only the file manager.

RELATED COMMANDS

mc

xfilemanager

zcat *file*

PURPOSE

The **zcat** command uncompresses a **gzip** compressed file and write it to standard output, usually the screen (in the same manner that **cat** works).

RELATED COMMANDS

gzip

zforce *filename(s)*

PURPOSE

The **zforce** command forces files compressed with the **gzip** command to have a file extension of **.gz**.

RELATED COMMANDS

gzip

GNU Command

znew *option(s) filename.Z filename.gz*

PURPOSE

The **znew** command takes existing compressed **.Z** files and recompresses them in the **gzip** (**.gz**) format. The old **.Z** file will then be deleted.

OPTIONS

-9	Optimal compression method; also the slowest.
-f	Compress new *filename.gz*, even if *filename.gz* already exists.
-K	Check if the new *filename.gz* file is smaller than the old *filename.Z* file; if not, then no recompression work is done.
-P	Pipe to conversion program, conserving disk space.
-t	Test new *filename.gz* before deleting old *filename.Z* file.
-v	Verbose mode.

RELATED COMMANDS

gzip

zoo *option(s) archivefile*

PURPOSE

The **zoo** command uses Lempel-Ziv compression algorithm to create file archives. See the voluminous online manual pages for more information.

TEXT-PROCESSING COMMANDS

These commands are designed to work directly with text files.

bpe *filename*

PURPOSE

The **bpe** command is used to modify or edit binary files, either in hexadecimal or ASCII. There are a number of commands available as the binary file is displayed; to go into editing mode, select **e** for ASCII edit or **E** for hex edit.

COMMANDS

D	Dumps one page from the current file position.
e	Edits the ASCII part of the file.
E	Edits the hex part of the file.
F	Finds a string in the file, after the current file position.
H	Locates hex bytes in the file, after the current file position.
N	Displays the next sector.
P	Displays the previous sector.
Q	Quits the program.
S	Sets the current file pointer.
W	Writes the modified sector to disk.
+	Scrolls forward two lines.
-	Scrolls backward two lines.
/	Finds a string in the file, after the current file position.
?	Displays Help.

RELATED COMMANDS

hd

od

cat *option(s) files*

PURPOSE

The **cat** command is the most useful command in the Linux operating system, thanks to the many (mostly) mundane functions that it performs. On a basic level, it reads a file and prints it to standard output (usually the screen, unless standard output has been piped to another command or file). The **cat** command can also be combined with the > operator to combine files into a single file, as well as the >> operator to append files to an existing file. Finally, the **cat** command can create a new text file when combined with the name of a new file.

OPTIONS

-A or **--show-all**	Prints nonprinting and control characters, except for linefeeds and tabs; places a dollar sign at the end of each line; and prints tabs as ^I. (The same as **-vET**.)
-e, **-E**, or **--show-ends**	Prints a dollar sign ($) at the end of each line.
-n	Numbers the lines, beginning with 1 at the beginning of the first line.
-s	Squeezes out blank lines.
-t	Prints each tab as ^I and form feeds as ^L.
-T or **--show-tabs**	Prints each tab as ^I.
-u	Doesn't do anything; exists for compatibility with other UNIX scripts.
-v	Shows nonprinting and control characters, except for linefeeds and tabs.

EXAMPLES

```
$ cat report
```

This displays the file named **report**.

```
$ cat report report2
```

This displays the file **report**, followed immediately by the file **report2**.

Continued

```
$ cat report report2 > report3
```

This combines **report** and **report2** into a new file called **report3**. The combination occurs in the order that the files are specified on the command line.

```
$ cat report > report2
```

This copies the contents of the file **report** into a new file named **report2**. The old file **report** remains unchanged.

```
$ cat > report
```

This creates a new file named **report** and sends your subsequent keyboard input into the file. You can end the input by pressing **Ctrl-D**.

```
$ cat report >> report2
```

This places the contents of the file **report** at the end of the existing file **report2**.

```
$ cat - >> report
```

This places keyboard input at the end of the existing file **report2**. You can end the input by pressing **Ctrl-D**.

RELATED COMMANDS

cp

more

page

cmp *option(s) filename1 filename2*

PURPOSE

The **cmp** command compares the contents of two files. If there's no difference between the files, there's no return from **cmp**. If the files are different, then **cmp** returns the line number and byte position of the first difference. This command can be used with binary files as well as text files, as opposed to text-only tools like **diff**.

OPTIONS

-c	Prints the differing bytes as characters.
-i *num*	Ignores the first *num* of bytes in the files.
-l	Displays the byte position and differing characters for all differences within the files.
-s	Works in silent mode, returning only the exit codes and not any instances of differences. The exit code is one of the following:

0	Files are identical.
1	Files are different.
2	One of the files cannot be read.

EXAMPLE

```
$ cmp report memo
report memo differ: char 12, line 1
```

RELATED COMMANDS

comm

diff

sdiff

Linux Commands,
Organized by Group

colrm *start stop file*

PURPOSE

The **colrm** command removes columns from a specified file, but there must be only one character in a line, separated by spaces.

column *option(s) file*

PURPOSE

The **column** command formats input into columns, whether from a *file* or from standard input.

OPTIONS

-c *num*	Sets the number of columns as *num*.
-s *char*	Sets *char* as the column delimiter. Must be used in conjunction with **-t**.
-t	Formats input as a table and not as a column. The default is to format with spaces, unless an alternative has been set with **-s**.
-x	Fills characters before filling the rows.

Linux Commands,
Organized by Group

comm *option(s) file1 file2*

PURPOSE

The **comm** command compares the contents of two files that have already been sorted with the **sort** command. The output is sorted into three columns:

Lines in *file1*   **Lines in** *file2*   **Lines in both files**

This command is similar to the **diff** and **uniq** commands, except that **comm** can be used with two sorted files to seek out duplicate or unique lines.

OPTIONS

-1	Suppresses the printing of the first column.
-2	Suppresses the printing of the second column.
-3	Suppresses the printing of the third column.
-12	Suppresses the printing of the first and second columns.
-13	Suppresses the printing of the first and third columns.
-23	Suppresses the printing of the second and third columns.

RELATED COMMANDS

cmp

diff

sdiff

sort

csplit *option(s) file arguments*

PURPOSE

The **csplit** command splits a long file into two or more smaller files. You can tell **csplit** to split files based on size or by content, using specific expressions as markers for splitting. The original file will be unchanged.

The new files will begin with **xx**. The first file is **xx00** (remember, Linux likes to begin everything with *0*), the next file is **xx01**, and so on. There's a limit of 100 files, so the highest filename numerically is **xx99**.

OPTIONS

-f *txt*	Uses *txt* instead of **xx** to begin the new filenames.
-k	Keeps files even if the command line fails.
-n *num*	Uses numbers that are *num* characters long in filenames, instead of two, the default.
-q	Suppresses character counts.
-s	Suppresses character counts.
-z	Doesn't create empty files, but does maintain numbering.

ARGUMENTS

/*expr*/	Creates a file that begins with a current line to the line containing *expr*. You can add a suffix that ends a file *num* lines before or after *expr*—either +*num* or -*num*.
%*expr*%	Creates a file that begins with *expr*. You can add a suffix that ends a file *num* lines before or after *expr*—either +*num* or -*num*.
line	Creates a file at the current line and ends one line before *line*.
{*n*}	Repeats an argument *n* number of lines. The default is to repeat an argument once.

EXAMPLE

```
$ csplit -k bonfire '/Chapter/' {20}
```

This splits a file named **bonfire** into 20 chapters, each beginning with *Chapter*.

Linux Commands, Organized by Group

cut *option(s) files*

PURPOSE

The **cut** command cuts columns or fields from a file or set of files and displays them. You can use the information to view parts of a file, or else you can take the information and send it to another new file.

OPTIONS

-c *list*	Cuts columns specified in *list*.
-d *character*	Specifies delimiter for determining columns or fields; the default is a tab. If a nonalphanumeric character is used (such as a space), then it must be enclosed in single quote marks. This option must be used with the **-f** option.
-f *list*	Cuts fields specified in *list*.
-s	Suppresses lines without a delimiter; used with the **-f** option.

EXAMPLE

```
$ cut -f1,4 payroll
```

This cuts the first and fourth fields from the file **payroll** and displays them on the screen.

```
$ cut -c1,4 payroll > payroll.old
```

This cuts the first and fourth columns from the file **payroll** and places then in a new file entitled **payroll.old**.

RELATED COMMANDS

grep

join

paste

diff *option(s) diroptions file1 file2*

PURPOSE

The **diff** command compares two files and returns the lines that differ. The line numbers of the differing files are marked with the < and > symbols: The differing line from *file1* is marked with < and the differing line from *file2* is marked with >. Three hyphens (---) separate the contents of the files.

The **diff** command can also be used to compare files in different directories. In this situation, use **diroptions**.

This command works best with smaller text files.

OPTIONS

-a	Compares all files, including binary files.
-b	Ignores blanks at the end of a line.
-B	Ignores blank lines within the files.
-c	Prints three lines of context for each difference.
-d	Speeds processing by ignoring areas with many changes.
-e	Returns commands to recreate *file2* from *file1* using the **ed** text editor.
-H	Scans for scattered small changes; will miss out on many other changes.
-i	Ignores the case when comparing files.
-I *expr*	Ignores file lines that match *expr*.
-n	Returns information in RCS **diff** format.
-N	Treats nonexistent files as empty.
-t	Expands tabs to spaces in output.
-T	Inserts tabs at the beginning of lines.
-u	Prints old and new versions of a file as a single line.
-w	Ignores tabs and spaces (white space).
-y	Returns information in two columns.

Linux Commands,
Organized by Group

Continued

DIROPTIONS

-l	Paginates the output to **pr**.
-r	Recursively runs **diff** to look at files in common subdirectories.
-s	Returns identical files.
-S*file*	Begins with *file* when comparing directories, ignoring files alphabetically listed before *file*.
-x *expr*	Ignores files that match *expr*; wildcards cannot be used.
-X *filename*	Ignores files that match *expr*; wildcards can be used.

EXAMPLE

```
$ diff letter.1212 letter 1213
1c1
< December 12, 1997
- - -
> December 13, 1997
...
```

RELATED COMMANDS

cmp

diff3

sdiff

diff3 *option(s) file1 file2 file3*

PURPOSE

The **diff3** command compares three files and returns the differences between them, as with **diff**, but does not automatically return the differences. Instead, one of the following codes is returned:

====	All three files differ.
====1	*file1* is different.
====2	*file2* is different.
====3	*file3* is different.

OPTIONS

-a	Treats all files as text; useful for determining if there are differences between binary files.
-A	Creates an **ed** script that shows all differences between the files in brackets.
-e	Creates an **ed** script that places differences between *file2* and *file3* into *file1*.
-E	Creates an **ed** script that incorporates unmerged changes, delineated by brackets.
-i	Adds the **w** (save) and **q** (quit) commands to the end of **ed** scripts.
-L *name*	Uses *name* instead of the filename in the output.
-m	Creates a new file with the changes merged; this is done directly and not with an **ed** script.
-T	Inserts a tab at the beginning of each line of differences, instead of the default two spaces.
-x	Creates an **ed** script that places all differences in the files in *file1*.
-X	Creates an **ed** script that places all differences in the files in *file1*. This is same as **-x**, except that the differences are surrounded by brackets.
-3	Creates an **ed** script that places differences between *file1* and *file3* into *file1*.

Linux Commands,
Organized by Group

Continued

RELATED COMMANDS

cmp

diff

sdiff

egrep *option(s) pattern file(s)*

PURPOSE

The **egrep** command searches files for text (referred to as *patterns* or *expressions*) in multiple files or a single file. It is a cousin to the **fgrep** and **grep** commands and usually is considered the most powerful and fastest of the three. However, it doesn't support all ASCII characters—it will search for +, |, (,), and ? as long as they are surrounded by quotation marks, but it will not search for patterns beginning with \.

OPTIONS

-A *num*	Displays *num* of lines after the matched pattern.
-B *num*	Displays *num* of lines before the matched pattern.
-b	Returns the block number of the matched line.
-c	Returns the number of matches without listing the actual matches.
-C	Displays two lines before and after the matched pattern.
-e *pattern*	Searches for *pattern* when *pattern* begins with a hyphen (-).
-f *file*	Uses a *pattern* from *file*.
-h	Lists lines with matches without listing the files that contain them.
-i	Ignores case when matching.
-l	Lists files with matches without listing the actual matches.
-L	Lists files that don't contain matching lines.
-n	Lists matched lines and their line numbers.
-s	Suppresses error messages about files that can't be read or accessed.
-v	Lists lines that do not match the pattern.x
-w	Lists only whole words that are matched.
-x	Lists only whole lines that are matched.

Linux Commands,
Organized by Group

Continued

EXAMPLES

```
$ egrep "Cogswell Cogs|Spacely Sprockets" *
```

This searches the current directory—as noted with *—for the strings *Cogswell Cogs* and *Spacely Sprockets*.

RELATED COMMANDS

grep

fgrep

elvis *option(s) filename*

PURPOSE

The **elvis** command launches a text editor. It's a clone of the popular **vi** text editor; on Linux systems, if you use **vi** on a command line, you'll really be invoking the **elvis** text editor. It responds to all the standard **vi** commands.

OPTIONS

-r	Invokes the **elvrec** command to recover files.
-R	Opens a file in read-only status.
-s	Works in safe mode, so neophytes can't do too much damage to files or a system.
-t *tag*	Opens the file with *tag* as the first line.
-m *file*	Searches through *file* for an error message from a compiler.
-e	Starts in colon command mode, similar to the UNIX **ex** command.
-v	Starts in visual command mode, similar to the UNIX **vi** command.

RELATED COMMANDS

elvrec

emacs

vi

emacs   Text Editor

 GNU Command

 X Window System Command

emacs *option(s) filename(s)*

PURPOSE

The **emacs** command launches a text editor. Most Linux distributions install **emacs** to work under the X Window System, but it can be installed and configured to work under a terminal interface.

The full documentation to **emacs** can be found online using the **info** command.

OPTIONS

+*number*	Opens the file on line *number*.
-font *font*	Specifies a fixed-width *font* for the window. (Used with X.)
-i	Uses the kitchen sink bitmap icon when iconifying the **emacs** window. (Used with X.)
-name *name*	Specifies a *name* for the initial X window.
-nw	Works with terminal interface under X.
-q	Doesn't load an **init** file.
-r	Displays in reverse video. (Used with X.)
-t *file*	Uses *file* as the terminal instead of standard input/output.
-title *title*	Specifies a *title* for the initial X window.
-u *user*	Loads *user*'s **init** file.

RELATED COMMANDS

elvis

vi

expand *option(s) file(s)*

PURPOSE

The **expand** command converts tabs to spaces.

OPTION

-i   Converts only tabs at the beginning of lines.

fgrep *option(s) pattern file(s)*

PURPOSE

The **fgrep** command searches files for text (referred to as *patterns* or *expressions*) in multiple files or a single file. It is a cousin to the **egrep** and **grep** commands and usually is considered the simplest of the three. It returns a 0 if any lines match, 1 if no lines match, and 2 if it encounters an error.

OPTIONS

-A *num*	Displays *num* of lines after the matched pattern.
-B *num*	Displays *num* of lines before the matched pattern.
-b	Returns the block number of the matched line.
-c	Returns the number of matches without listing the actual matches.
-C	Displays two lines before and after the matched pattern.
-e *pattern*	Searches for *pattern* when *pattern* begins with a hyphen (-).
-f *file*	Uses a *pattern* from *file*.
-h	Lists lines with matches without listing the files that contain them.
-i	Ignores case when matching.
-l	Lists files with matches without listing the actual matches.
-L	Lists files that don't contain matching lines.
-n	Lists matched lines and their line numbers.
-v	Lists lines that do not match the pattern.
-w	Lists only whole words that are matched.
-x	Lists only whole lines that are matched.
-*num*	Displays *num* lines before and after the matched pattern.

RELATED COMMANDS

egrep

grep

fmt *option(s) files*

PURPOSE

The **fmt** command formats files by justifying the text to the right margin and eliminating newlines. However, the **fmt** command does preserve spacing, indentations, and blank lines from the original file.

Since this function is not performed by text editors, it's usually invoked within the text editor (**elvis** has a mechanism for doing this) or piped from a text editor. In addition, because it's often used to format a file and then sent directly to a printer, it usually exists as one step in a pipeline.

OPTIONS

-c	Overrides formatting of the first two lines.
-p *prefix*	Formats lines beginning with *prefix*.
-s	Overrides joining lines.
-t	Tags paragraphs.
-u	Applies uniform spacing of only one space between words and two spaces between sentences.
-w *num*	Sets the line width to *num* characters; the default is 72.

fold *option(s) file(s)*

PURPOSE

The **fold** command formats text to a specific width, breaking words in the middle to achieve that width. The default is 80 characters.

OPTIONS

-b	Counts bytes instead of characters. Here, tabs and formatting commands (like backspace commands and carriage returns) are considered countable.
-s	Breaks only on spaces.
-w *num*	Sets the line width to *num* characters; the default is 80.

X Window System Command

ghostview *option(s) filename*

PURPOSE

The **ghostview** command displays PostScript files, using the **ghost-script** interpreter. A large number of options are associated with this command, but generally it is just invoked with a filename. (See the online-manual pages for more information on the many options.)

grep *option(s) pattern file(s)*

PURPOSE

The **grep** command searches a file or multiple files for text strings (referred to as *patterns* or *expressions*), and displaying the results of the search on the screen.

The **grep** command is a relative of the **fgrep** and **egrep** commands and is considered the most limited of the lot.

OPTIONS

-A *num*	Displays *num* of lines after the matched pattern.
-b	Returns the block number of the matched line.
-B *num*	Displays *num* of lines before the matched pattern.
-c	Returns the number of matches without listing the actual matches.
-C	Displays two lines before and after the matched pattern.
-e *pattern*	Searches for *pattern* when *pattern* begins with a hyphen (-).
-f *file*	Uses a *pattern* from *file*.
-h	Lists lines with matches without listing the files that contain them.
-i	Ignores case when matching.
-l	Lists files with matches without listing the actual matches.
-L	Lists files that don't contain matching lines.
-n	Lists matched lines and their line numbers.
-s	Suppresses error messages.
-v	Lists lines that do not match the pattern.
-w	Lists only whole words that are matched.
-x	Lists only whole lines that are matched.
-*num*	Displays *num* lines before and after the matched pattern.

Continued

EXAMPLE

```
$ grep "mail pixmap" *
```

This searches the current directory—as noted with *—for the
string *mail pixpap.*

RELATED COMMANDS

egrep

fgrep

Linux Commands,
Organized by Group

grodvi *option(s) filename(s)*

PURPOSE

The **grodvi** command converts **groff** output to the TeX DVI format.

OPTIONS

-d   Does not use tpic specials to implement drawing commands.

-F*dir*   Searches the directory ***dir*/*devdvi*** for font and device description files.

-w*n*   Sets the default line thickness to *n* thousandths of an em.

RELATED COMMANDS

eqn

groff

tfmtodit

troff

groff *option(s) filename(s)*

PURPOSE

The **groff** command is a front end to the **groff** document-formatting commands. It typically runs the **troff** program and a postprocessor to prepare documents for a specific device.

The postprocessor is specified by the **postpro** command in the device-description file.

DEVICES

ps	PostScript printers and previewers (default)
dvi	TeX DVI format
X75	X Window 75-dpi previewer
X100	X Window 100-dpi previewer
ascii	Line printers with no formatting
latin1	Line printers with the ISO Latin-1 character set.

OPTIONS

-e	Preprocesses with **eqn**.
-p	Preprocesses with **pic**.
-R	Preprocesses with **refer**.
-s	Preprocess with **soelim**.
-t	Preprocesses with **tbl**.
-V	Prints a pipeline without executing it.
-z	Suppresses output from **troff**; prints error messages.
-Z	Overrides postprocessing output from **troff**.
-P*arg*	Passes *arg* to the postprocessor.
-l	Sends output to a printer.
-L*arg*	Passes *arg* to the spooler.
-T*dev*	Prepares output for *dev*. The default is **ps**.
-X	Previews with **gxditview** instead of using the usual postprocessor.
-N	Doesn't allow newlines with **eqn** delimiters.
-S	Runs in safer mode.

Continued

RELATED COMMANDS

eqn

troff

tbl

grolj4 *option(s) filename(s)*

PURPOSE

The **grolj4** is a **groff** driver for the H-P Laserjet 4 family, producing output in PCL5 format.

OPTIONS

-c*n*	Prints *n* copies of each page.
-F*dir*	Searches directory ***dir/devlj4*** for font and device-description files.
-l	Prints the document with a landscape orientation.
-p *size*	Sets the paper size to *size*: letter, legal, executive, a4, com10, monarch, c5, b5, or dl.
-w*n*	Sets the default line thickness to *n* thousandths of an em.

RELATED COMMANDS

eqn

groff

tfmtodit

troff

grops *option(s) filename(s)*

PURPOSE

The **grops** command is a PostScript driver for **groff**. It's a somewhat redundant command, since the default output for **groff** is PostScript.

OPTIONS

-b*n*	Works with previewers and spoolers that don't conform to the Document Structuring Conventions 3.0. The *n* specifies how **grops** deals with this; see the online manual pages for the specific values.
-c*n*	Prints *n* copies of each page.
-F*dir*	Searches directory ***dir/devname*** for font and device-description files.
-g	Guesses the page length.
-l	Prints the document with a landscape orientation.
-m	Turns on manual feed.
-w*n*	Sets the default line thickness to *n* thousandths of an

em.

RELATED COMMANDS

eqn

groff

tfmtodit

troff

grotty *option(s) filename(s)*

PURPOSE

The **grotty** command formats output for a typewriter-type device.

OPTIONS

-b	Suppresses overstriking for bold characters.
-B	Uses overstriking for bold-italic characters.
-d	Ignores all **\D** commands.
-f	Uses form feeds.
-F*dir*	Searches directory ***dir/devname*** for font and device-description files.
-h	Imposes horizontal tabs.
-o	Suppresses overstriking, other than for bold or underlined characters.
-u	Suppresses underlining for italic characters.
-U	Uses underlining for bold-italic characters.

RELATED COMMANDS

eqn

groff

tfmtodit

troff

Linux Commands, Organized by Group

head *option file(s)*

PURPOSE

The **head** command displays the beginning of a file. The default is 10 lines. If you specify more than one file, a header will be placed at the beginning of each file.

OPTIONS

-c *num*	Prints the first *num* bytes of the file.
-c *num*k	Prints the first *num* kilobytes of the file.
-c *num*m	Prints the first *num* megabytes of the file.
-n *num*	Prints the first *num* lines of the file.
-v	Prints a header at the beginning of each file.

GNU Command

ispell *option(s) file(s)*

PURPOSE

The **ispell** command checks the spellings of words in a *file* or *files*
against the system dictionary. If **ispell** runs across a word not in
the dictionary, it asks you what to do with the word and displays
correctly spelled words, at which point you enter a command. The
ispell command also creates a personal dictionary file that's also
checked, allowing you to place frequently used words there. (You
cannot change the system dictionary file.) If you override the **ispell**
suggestion, the word is then added to a personal dictionary.

The **ispell** command is used as the spelling checker in the
emacs text editor.

OPTIONS

-b	Creates a backup file, adding *.bak* to the original file-name.
-B	Searches for missing blank spaces, where words are jammed together (concatenated).
-C	Ignores concatenated strings.
-d *file*	Uses *file* as the dictionary file, instead of the standard **ispell** dictionary.
-L *num*	Shows *num* lines around the misspelled word.
-M	Displays interactive commands at the bottom of the screen.
-N	Suppresses display of interactive commands.
-n	Checks the spelling of **nroff** or **troff** files.
-p *file*	Uses *file* as the personal dictionary file, instead of your standard **ispell** personal dictionary.
-P	Suppresses suggestion of root/affix combinations.
-S	Sorts replacement words by level of likelihood of correctness.

Continued

-t	Checks the spelling of **tex** or **latex** files.
-T *type*	Assumes that files are formatted by *type*.
-w *chars*	Exempts *chars* from the spelling check.
-W *num*	Skips words that are *num* characters or less.
-V	Displays control characters in hat notation (^C, for example) and - to denote high bits.

COMMANDS

a	Designates the word as spelled correctly, but doesn't add it to the personal dictionary.
i	Adds the word to your personal dictionary.
l	Searches the system dictionary.
q	Quits **ispell** without saving the spelling changes.
r	Replaces the word with the suggestion.
u	Adds a lowercase version of the word to your personal dictionary.
x	Skips to the next file when multiple files are designated.
number	Replaces misspelled word with *number* word.
!*command*	Runs *command* after launching a shell.

RELATED COMMAND

wc

GNU Command

join *option(s) file1 file2*

PURPOSE

The **join** command joins lines of two files (*file1* and *file2*) on a common join field.

OPTIONS

-1 *field*	Joins on field *field* of *file1*.
-2 *field*	Joins on field *field* of *file2*.
-a *file-number*	Prints a line listing each unpairable line in *file1* or *file2*.
-e *string*	Replaces empty output fields with *string*.
-o *field-list*	Uses the format in *field-list* to construct the output lines.
-t *char*	Inserts *char* as the input and output field separator.
-v *file*	Prints a line for each unpairable line in *file* (either *file1* or *file2*), instead of the normal output.

Linux Commands,
Organized by Group

GNU Command

less *option(s) file(s)*

PURPOSE

The **less** command displays portions of a file interactively. It's designed as a more advanced version of the old UNIX **more** command—it allows you to move backward in the file as well as forward—and it reads in portions of files, not entire files, so it's quicker than text editors.

You may find that the **less** command is one of your most frequently used commands, since it's so flexible and provides the best aspects of the **cat** command and your text editors.

OPTIONS

-?	Displays available commands, along with a summary of their functionality.
-h	Displays available commands, along with a summary of their functionality.
-a	Creates a new display after the last line displayed. (The default is two lines.)
-b*buffers*	Displays by *buffers* bytes of size. A buffer is 1 kilobyte, and 10 buffers are used for each file.
-B	Allocates buffers automatically as needed if data is read through a pipe.
-c	Redraws the screen from the top, not the bottom.
-C	Redraws the screen from the top, not the bottom, and clears the screen before repainting.
-d	Suppresses error messages displayed on dumb terminals, such as noting that the terminal lacks the ability to clear the screen.
-e	Exits **less** the second time it reaches the end of the file.
-E	Exits **less** the first time it reaches the end of the file.
-f	Forces **less** to open nonregular files, such as directories or device drivers, and also suppresses error messages when binary files are opened.

Continued

-g	Highlights strings matching only the last search command, not all search commands.
-G	Suppresses highlighting of strings.
-h*num*	Specifies the maximum *num* of lines to scroll backward.
-i	Disregards case when searching. If an uppercase letter is included in a search pattern, then case is taken into account.
-I	Disregards case when searching, even if an uppercase letter is included in a search pattern.
-j*num*	Specifies a "target" line to be positioned at the top of the screen. This can be the object of a text search, tag search, line number, a file percentage, or marked position. A negative number would position the "target" line relative to the bottom of the screen.
-k*filename*	Opens a file as a **lesskey** file, not as a normal text file.
-m	Opens in verbose mode a la the **more** command, with percentages listed at the bottom of the screen.
-M	Opens in verbose mode a la the **more** command, with percentages, line numbers, and total lines listed at the bottom of the screen.
-n	Turns off listing line numbers.
-N	Lists line numbers at the beginning of each line in the display.
-o*filename*	Copies output to *filename* from a pipe. If *filename* exists, **less** asks for permission before overwriting it.
-O*filename*	Copies output to *filename* from a pipe. If *filename* exists, **less** will not ask for permission before overwriting.
-p*pattern*	Starts **less** at the first occurrence of *pattern*.
-P*prompt*	Defines prompt in one of three ways:

-P*string*	Prompt is **string**.
-Pm*string*	Medium prompt is **string**.
-Pm*string*	Long prompt is **string**.

Linux Commands,
Organized by Group

Continued

-q	Works in quiet mode, where no sounds are made if there is an attempt to scroll past the end of the file or before the beginning of the file.
-Q	Works in totally quiet mode, where no system sounds are made.
-r	Displays "raw" characters, instead of using carets. Can cause display errors.
-s	Squeezes consecutive blank lines into a single blank line. Usually used with **nroff** files.
-S	Chops off lines longer than the screen, discarding them instead of folding them into the next line.
-t_tag_	Edits a file containing _tag_, contained in **./tags** and generated by the **ctags** command.
-T_tagfile_	Specifies a tags file to be used instead of ./tags.
-u	Treats backspaces and carriage returns as printable characters.
-U	Treats backspaces and carriage returns as control characters.
-V	Displays the version number of **less**.
-w	Represents lines after the end of the file as blank lines instead of tilde (~) characters.
-x_num_	Sets the tab every _num_ positions; the default is eight.
-X	Disables sending the termcap initialization and deinitialization strings to the terminal.
-y_num_	Specifies a maximum number of lines to scroll forward.
-[z]_num_	Changes the default scrolling window size to _num_ lines; the default is one screen.

COMMANDS

h	Displays Help information.
Space, Ctrl-V, f, Ctrl-F	Scrolls forward the default number of lines (one window; this can be changed by the **-z** option)..
z _num_	Scrolls forward the default number of lines; if _num_ is specified, then it becomes the new window size.

Continued

Enter, Ctrl-N, e, Ctrl-E, j, Ctrl-J	Scrolls forward one line.
d, Ctrl-D *num*	Scrolls forward one-half of the screen; if *num* is specified, **less** scrolls forward that number of lines, and it becomes the default.
b, Ctrl-B, Esc-v	Scrolls backward the default number of lines (one window; this can be changed by the **-z** option or **w** command).
w *num*	Scrolls backward the default number of lines (one window; this can be changed by specifying *num*).
y, Ctrl-Y, Ctrl-P, k, Ctrl-K	Scrolls backward the default number of lines (one).
u, Ctrl-U *num*	Scrolls backward the default number of lines (one-half of one screen). If *num* is specified, it becomes the default for the **d** and **u** commands.
r, Ctrl-R, Ctrl-L	Redraws the screen.
R	Redraws the screen and discards the input in the buffer.
F	Scrolls forward, even when the end of the file is reached (similar to **tail -f**).
g, <, Esc-<	Scrolls to the beginning of the file.
G, >, Esc->	Scrolls to the end of the file.
p, % *num*	Scrolls to a position *num* percent into the file. *Num* must be between 0 and 100.
{	Scrolls to the matching **}** if **{** appears in the top line of the screen.
}	Scrolls back to the matching **{** if **}** appears in the top line of the screen.
(	Scrolls to the matching **)** if **(** appears in the top line of the screen.
)	Scrolls back to the matching **(** if **)** appears in the top line of the screen.
[	Scrolls to the matching **]** if **[** appears in the top line of the screen.
]	Scrolls back to the matching **[** if **]** appears in the top line of the screen.

Continued

Esc-Ctrl-F the **char1 char2**	Scrolls to the matching *char2* if *char1* appears in top line of the screen.
Esc-Ctrl-B **char1 char2**	Scrolls back to the matching *char1* if *char2* appears in the top line of the screen.
m *letter*	Marks the current position with lowercase *letter*.
' *letter*	Returns to the position marked with lowercase *letter*.
Ctrl-X Ctrl-X	Returns to the position marked with lowercase *letter*.
/pattern	Searches for next occurrence of *pattern*, starting at the second displayed line.
/!pattern	Searches for lines that do not contain *pattern*.
/*pattern	Searches for next occurrence of *pattern*, starting at the second displayed line, and extending the search through the next files in the command-line list.
/@pattern	Searches for next occurrence of *pattern*, starting at the first line of the first file listed on the command line.
?pattern	Searches backward in the file for the next occurrence of *pattern*, starting with the line immediately before the top line of the screen.
?!pattern	Searches backward for lines that do not contain *pattern*.
?*pattern	Searches backward for next occurrence of *pattern*, starting at the line immediately before the top line of the screen, and extending the search backwards through the previous files in the command-line list.
?@pattern	Searches for next occurrence of *pattern*, starting at the last line of the last file listed on the command line.
Esc-/pattern	Searches for next occurrence of *pattern*, starting at the second displayed line, and extending the search through the next files in the command-line list.
Esc-*pattern	Searches backward for next occurrence of *pattern*, starting at the line immediately before the top line of the screen, and extending the search backwards through the previous files in the command-line list.
n	Repeats the previous search.
N	Repeats the previous search, but in the reverse direction.
Esc-n	Repeats the previous search and extends the search to files specified on the command line.

Continued

Esc-N	Repeats the previous search, but in the reverse direction, and extends the search to files specified on the command line.
Esc-u	Turns off highlighting of patterns matched by the searches.
:e *filename*	Opens a new *filename*. If no new file is specified, the current file is reloaded.
Ctrl-X, Ctrl-V, **E** *filename*	Opens a new *filename*. If no new file is specified, the current file is reloaded.
:n *num*	Opens the next file on the command line. If *num* is present, then that number of file(s) on the command line will be opened.
:p *num*	Opens the previous file on the command line. If *num* is present, then that number of previous file on the command line will be opened.
:x *num*	Opens the first file on the command line. If *num* is present, then that number of file on the command line will be opened.
=, Ctrl-G, :f	Returns information about the file being viewed: name, line number, byte offset of the bottom line being displayed, length of the file, the number of lines in the file and the percent of the file above the last displayed line.
-option	Changes a command-line option while **less** is running. If a value is required, you are asked for it; if no new value is entered, the current value is displayed.
-+option	Resets a command-line option to default value.
--option	Resets a command-line option to the opposite of the default value. Useless when working with options that require numerical or string-based input.
_option	Returns the current value of *option*.
+command	Runs *command* every time a new file is loaded.
V	Prints version number.
q, :q, :Q, ZZ	Quits **less**.
v	Launches an editor (defined by VISUAL or EDITOR) to edit the current file.

Continued

! *shell-command*   Runs the specified *shell-command*. To list the current file in the command, use the percent sign (%). To list the previously viewed command in the command line, use the pound sign (#). To repeat the previous shell command, use **!!** . To launch a shell with no command, use **!** .

| *mark_letter*   Uses *mark_letter* to send a section of the file via pipe
** *shell-command***   to the specified *shell-command*. (Use the **m *letter*** command to mark a file.) The beginning of the section is the top of the screen, while the end of the section is the *mark-letter*.

EDITING COMMANDS

Left arrow, Esc-h	Moves the cursor one space to the left.
Right arrow, Esc-l	Moves the cursor one space to the right.
Ctrl-left-arrow, Esc-b, Esc-left-arrow	Moves the cursor one word to the left.
Ctrl-right-arrow, Esc-w, Esc-right-arrow	Moves the cursor one word to the right.
Home, Esc-0	Moves the cursor to the beginning of the line.
End, Esc-$	Moves the cursor to the end of the line.
Backspace	Deletes the character to the left of the cursor, or cancels a command.
Delete, Esc-x	Deletes the character under the cursor.
Ctrl-Backspace, Esc-Backspace	Deletes the word to the left of the cursor.
Ctrl-Delete, Esc-X, Esc-Delete	Deletes the word under the cursor.
Up arrow, Esc-k	Retrieves the previous command line.
Down arrow, Esc-j	Retrieves the next command line.
Tab	Completes a partial filename. If more than one filename matches, the potential filenames are cycled through every time **tab** is used.

Continued

Esc-tab	Completes a partial filename. If more than one filename matches, the potential filenames are cycled in reverse through every time **tab** is used.
Ctrl-L	Complete a partial filename. If more than one filename matches, all the potential filenames are displayed.
Ctrl-U	Deletes a command line or cancels a command.

RELATED COMMAND

more

look *option(s) string file*

PURPOSE

The **look** command looks for lines beginning with *string*. If *file* isn't specified, then **/usr/dict/words** is used.

OPTIONS

-a	Uses the alternate dictionary **/usr/dict/web2**.
-d	Compares only alphanumeric characters.
-f	Ignore case.
-t	Sets a string termination character.

RELATED COMMANDS

grep

sort

lpq *option(s) user*

PURPOSE

The **lpq** checks the print spool (used by **lpd**) and also reports on the status of specified jobs, either by job-ID or user. By itself on a command line, **lpq** returns information about all jobs in the queue.

The **lpq** command reports the user's name, current rank in the queue, the names of files comprising the job, the job identifier, and the total size in bytes.

OPTIONS

-l	Prints information about each of the files in a job entry; the default is to truncate information at a single line.
-P*printer*	Designates a specific printer; the default is the value of the PRINTER environment variable or the default line printer.

RELATED COMMANDS

lpc

lpd

lpr

lprm

lpr option(s) file(s)

PURPOSE

The **lpr** sends files to a print-spool daemon, when then sends files to the printer when it is available. The file options are used to designate specific types of files (the assumption is that a text file is on the way), so the printer can adjust accordingly.

FILE OPTIONS

-c	Assumes the files are produced by **cifplot**.
-d	Assumes the files are produced by TeX (DVI format).
-f	Uses a filter that interprets the first character of each line as a standard FORTRAN carriage-control character.
-g	Assumes the files are produced by **plot** routines.
-l	Filters control characters as printable characters and suppresses page breaks.
-n	Assumes the files are produced by **ditroff**.
-p	Uses the **pr** command to format the files (same as **print**).
-t	Assumes the files are produced by **troff**.
-v	Assumes the files contain a raster image for devices like the Benson Varian.

GENERAL OPTIONS

-C *class*	Specifies a job classification on the burst page.
-h	Suppresses printing of the burst page.
-i [*cols*]	Indents the output *num* number of columns. If no *num* is specified, then each line will be indented eight characters.
-m	Sends mail when print job is complete.
-P*printer*	Sends output to *printer.*
-r	Removes file upon completion of spooling or upon completion of printing (with the **-s** option).
-s	Uses symbolic links, instead of copying files to the spool directory. If you do this, do not change files until they have been printed.

Continued

-T *title*	Specifies a *title* name for **pr**, instead of the filename.
-U *user*	Specifies a *user* name to print on the burst page.
-wnum	Uses *num* as the page width for **pr**.
-#num	Prints *num* copies of each file.
-[num**]**font	Specifies a *font* to be mounted on font position *num*.

RELATED COMMANDS

lpc

lpd

lpq

lprm

pr

lprm *option(s) job-ID username*

PURPOSE

The **lprm** command removes print jobs from the print spool. Use the **lpq** command to determine the job-IDs. You must own the job or be the superuser in order to remove print jobs.

OPTIONS

-P*printer*	Specifies a *printer* queue instead of the default.
-	Removes jobs owned by *user*.

RELATED COMMANDS

lpd

lpq

lpr

more *option(s) file(s)*

PURPOSE

The **more** command displays all or parts of a file, one screenful at a time. It has largely been superseded by the **less** command in functionality.

Type **q** to quit **more**. Press the space bar to continue scrolling through a file.

OPTIONS

+*num*	Starts display at line number *num*.
+/*pattern*	Searches for *string* before file is displayed.
-*num*	Sets the screen size to *num* of lines.
-c	Turns off scrolling; instead, the screen is cleared and the new text is painted from the top of the screen.
-d	Displays the following prompt at the bottom of the screen: *[Press space to continue, 'q' to quit.]*
-f	Counts logical lines, not screen lines.
-l	Ignores the ^L (form feed) as a special character.
-p	Turns off scrolling; instead, the screen is cleared and the new text is displayed.
-s	Squeezes multiple blank lines into one.
-u	Suppresses underlining.

COMMANDS

The following commands are used when **more** is displaying a file. They're entered at the bottom of the screen as with the **vi** text editor.

RETURN	Displays the next line of text. If an argument is provided, that becomes the new default.
b or **^B**	Moves backwards one screen of text. If an argument is provided, that becomes the new default.
d or **^D**	Scrolls 11 lines of text. If an argument is provided,

Continued

that becomes the new default.

f	Skips forward one screen of text. If an argument is provided, that becomes the new default.
h or **?**	Displays a summary of commands.
Ctrl-L	Redraws the screen.
n	Repeats the last search.
q or **Q**	Exits **more**.
s	Skips forward one line of text. If an argument is provided, that becomes the new default.
v	Launches **vi** at the current line.
z	Displays the next screen of text. If an argument is provided, that becomes the new default.
'	Reverts to where the previous search started.
=	Displays the current line number.
/pattern	Searches for the next occurrence of *pattern*. If an argument is provided, that becomes the new default.
!cmd or **:!cmd**	Runs *cmd* in a subshell.
:f	Displays the current file and line number.
:n	Opens the next file.
:p	Opens the previous file.
.	Repeats the previous command.

RELATED COMMAND

less

nroff *option(s) filename*

PURPOSE

The **nroff** command calls on the **groff** command to emulate the
nroff command found on other UNIX systems. See the **groff** command for details and command-line options.

Linux Commands,
Organized by Group

GNU Command

paste *option(s) file(s)*

PURPOSE

The **paste** options merges files and places the files side by side. The first line of *file1* will be followed by the first line of *file2*, separated by a tab and ending with a newline.

OPTIONS

-d*char*   Uses *char* instead of a tab to separate lines.

-s   Merges lines from files, instead of printing both on the same line.

RELATED COMMANDS

cut

join

pico *option(s) filename*

PURPOSE

The **pico** text editor is a slim tool based on the composing tools found in the **pine** mail manager. If you work a lot with **pine** and want to maintain some consistency in your tools, you might want to use **pico** for your basic editing needs.

OPTIONS

+*n*	Loads a file with the cursor *n* lines into the file.
-d	Rebinds the **Delete** key so the character the cursor is on is rubbed out rather than the character to its left.
-e	Enables filename completion.
-g	Shows cursor before the current selection, rather than the lower left of the display.
-k	Removes text from the cursor to the end of the line, rather than the entire line.
-m	Enables mouse functionality; available only when running under X Window.
-n*n*	Notifies you when new mail arrives; check for mail every *n* seconds.
-o *dir*	Works in *dir* directory.
-r*n*	Sets *n* column used to limit the right margin.
-t	Enables tool mode, where there's no prompting for a save on an exit, and there's no renaming of the buffer. Used when composing text in other tools, such as **elm** or **Pnews**.
-v	Views the file without editing.
-w	Disables word wrap.
-x	Disables the keymenu at the bottom of the screen.
-z	Enables ^Z suspension.

RELATED COMMAND

pine

GNU Command

pr *file*

PURPOSE

The **pr** command prepares a file for printing. It doesn't actually print
the file—you need to send the file to the printer to do that—but the
pr command creates a paginated, columned file suitable for printing.

OPTIONS

+*page*	Begins printing with page *page*.
-*column*	Prints *column* number of columns.
-a	Prints columns across, rather than down.
-b	Evens columns on the last page.
-c	Prints control characters using carets (^**G**); prints other unprintable characters in octal backslash notation.
-d	Prints output doublespaced.
-e *width*	Expands tabs to spaces on input; if *width* is specified, exchange tab for *width*.
-F	Uses formfeeds instead of newlines between pages.
-h *header*	Replaces the filename in the header with *header*.
-i[*out-tab-char*] [*out-tab-width*]	Replaces spaces with tabs. You can specify an output tab character (*out-tab-char*) or the output tab character's width (*out-tab-width*), which has a default of 8.
-l *page-length*	Sets the page length to *page-length* lines; the default is 66.
-m	Print all files in parallel, one in each column.
-n[*number-separator*[*digits*]]]	Precedes each column with a line number; with parallel files, precedes each line with a line number. The optional argument *number-separator* is the character to print after each number. The optional *digits* is the number of digits per line number; the default is 5.

Continued

-o *left-margin*	Offsets each line with a margin *left-margin* spaces wide.
-r	Ignores warnings when an file cannot be opened.
-s[*column-separator***]**	Separates columns by the single character *col-umn- separator*.
-t	Suppresses printing the header and trailer on all pages.
-v	Print unprintable characters in octal backslash notation.
-w *page-width*	Sets the page width to *page-width* columns; the default is 72.

Linux Commands,
Organized by Group

GNU Command

printf *argument*

PURPOSE

The **printf** command prints a *string*, using % directives and \
escapes in the same manner as the C-language **printf** command.

psbb *file*

PURPOSE

The **psbb** returns the dimensions of a bounding box from a PostScript document. If it finds one, it prints a line:

llx lly urx ury

and exits. If it does not find one, it prints a message saying so and exits.

GNU Command

refer *option(s) filename*

PURPOSE

The **refer** preprocesses bibliographic references for the **groff** command. It copies the contents of *filename* to standard output, except that lines between **.[** and **.]** are interpreted as citations, and lines between **.R1** and **.R2** are interpreted as commands about how citations are to be processed. A longer description of citations and their significance, as well as references to obscure options, can be found in the manual pages.

rev *filename*

PURPOSE

The **rev** command reverses the lines of a file. It copies the file to standard output, reversing the order of characters in every line.

GNU Command

sdiff *option(s) file1 file2*

PURPOSE

The **sdiff** command merges two files and prints the results to a third file.

OPTIONS

-a	Treats all files as text and compares them line-by-line, even if they do not appear to be text.
-b	Ignores changes in amount of white space.
-B	Ignores changes that only insert or delete blank lines.
-d	Changes the algorithm to find a smaller set of changes.
-H	Uses heuristics to speed handling of large files that have numerous scattered small changes.
--expand-tabs	Expands tabs to spaces in the final file.
-i	Ignores changes in case.
-I *regexp*	Ignores changes that only insert or delete lines that match *regexp*.
--ignore-all-space	Ignores white space when comparing lines.
--ignore-blank-lines	Ignores changes that only insert or delete blank lines.
--ignore-case	Ignores case.
--ignore-matching-lines=*regexp*	Ignores changes that inserts or deletes lines that match *regexp*.
--ignore-space-change	Ignores changes in the amount of white space.
-l	Prints only the left column of two common lines.
--minimal	Changes the algorithm to seek a smaller set of changes.

334

Continued

-o *file*	Saves the merged output to *file*.
-s	Doesn't print common lines.
--speed-large-files	Uses heuristics to speed handling of large files with numerous scattered small changes.
-t	Expands tabs to spaces.
--text	Treats all files as text.
-w *columns*	Sets an output width of *columns*.
-W	Ignores horizontal white space when comparing lines.

RELATED COMMANDS

cmp

comm

diff

diff3

Linux Commands,
Organized by Group

sed *option(s) filename(s)*

PURPOSE

The **sed** command reads files and modifies the input as specified by a list of commands. The input is then written to the standard output.

OPTIONS

-a	Files listed as parameters for the **w'** functions are created (or truncated) before any processing begins.
-e *command*	Appends the editing commands specified by *command* to the list of commands.
-f *command_file*	Append the commands from *command_file* to the list of commands.
-n	Suppresses echoing of each line of input.

selection *option(s)*

PURPOSE

The **selection** command takes characters from the current Linux console and pastes them into another section of the current console. The command is typically launched at boot time from the **/etc/rc.local** file and run as a background process.

OPTIONS

-a*accel*   Movements of more than *delta* pixels are multiplied by *accel* (the default is 2).

-b*baud-rate*   Sets the baud rate of the mouse. WARNING: This is an option to be avoided, as setting the incorrect baud rate can cause your mouse to freeze, and there are other mechanisms for setting the baud rate elsewhere in Linux and XFree86.

-c*l\m\r*   Sets the copy button to left (*l*), middle(*m*), or right (*r*). (The default is left.)

-d*delta*   Movements of more than *delta* pixels are multiplied by *accel* (the default is 25).

-m*mouse-device* Sets the mouse (the default is **/dev/mouse**).

-p*l\m\r*   Sets the paste button to left (*l*), middle(*m*), or right (*r*). (The default is right.)

-s*sample-rate* Sets the sample rate of the mouse (the default is 100).

-t*mouse-type*   Sets the mouse type: Microsoft is *ms*, Mouse Systems is *msc*, MM Series is *mm*, Logitech is *logi*, Bus Mouse is *bm*, MSC 3-bytes is *sun*, and PS/2 mouse is *ps2*. The default is *ms*. WARNING: This is an option to be avoided, as setting the mouse type can cause your mouse to freeze, and there are other mechanisms for setting the mouse type elsewhere in Linux and XFree86.

-w*slack*   Sets the amount of slack before the pointer reappears at the other side of the screen.

Linux Commands, Organized by Group

soelim *option filename(s)*

PURPOSE

The **soelim** command interprets **.so** requests in groff input. It reads a specified *filename* and replaces lines of the form:

.so file

with the contents of *filename*.

OPTION

-C   Recognizes **.so** even when it is followed by a charac-
                    ter other than space or newline.

RELATED COMMAND

groff

GNU Command

sort *option(s) filename(s)*

PURPOSE

The **sort** command sorts, merges, or compares the lines of text files. The results are written to the screen.

MODE OPTIONS

You can change the mode with the following options:

-c	Checks whether files are sorted; if not, an error message is printed.
-m	Merges files by sorting them as a group, but the files must already be sorted.

GENERAL OPTIONS

+POS1 [-POS2]	Within each line, sets the field to use as the sorting key.
-b	Ignores leading blanks in lines.
-d	Sorts in phone directory order, ignoring all characters except letters, digits, and blanks when sorting.
-f	Folds lowercase characters into the equivalent uppercase characters when sorting.
-i	Ignores non-ASCII characters.
-k POS1[,POS2]	Sets the field within each line to use as the sorting key.
-M	Month abbreviations are changed to uppercase and sorted in order.
-n	Compares in arithmetic value.
-o *file*	Writes output to *file*.
-r	Reverses the order.
-t *separator*	Specifies *separator* as the field separator.
-u	Displays only the first of a sequence of lines that compare equal when using the **-m** option, or checks that no pair of consecutive lines compares equal when using the **-c** option.

Linux Commands, Organized by Group

GNU Command

split *option(s) infile outfile*

PURPOSE

The **split** command splits a file into two or more output files. The default is to split a file after each 1,000 lines, but that can be changed with a command-line option.

OPTIONS

-lines	Uses *lines* as the number of lines in file (the default is 1000).
-b *bytes*[*bkm*]	Separates files by *bytes* number of bytes. You can add a character to specify different units:

b	512-byte blocks
k	1-kilobyte blocks
m	1-megabyte blocks

-C *bytes*[*bkm*]	Separates files by *bytes* number of bytes, but makes sure that the file ends on a complete line. You can add a character to specify different units:

b	512-byte blocks
k	1-kilobyte blocks
m	1-megabyte blocks

GNU Command

tac *option(s) filename*

PURPOSE

The **tac** command (opposite of **cat**) is used to display files in reverse order; that is, the ending line of a file is displayed first, followed by the second-to-the-last line, and so on.

OPTIONS

-b	Attaches the separator to the beginning of the record that precedes it.
-r	Sets the separator to a regular expression.
-s string	Sets *string* as the record separator.

RELATED COMMAND

cat

Linux Commands,
Organized by Group

GNU Command

tail *option(s) filename*

PURPOSE

The **tail** command prints the last 10 lines of *filename* to the screen. You can display more or less of the file using options. The command is the opposite of the **head** command, used to display the first 10 lines of a file.

OPTIONS

-c *num*	Displays *num* number of bytes.
-f	Loops forever trying to read more characters at the end of the file, on the assumption that the file is growing.
-l *num*	Displays *num* number of lines.
-q	Does not print filename headers.
-v	Prints filename headers.

RELATED COMMAND

head

GNU Command

tr *option(s) [string1 [string2]]*

PURPOSE

The **tr** command translates or deletes characters, replacing *string1* with *string2*.

GNU Command

GNU COMMAND

troff *option(s) filename*

PURPOSE

The **troff** command is a text formatter, part of the **groff** family of formatters. You usually don't use it on your own. Rather, it is invoked by the **groff** command on its own. Check the **groff** command for more information.

RELATED COMMANDS

groff

GNU Command

unexpand *option(s) filename*

PURPOSE

The **unexpand** command converts spaces to tabs in a textfile.

OPTIONS

-a	Converts all strings of two or more spaces or tabs, not just initial ones, to tabs.
-t *tab1*	Set the tabs *tab1* spaces apart, instead of the default 8.

345

GNU Command

uniq *option(s) filename1 filename2*

PURPOSE

The **uniq** command strips duplicate lines from a specified file (*filename1*) and then sends them either to another file (*filename2*) or to standard output is no other file is named.

OPTIONS

-c	Counts duplicate lines.
-d	Returns duplicate lines, but no unique lines.
-f*n*	Skips the first *n* fields of a line; fields are separated by spaces or tabs.
-s*n*	Skips the first *n* characters of a field; fields are separated by spaces or tabs.
-u	Returns unique lines, and duplicate lines are sent to the ether.
-w *n*	Compares the first *n* characters of a line.
-*n*	Skips the first *n* fields of a line; fields are separated by spaces or tabs.
+*n*	Skips the first *n* characters of a field; fields are separated by spaces or tabs.
--check-chars=*n*	Compares the first *n* characters of a line.
--skip-chars=*n*	Skips the first *n* characters of a field; fields are separated by spaces or tabs.
--skip-fields=*n*	Skips the first *n* fields of a line; fields are separated by spaces or tabs.

RELATED COMMANDS

comm

sort

vi option(s) filename

PURPOSE

The **vi** command is actually a shortcut to the **elvis** text editor. (Technically, the **vi** editor found on other UNIX systems is not the same **vi** as this one.) See **elvis** for more information.

vim *option(s) filename*

PURPOSE

The **vim** text editor is an **vi-**compatible text editor useful for editing text files. See the online-manual pages for a list of the available
options.

wc option(s) filename

PURPOSE

The **wc** command counts the words in a text file; if no *filename* is specified, then standard input is counted. This is a handy command when combined with other text-processing commands within a pipeline.

OPTIONS

-bytes	Prints the character count.
-c	Prints the character count.
--chars	Prints the character count.
-l	Prints the number of lines in the file.
--lines	Prints the number of lines in the file.
-w	Prints the number of words in the file; this is the default.
--words	Prints the number of words in the file; this is the default.

EXAMPLE

```
$ wc textfile
324
```

X Window System Command

xedit *filename(s)*

PURPOSE

The **xedit** command launches a simple text editor running under the X Window System.

zcmp *option(s) file(s)*

PURPOSE

The **zcmp** command uncompresses a **gzip** compressed file and calls on **cmp**. The options associated with this command are actually **cmp** options, which are passed along to **cmp** along with the compressed file.

RELATED COMMANDS

cmp

gzip

zegrep

zfgrep

zdiff *option(s) file(s)*

PURPOSE

The **zdiff** command uncompresses a **gzip** compressed file and calls on **diff**. The options associated with this command are actually **diff** options, which are passed along to **diff** along with the compressed file.

RELATED COMMANDS

diff

gzip

zegrep *option(s) file(s)*

PURPOSE

The **zegrep** command uncompresses a **gzip** compressed file and calls on **egrep**. The options associated with this command are actually **egrep** options, which are passed to **egrep** along with the compressed file.

RELATED COMMANDS

egrep

gzip

zgrep

zfgrep

zfgrep *option(s) file(s)*

PURPOSE

The **zfgrep** command uncompresses a **gzip** compressed file and calls on **fgrep**. The options associated with this command are actually **fgrep** options, which are passed to **fgrep** along with the compressed file.

RELATED COMMANDS

fgrep

gzip

zgrep

zegrep

zgrep *option(s) file(s)*

PURPOSE

The **zgrep** command uncompresses a **gzip** compressed file and calls on **grep**. The options associated with this command are actually **grep** options, which are passed to **grep** along with the compressed file.

RELATED COMMANDS

grep

gzip

zegrep

zfgrep

GNU Command

GNU COMMAND

zmore *file(s)*

PURPOSE

The **zmore** command is the GNU version of the venerable UNIX **more** command. **Zmore** prints files to the screen, one screen at a time. The twist here is that **zmore** will display files compressed with **gzip**. There are no command-line options to **zmore**, only commands that can be invoked when **zmore** is running.

COMMANDS

space	Prints the next screen of the file.
d or **^D**	Prints the next 11 lines, or the *num* set with **i[num]**.
i	Prints the next screen of the file.
i[num]	Sets the number of lines to be displayed as *num*, instead of a full screen.
Q	Quits reading the current file and moves to the next (if any).

RELATED COMMANDS

more

less

INTERNET/ELECTRONIC-MAIL COMMANDS

These commands are used to read and send electronic mail, read and send Usenet postings, download from FTP servers, and surf the World Wide Web.

answer *option(s)*

PURPOSE

The **answer** command is a secretarial tool used to transcribe telephone messages to an electronic mail message in **elm**. After launching, **answer** checks the **.elm/aliases** file for a list of users and then guides the user through a form designed to mimic phone-message slips (with fields like "Message-To:" and "Please Call").

OPTIONS

-p   Prompts for message fields.

-u   Allows for names that aren't in the **.elm/aliases** file.

RELATED COMMANDS

mail

printmail

audiocompose *filename*

PURPOSE

The **audiocompose** command records audio. If you want to record audio clips to attach to your outgoing mail messages, this is the command to use. Run this command on the command line with a filename; you'll be prompted to record a file, and then asked if you want to listen to the file after recording it.

Then, you'll need to use the **audiosend**, **mailto**, or **metamail** command to attach the file to an outgoing mail message.

You must have an audio device installed on your Linux system, usually as **/dev/audio**.

If you want to make this format the default for your system, you'll need to set up a RECORD_AUDIO environment variable to audiocompose.

EXAMPLE

```
$ audiosend hello
```

RELATED COMMANDS

audiosend

mailto

metamail

showaudio

audiosend *e-mail_address*

PURPOSE

The **audiosend** command, unlike **audiocompose**, can be used to both record the audio and e-mail it to another user. The audio segment makes up the entire e-mail message; you can't attach text or other files to the mail message.

The command is simple: You use **audiosend** on a command line, along with an e-mail address. (If you don't specify an address, the command will prompt you for one.) The command then prompts you for *Subject* and *Cc* fields, after which you record your message. Before sending the message, **audiosend** asks if you want to rerecord the message or listen to it.

You must have an audio device installed on your Linux system, usually as **/dev/audio**.

If you want to make this format the default for your system, you'll need to set up a RECORD_AUDIO environment variable to **audiocompose**.

EXAMPLE

```
$ audiosend hello
```

RELATED COMMANDS

audiocompose

showaudio

biff *option*

PURPOSE

The **biff** command notifies you that new mail has been received, as long as your system uses **sendmail** or **smail** as a mail-transport agent. To see the current status of **biff**, type it alone on a command line. To enable **biff**, use the **y** option; to disable **biff**, use the **n** option.

OPTIONS

n   Turns **biff** off.
y   Turns **biff** on.

RELATED COMMAND

xbiff

Linux Commands,
Organized by Group

checknews

PURPOSE

The **checknews** command is usually used in a user profile (**.profile**) or a shell script (**.login**) to call the **readnews** command in order to check for unread Usenet news messages when a user logs in. The **readnews** command is used with the **-c** option.

RELATED COMMANDS

readnews

chfn *option(s)*

PURPOSE

The **chfn** command changes the information stored in your finger profile. This information is returned over the network to anyone requesting information about you via the finger command. This information includes your name, your office number, your office phone, and your home phone. (By default, this information is not stored on a Linux system; you must enter it yourself.) The existing finger information is returned in brackets if you decide to enter the new finger information interactively (the process if you run **chfn** on a command line by itself).

OPTIONS

-f *name*	Enters your full name.
-h *number*	Enters your home phone number.
-o *office*	Enters your office number.
-p *number*	Enters your office phone number.
-u	Returns Help information.
-v	Prints the version number.

EXAMPLE

```
$ chfn
Changing finger information for Kevin.
Name [Kevin]:
Office [101]:
Office Phone [555-1212]:
Home Phone [555-1213]:
```

RELATED COMMAND

finger

passwd

Linux Commands,
Organized by Group

elm *option(s)*

PURPOSE

The **elm** command is an interactive mail system, more advanced in its capabilities than the **mail** command. You can use **elm** to send a message from a command line (with text input from the command line), send a file to a user from a command line, or specify nothing and use the **elm** interface to read and send mail.

OPTIONS

-a	Uses an arrow cursor.
-c	Expands an alias.
-d *level*	Sets the debugging level.
-f *folder*	Reads mail from *folder* rather than the inbox.
-i *file*	Includes *file* in the outgoing mail message.
-m	Turns the menu off and uses the space to display more message headers.
-s *subj*	Specifies a subject.

RELATED COMMANDS

fastmail

mail

metamail

pine

fastmail *option(s) filename address-list*

PURPOSE

The **fastmail** command sends batch mail to a large group of people in staggered fashion so that the mail system is not overwhelmed. Basically, it's a simplified mail system for the general user.

OPTIONS

-b *bcc-list*	Sends blind carbon copies (BCC) to the e-mail addresses in *bcc-list*.
-c *cc-list*	Sends carbon copies (CC) to the e-mail addresses in *cc-list*.
-C *comments*	Adds *comments* as a Comments: line, added to the RFC822 header.
-d	Lists errors in debugging mode.
-f *from*	Sets *from* as the user name in the From: line.
-i **msg-id**	Adds a message-ID to the mail message.
-r *replyto*	Sets *reply-to* field.
-R *references*	Sets descriptive/reference text for the message.
-s *subject*	Sets the Subject: line of the message with *subject*.

RELATED COMMANDS

elm

rmail

sendmail

finger *option(s) user*

PURPOSE

The **finger** command returns information about a user, stored in their **.plan** and **.project** files. (Most users don't bother to set up these files, so don't be surprised if no information is returned.) You can specify *user* as a login name (which must be exact) or as a first or last name (where all matches are returned; this can be a long list in a networked environment).

OPTIONS

-l   Displays information in the long format. In addition to the information provided in the **-s** option (login name, real name, terminal name, write status, idle time, office location, and office phone number), this option adds the home directory, home phone number, login shell, mail status, and the contents of the **.plan**, **.project**, and **.forward** files.

-m   Overrides matching of first and last names.

-p   Cancels delivery of **.plan** and **.project** files.

-s   Displays information in the short format: login name, real name, terminal name, write status, idle time, office location, and office phone number.

formail *option(s)*

PURPOSE

The **formail** command formats standard input (usually a file, in this instance) into a mailbox format, which can then be manipulated by mail programs.

OPTIONS

+*num*	Skips the first *num* messages.
-*num*	Splits only *num* number of messages.
-a *headerfield*	Adds *headerfield* to messages lacking headers.
-b	Ignores bogus **From:** fields.
-c	Concatenates header fields that are more than one line long.
-d	Allows loose formatting.
-e	Places messages immediately after one another, instead of inserting blank lines between them.
-f	Ignores nonmailbox-format lines.
-i *headerfield*	Adds new *headerfield* even if one already exists; old headerfield is renamed **Old-*headerfield***.

Linux Commands,
Organized by Group

frm *option(s)* [*folder* I *username*]

PURPOSE

The **frm** command list the From: and Subject: fields of selected messages in a mailbox or folder.

OPTIONS

-n	Uses the same numbering scheme as **readmsg**.
-q	Works in quiet mode, producing only a one-line summary for each mailbox or folder specified.
-Q	Works in very quiet mode, returning only error messages.
-s *status*	Uses *status* to specify messages; *status* can be new, unread, old, or read.
-S	Summarizes the number of messages.
-t	Displays full From: field, even if it means displacing the Subject: field.
-v	Prints a header before listing the contents.

RELATED COMMANDS

readmsg

elm

mail

mailx

ftp *option(s) hostname*

PURPOSE

The **ftp** command connects to a remote computer—either on your own network or on the wider Internet. After you're connected to the remote computer, you can copy files back and forth, delete files, and view directory contents so long as you have the proper permissions on the remote computer to do so.

There are two different levels of FTP access usually found on the Internet. *Anonymous FTP* is one level. It occurs when certain portions of a computer are opened to the Internet at large, and anyone can download files from the FTP server. In these cases, you pass along a username of *anonymous* and a password of your electronic-mail address. The second level of access occurs when FTP servers are set up to allow access to specific people. In these cases, you'll need an account on the FTP server, complete with username and password.

Using the FTP command is rather simple—you merely use it on a command line (with or without options; options are usually unnecessary) with or without a hostname. A new FTP prompt replaces the system prompt (as you will see later in the Examples), and from there you enter commands that are executed on the remote machine.

Most Linux distributions, including Slackware Linux, come with the WU-FTP FTP server. This subject is covered under the **ftpd** command.

OPTIONS

-d	Turns on debugging.
-g	Turns off filename globbing.
-i	Turns off interactive mode.
-n	Turns off auto-login after connecting to remote site.
-v	Turns on verbose mode, where all information from the remote server is displayed.

Continued

COMMANDS

! *command arg(s)*	Runs a shell on the local machine, along with optional *argument(s)*.
$ *macro arg(s)*	Runs a *macro* on the local machine.
? *command*	Displays Help information for the specified FTP *command*.
account *password*	Specifies a password that will be required after you login a remote system. This is used with FTP server that are not anonymous in nature.
append *file1 file2*	Appends the local *file1* to the remote *file2*.
ascii	Sets transfer mode to ASCII (text) format, which is the default. If you transfer binary files in ASCII format, you'll find that the binary files have been reduced to rubbish.
bell	Launches a system sound every time a file is transferred.
binary	Sets transfer mode to binary (file) format. This can be used to transfer any file; it's the opposite of the **ascii** setting.
bye	Ends the remote FTP session and the local **ftp** program.
case	Changes the case of all incoming files to lowercase.
cd *directory*	Changes the current directory on the remote machine to *directory*. This only works if you have access to the **cd** command on the remote FTP server.
cdup	Changes the current directory on the remote machine to one level up in the hierarchy.
chmod *options file*	Changes the permissions on the specified *file* on the remote machine. If you don't specify new permissions with *options*, the **ftp** command will prompt you for new permissions.
close	Ends the remote FTP sessions, but leaves the **ftp** program running locally.
cr	Changes carriage-return stripping to **on**.
delete *filename*	Deletes *filename* from the remote FTP server.
debug	Turns on debugging mode.

Continued

dir *directory filename*	Returns the contents of the specified *directory* (or the current working directory if no *directory* is specified) on the remote machine, either to the screen or to a specified *filename* on the local machine.
disconnect	Ends the remote FTP sessions, but leaves the **ftp** program running locally.
get *file1 file2*	Downloads *file1* from the remote machine and stores it locally as *file2*. If *file2* is not specified, the file will be stored locally as *file1*.
glob	Turns on filename expansion for the **mget**, **mdelete**, and **mput** commands.
hash	Returns hash marks (#) for each block transferred.
help *command*	Returns help information for the specified *command*.
idle *seconds*	Sets the **idle** setting on the remote machine in *seconds*.
image	Sets transfer mode to binary (file) format. This can be used to transfer any file; it's the opposite of the **ascii** setting.
lcd *directory*	Changes the current local directory to *directory*. If a *directory* is not specified, the current local directory is changed to your home directory.
ls *directory filename*	Lists the contents of *directory* (or the current working directory if no *directory* is specified) on the remote machine, either to the screen or to a specified *filename* on the local machine.
macdef *macrofile*	Defines a macro, ending with a blank line; the result is stored in *macrofile*.
mdelete *filename(s)*	Deletes *file(s)* on the remote machine.
mdir *filename(s)*	Returns directory information for multiple, specified *filename(s)*.
mget *filename(s)*	Gets the specified *filename(s)* from the remote machine.
mkdir *directory*	Creates a new *directory* on the remote machine.
mls *directory localfile*	Lists the contents of the remote *directory* into *localfile*.

371

Continued

mode *modename*	Changes the mode to the new *modename*. The default is streaming mode.
modtime *filename*	Displays the last modification time of specified *filename*.
mput *filename(s)*	Uploads specified *filename(s)* from local machine to FTP server.
newer *remotefile*	Downloads *remotefile* if it is newer than the version on the local machine.
nlist *directory localfile*	Lists the contents of the remote *directory* into *localfile*.
open *host (port)*	Opens a connection to the specified *host* and optional *port*. If you don't specify a host, the command will prompt you for one.
prompt	Turns off (or on) interactive prompting.
proxy *command*	Runs *command* on another connection.
put *file1 file2*	Copies local file *file1* to the remote machine as *file2*. If *file2* is not specified, then the name *file1* will be used.
pwd	Prints the current (working) directory on the remote machine.
quit	Ends the remote FTP session and the local **ftp** program.
recv *file1 file2*	Downloads *file1* from the remote machine and stores it locally as *file2*. If *file2* is not specified, the file will be stored locally as *file1*.
reget *file1 file2*	Downloads *file1* from the remote machine and stores it locally as *file2*. If there was an interruption in the transfer, the new transfer will start where the old one was interrupted.
remotehelp *command*	Returns help information about *command* from the remote machine.
remotestatus *file*	Returns the status of the remote machine or *file* on the remote machine.
rename *file1 file2*	Renames *file1* on the remote system to *file2*.
reset	Resets the transfer queue.
restart *byte*	Restarts a transfer, beginning with a specific *byte* count.
rmdir *directory*	Deletes *directory* on the remote machine.

Continued

runique	Turns on unique local file naming; if you're attempting to grab a file from a remote machine and one already exists with the same name locally, the remote filename will be grabbed and a number (**.1**, **.2**, etc.) added to the new file.
send *file1 file2*	Copies local file *file1* to the remote machine as *file2*. If *file2* is not specified, then the name *file1* will be used.
site *command*	Returns information about the remote site.
size *file*	Returns the size of the remote *file*.
status	Returns information about the current session.
struct *name*	Changes the file-transfer structure to *name*. The default is streaming.
sunique	Turns on unique remote file naming; if you're attempting to upload a file to a remote machine and one already exists with the same name, the file will be uploaded and a number (**.1**, **.2**, etc.) added to the new file.
system	Returns the name of the operating system running on the remote machine.
trace	Turns on packet tracing.
type *type*	Sets the file-transfer type to *type*; the default is ASCII. Without *type* specified, the current type is returned.
umask *mask*	Sets the mode mask on the remote machine. Without *mask* specified, the current mask is returned.
user *name password account*	Sends your name, password, and account number to the remote server. If you don't specify *password* or *account*, the remote server will prompt you for the information.
verbose	Turns on verbose mode.

RELATED COMMANDS

ftpd

ftpcount

PURPOSE

The **ftpcount** shows the current number of users for each class defined in the **ftpaccess** file.

RELATED COMMAND

ftpwho

getlist *option list*

PURPOSE

The **getlist** gets a list from an NNTP server. The list can be one of *active*, *active.times*, *distributions*, or *newsgroups*. These values request the **active**, **active.times**, **/usr/lib/news/distributions**, or **/usr/lib/news/newsgroups** files, respectively.

OPTION

-h *hostname*   Connects to specified *hostname*.

RELATED COMMANDS

active

nnrpd

lynx *option(s) URL*

PURPOSE

The **lynx** command launches a character-based World Wide Web browser. It doesn't display images in a graphics-rich environment. As a result, it's a fairly speedy Web browser because there is no wait for graphics.

OPTIONS

-anonymous	Specifies an the anonymous account.
-ascii	Disables Kanji translation when Japanese mode is on.
-auth=*ID passwd*	Sets the *ID* and *password* for sites that require such authentication.
-book	Launches **lynx** with the bookmark pages as the initial document.
-cache=*number*	Sets the *number* of cached documents; the default is 10.
-case	Turns on case-sensitive string searching.
-cfg=*filename*	Specifies a new configuration file.
-crawl	Outputs each page to a file if used with **-traversal**; outputs each page to standard output if used with **-dump**.
-display=*display*	Set the display variable for X **rexeced** programs.
-dump	Sends the formatted output of the default document to standard output.
-editor=*editor*	Launches edit mode with the specified *editor*.
-emacskeys	Uses **emacs**-like key movement.
-force_html	Interprets the first document as an HTML page, no matter what.
-ftp	Disables FTP access.
-get_data	Sends form data from standard input using GET method and dump results.
-head	Sends a HEAD request for the mime headers.
-homepage=*URL*	Sets a homepage separate from start page.
-image_links	Toggles inclusion of links for all images.
-index=*URL*	Set the default index file to the specified URL.

376

Continued

-localhost	Disables URLs that point to remote hosts.
-locexec	Enables local-program execution from local files only.
-mime_header	Displays a MIME header of a fetched document along with its source.
-nobrowse	Disables directory browsing.
-noexec	Disables local program execution.
-nolist	Disables the link-list feature in dumps.
-nolog	Disables mailing of error messages to document owners.
-noprint	Disables print functions.
-noredir	Prevents automatic redirection and prints a message with a link to the new URL.
-nostatus	Disable the retrieval status messages.
-number_links	Starts numbering of links.
-post_data	Sends form data from standard input using POST method and dump results.
-realm	Restricts access to URLs in the starting realm.
-reload	Flushes the cache on a proxy server (only the first document is affected).
-restrictions= *option*	Disables services; *option* is one of the following:

all	Restricts all options
bookmark	Disallows changing the location of the bookmark file.
bookmark_exec	Disallows execution links via the bookmark file.
change_exec_ perms	Disallows changing the execute permission on files (but still allows it for directories).
default	Disables default services for anonymous users.
dired_support	Disallows local file management.
disk_save	Disallows saving binary files to disk.
download	Disables downloads.

Continued

editor	Disallows editing.
exec	Disables execution scripts.
exec_frozen	Disallow the changing of the local execution option.
file_url	Disables the opening of files via URLs.
goto	Disables the **goto** command.
inside_ftp	Disallows FTP connections for people from inside your domain.
inside_news	Disallows Usenet new posts from people from inside your domain.
inside_rlogin	Disallows rlogins for people from inside your domain.
inside_telnet	Disallows telnets for people from inside your domain.
jump	Disables the **jump** command.
mail	Disables outgoing mail.
news_post	Disable news posting.
options_save	Disallow saving options in **.lynxrc**.
outside_ftp	Disallow FTPs for people coming from outside your domain.
outside_news	Disallows news postings for people from outside your domain.
outside_rlogin	Disallows rlogins for people from outside your domain.
outside_telnet	Disallows telnets for people from outside your domain.
print	Disallows most print options.
shell	Disallows shell escapes,
suspend	Disallows Linux **Ctrl-Z** suspends with escape to shell.
telnet_port	Disallows specifying a port in telnet connections.

Continued

-rlogin	Disable recognition of **rlogin** commands.
-selective	Requires **.www_browsable** files to browse directories.
-show_cursor	Positions the cursor at the start of the currently selected link, not hidden in the right-hand corner.
-source	Sends the raw HTML code of the default document to standard output.
-telnet	Disables recognition of **telnet** commands.
-term=TERM	Sets terminal type.
-trace	Turns on WWW trace mode.
-traversal	Traverses all HTTP links derived from *startfile*.
-underscore	Toggles use of underline format in dumps.
-validate	Accepts only HTTP URLs for validation.
-vikeys	Enable **vi**-like key movement.

Linux Commands,
Organized by Group

mail *option(s) users*

PURPOSE

The **mail** command (also known in Linux as the **mailx** command) is used to send and receive electronic mail, either from other users on the system or users from the Internet at large (if your system has Internet capabilities).

Mail is only one of many electronic-mail options under Linux; virtually all distributions include the easier-to-use **pine** and **elm** programs, and other distributions include more advanced graphical mail tools.

EXAMPLES

```
$ mail
```
This displays your mail.
```
$ mail reichard@mr.net
```
This begins the process of sending electronic mail to *reichard@mr.net*.

OPTIONS

-b *list*	Sends blind carbon copies to *list*, which is a comma-separated list of names.
-c *list*	Sends copies to users in *list*.
-f *file*	Uses **mbox** (or *file*, if specified) when launching **mail**; used as an alternative mailbox.
-i	Ignores interrupt signals, which is useful when you're using a Linux machine on a noisy dial-up line.
-I	Forces interactive mode.
-n	Doesn't read **/etc/mail.rc** when starting.
-N	Suppresses display of message headers when reading mail or editing a mail folder.
-s *arg*	Uses *arg* as the subject of the mail message.
-v	Works in verbose mode, where the details of delivery are displayed.

Continued

COMMANDS

-num	Displays the preceding message; if *num* is specified, then the *num* number of previous messages is printed.
?	Displays a summary of commands.
!command	Executes shell *command*.
alias (a) alias	Prints all aliases if *alias* is not specified. If *alias* is specified, then information about that alias is listed. If multiple *alias*es are specified, a new one is created or an old one is changed.
alternates (alt)	Manages accounts on multiple machines, informing you about the status of listed addresses or alternates.
chdir dir (c)	Changes your current directory to *dir*. If no directory is specified, then the current directory changes to your home directory.
copy (co)	Copies a message, but does not delete the original.
delete (d)	Deletes messages.
dp, dt	Deletes the current message and displays the next message.
edit (e)	Launches text editor to edit message; after editing, the message is reentered into **mail**.
exit (ex or x)	Quits **mail** without saving changes to the mailbox.
file (fi)	Lists all folders in the folder directory.
folder (fo)	Opens a new mail file or folder. If you don't specify a new folder, the name of the current file is displayed. If you do switch to a new mail file or folder, the changes in the old mail file or folder will be written before switching. Shortcuts for the name of the new mail file or folder are:

#	previous file
%	system mailbox
%*user*	*user*'s system mailbox
&	your **mbox** file
+*folder*	file in your *folder* directory

folders	Lists all folders in the folder directory.

Linux Commands, Organized by Group

Continued

from (f)	Prints message headers of messages.
headers (h)	Lists the current range of headers, which is an 18-message group.
help	Displays a summary of commands.
hold (ho, preserve)	Marks messages that are to be stored in your system mailbox instead of in **mbox**.
ignore *header*	Adds a header field to a list of fields to be ignored. If *header* is not specified, then the current list of fields to be ignored is displayed.
mail (m) *user*	Sends mail to *user*; a list of users can also be specified.
mbox	Moves messages to **mbox** when exiting. Default.
next (n)	Displays next message in the sequence.
preserve (pre)	Marks messages that are to be stored in your system mailbox instead of in **mbox**.
print *list* **(p)**	Prints messages in *list*.
Print *list* **(P)**	Prints *list* of files, as well as ignored header fields.
quit (q)	Ends **mail** session, saving all undeleted, unsaved messages in the **mbox** file, preserving all messages marked with **hold** or **preserve** or never referenced in the system mailbox, and removing all other messages from the system mailbox.
reply (r)	Composes a reply to the originator of the message and the other recipients.
Reply (R)	Composes a reply to the originator of the message, but none of the other recipients.
respond	Composes a reply to the originator of the message and the other recipients.
retain *header*	Adds *header* to the list of fields named in **retained_list**, which are shown when you view a message.
save (s)	Saves a message to a specific folder.
set (se)	Displays all variables. If an argument is presented, it is used to set an option.
saveignore	Removes ignored fields when saving a message.
saveretain	Retains specified fields when saving a message.
shell (sh)	Launches shell.
size	Lists messages by size.

Continued

source *file*	Reads commands from *file*.
top	Displays the first five lines of a message.
type *list* (t)	Prints messages in *list*.
Type (T)	Prints *list* of files, as well as ignored header fields.
unalias	Discards previous aliases.
undelete (u)	Undeletes a message that was previously marked for deletion.
unread (U)	Marks previously read messages as being unread.
unset	Discards previous variables set with the **set** command.
visual (v)	Launches visual editor and edits each message in a list.
write *file* (w)	Writes the message body, without headers, to *file*.
xit (x)	Quits **mail** without saving changes to the mailbox.
z	Display next window of messages.
z-	Displays previous window of messages.

TILDE COMMANDS

These commands are used when composing messages. They must be placed at the beginning of lines.

~!*command*	Runs *command*, then returns to the message.
~b*name(s)*	Adds *name(s)* to the blind carbon-copy field.
~c*name(s)*	Adds *name(s)* to the carbon-copy field.
~d	Reads the **dead.letter** file from your home directory.
~e	Launches the text editor for further editing.
~f*message(s)*	Inserts *message(s)* into the message being sent.
~F*message(s)*	Inserts *message(s)* into the message being sent, including headers.
~h	Edits the header fields.
~m*message(s)*	Inserts *message(s)* into the message being sent, indented by a tab.
~M*message(s)*	Inserts *message(s)* into the message being sent, including headers, indented by a tab.
~p	Prints current message and the header fields.
~q	Quits current message and sends it to **dead.letter** file.

Continued

~r*filename*	Inserts *filename* into the message.
~s*string*	Sets subject as *string*.
~t*name(s)*	Adds *name(s)* to list of recipients.
~v	Starts the VISUAL editor for editing the message.
~w*filename*	Writes the message to *filename*.
~l*command*	Pipes the message through the *command* (usually **fmt**).
~:*mail-command*	Executes *mail-command*.
~~*string*	Inserts *string* into message, prefaced by ~.

MAIL OPTIONS

You can set the following options either via the **set** and **unset** commands or else you can set them in the **mail.rc** file.

append	Appends messages saved in **mbox**, rather than prepending them.
ask, asksub	Asks you for the subject of a message.
askcc	Asks you for additional carbon-copy recipients.
askbcc	Asks you for additional blind carbon-copy recipients.
autoprint	Displays the next message after deleting the current message.
debug	Displays debugging information.
dot	Inserts a dot (.) alone on the last line of a message.
hold	Holds messages in the system mailbox.
ignore	Ignores interrupt signals; displays them as @.
ignoreeof	Ignores **Ctrl-D** at the end of a file.
metoo	Includes the sender as part of a group.
noheader	Suppresses display of message headers when reading mail or editing a mail folder.
nosave	Does not send deleted letter to **dead.letter** file.
Replyall	Switches **reply** and **Reply** commands (covered under "Commands.")
quiet	Suppresses printing the version when first invoked.
verbose	Works in verbose mode, where the details of delivery are displayed.

384

Continued

OPTION STRING VALUES

EDITOR	Editor to use with the **edit** command and ~**e** escape.
LISTER	Pathname of the directory lister to use in the **folders** command. The default is **/bin/ls.**
PAGER	Pathname of the program to use in the **more** command or when the **crt** variable is set. The default paginator is **more**.
SHELL	Pathname of the shell to use in the ! command and the ~! escape. The default system shell is used if this option is not defined.
VISUAL	Pathname of the text editor to use in the **visual** command and ~**v** escape.
crt	Determines how long a message must be before **PAGER** is used to read it. The default is the height of the terminal screen.
escape	Defines the escape character; the default is ~.
folder	Defines the directory storing folders of messages. If it begins with /, then it's considered an absolute pathname; otherwise, it's considered relative to your home directory.
MBOX	Your **mbox** file; the default is **mbox** in your home directory.
record	Pathname of the file used to store outgoing mail; if not defined, outgoing mail is not stored.
indentprefix	String used for indenting message via the ~**m** escape, instead of tabs.
toplines	Defines the number of lines to be printed out with the **top** command.

RELATED COMMANDS

fmt

sendmail

messages *foldername*

PURPOSE

The **messages** command counts the number of messages in a *foldername*, keying off of the number of times the **From:** field appears.

metamail *option(s)*

PURPOSE

The **metamail** command works with multimedia mail messages, as defined by the Multipurpose Internet Mail Extension (MIME) format. It reads a mailcap file to determine how to display nontext message. It's also called by other mail programs that need to display nontext messages.

Unless you run into unusual circumstances, you'll never use **metamail** directly; instead, your mail package will invoke it to display nontext messages. Since users won't use this command directly, we devote little space to it; instead, we encourage you to check the online-manual pages to see how to add metamail support to a mail-reading program or add lines.

Linux Commands,
Organized by Group

387

metasend *option(s)*

PURPOSE

The **metasend** command sends an existing data file as a nontext multimedia mail message. You can specify a message recipient, subject, carbon-copy recipients, MIME content-type, filename, and encoding on the command line; if you don't, you'll be prompted for this information after you launch the command.

OPTIONS

-b	Works in batch mode, exiting if information is missing from the command line.
-c *cc*	Sets the carbon-copy (CC) address.
-D	Sets the Content-description value.
-e *encoding*	Sets the encoding type: *base64*, *quoted-printable*, *7bit*, or *x-uue*.
-E	Specifies that the file is already a MIME entity, not requiring a Content-description header.
-f *filename*	Sets the data file.
-F *from*	Sets the From address.
-i *<content-id>*	Sets the *content-id* for the MIME entity, enclosed in angle brackets.
-I *<content-id>*	Sets the *content-id* for the multipart entity created by **metasend**,
-m *MIME-type*	Sets the MIME content -type.
-n --	Specifies that an additional file is to be included.
-o *outputfile*	Sends the output to *outputfile*.
-P *preamblefile*	Specifies a file to be used as the preamble of the MIME message.
-s *subject*	Sets the Subject field.
-S *splitsize*	Sets the maximum size before splitting a message into parts via **splitmail**.
-t *to*	Sets the To: address,
-z	Deletes temporary files, even if delivery fails.

Continued

RELATED COMMAND

audiosend

mailto

mmencode

splitmail

mimencode *option(s)*

PURPOSE

The **mimencode** command translates to and from the Multipurpose Internet Mail Encoding (MIME) standard. Since MS-DOS/Windows/Windows 95/Windows NT doesn't support uuencoding, MIME encoding is preferable.

OPTIONS

-b	Specifies base64 encoding (the default).
-q	Specifies quoted-printable encoding instead of base64.
-u	Decodes input, not encodes it.
-p	Translates carriage return/line feed sequences into newlines.
-o *filename*	Sends output to *filename*.

mmencode *option(s)*

PURPOSE

The **mmencode** command translates to and from the Multipurpose Internet Mail Encoding (MIME) standard. Since MS-DOS/Windows/Windows 95/Windows NT doesn't support uuencoding, MIME encoding is preferable.

OPTION

-b	Specifies base64 encoding (the default).
-q base64.	Specifies quoted-printable encoding instead of
-u	Decodes input, not encodes it.
-p	Translates carriage return/line feed sequences into newlines.
-o *filename*	Sends output to *filename*.

pine *option(s) address*

PURPOSE

The **pine** command is used to read electronic mail and Usenet news. It supports MIME (Multipurpose Internet Mail Extensions), allowing you to save MIME objects to files. In some cases, it can also initiate the correct program for viewing the object.

Outgoing mail is usually handed off to **sendmail**, but it can be posted directly via SMTP. There are many command-line options; see the online-manual pages for more information.

RELATED COMMANDS

elm

mail

sendmail

Pnews

Pnews *newsgroup title*

Pnews *-h headerfile*

PURPOSE

The **Pnews** command posts news articles to specific newsgroups. It's an interactive program, which means that it guides you through the process of adding an item to a newsgroup. After you've entered the relevant information, the new news item is sent to the Usenet via the **inews** program.

Pnews will include a signature file, if the file is **.news_sig** and stored in your home directory. The **inews** program adds a signature via the **.signature** file stored in your home directory. (If both files exist, then they both will be added to a news item.)

Pnews will use the default system editor to compose messages, which is defined with the EDITOR variable. This program also interacts with the **trn** newsreader; you'll want to look through the online manual pages for more information.

EXAMPLES

```
$ Pnews
I see you've never used this version of Pnews before. I
   will give you extra help this first time through, but
   then you must remember what you learned.

$ Pnews alt.linux.slackware
```

OPTION

-h   When used with **trn**, **Pnews** will insert a previous
                    article that is the subject of the current article.

RELATED COMMANDS

inews

Rnmail

trn

popclient *option(s) host*

PURPOSE

The **popclient** retrieves electronic mail from a mail server running the Internet Post Office Protocol (POP). It supports both POP2 (as specified in RFC 937) and POP3 (RFC 1725).

   This command is used to grab the mail from the remote server (specified by *host*) and store it in a mail folder on your hard disk. From there you'll read it with a mail program like **mail** or **elm**.

OPTIONS

-2	Uses Post Office Protocol version 2 (POP2).
-3	Uses Post Office Protocol version 3 (POP3).
-a	Uses POP3 and retrieves old (previously retrieved) and new messages from the mail server.
-c	Writes messages to standard output instead of disk.
-F	Uses POP3 and deletes old (previously retrieved) messages from the mail server before retrieving new messages.
-f *pathname*	Sets an alternate name for the **.poprc** file.
-k	Keeps old messages on mail server.
-K	Deletes messages on mail server after retrieval.
-l *lines*	Retrieves *lines* of each message body and headers.
-p *string*	Passes *string* as password when logging on the mail server. If you don't specify one, you'll be prompted for a password when you actually login the mail server.
--protocol *proto*	Sets the protocol to use with the remote mail server. The protocol can be:
	POP2 (Post Office Protocol 2)
	POP3 (Post Office Protocol 3)
	APOP (POP3 with MD5 authentication)
	RPOP (POP3 with trusted-host-based authentication, like rlogin/rsh)

Continued

-o *folder*	Appends messages to file in *folder*.
-r *folder*	Grabs messages from *folder*, an alternative folder on the mail server.
-s	Works in silent mode.
-u *name*	Passes *name* as the user to the mail server; by default, this is your login name on your machine.
-v	Works in verbose mode, with all messages between you and the server displayed.

RELATED COMMANDS

fetchmail	(a newer version of popclient-most Linux distributions will contain one or the other)

postnews *option headerfile newsgroup(s)*

PURPOSE

The **postnews** command posts a news item to a Usenet newsgroup. You can specify the newsgroup (or newsgroups) on the command line; if you don't, the **postnews** command will prompt you for a newsgroup. If you do specify newsgroups, you need to separate them with commas but no spaces. After you specify the newsgroup, a text editor allows you to create the posting.

At any point you can terminate the posting by entering nonconforming input, such as a fictional newsgroup name.

OPTION

-h   Specifies that the header is in *headerfile*.

RELATED COMMAND

inews

printmail *option filename*

PURPOSE

The **printmail** command formats mail in anticipation of printing. It copies your messages from your user mailbox or a specified *filename*, with each message separated by a line of dashes. It's actually a call to the **readmsg** command, and it's usually part of a pipeline (like **printmail | lpr**).

OPTION

-p   Uses a form feed instead of dashes to separate messages.

RELATED COMMANDS

elm

readmsg

procmail *option(s) argument(s)*

PURPOSE

The **procmail** command works under the hood to process mail, usually through the **.forward** file mechanism as soon as mail arrives. It can also be installed to work immediately through the mail program.

The **procmail** command sets some environment variables to default values, reads the mail message from **stdin** until an end-of-file marker appears, separates the body from the header, and then, if no command-line arguments are present, looks for a file named **$HOME/.procmailrc**. This file routes the message to the correct folder.

Arguments containing = are considered to be environment-variable assignments. Any other arguments are presumed to be **rcfile** paths.

This is a complex command that can cause some damage to mail processing if not configured properly. Check the online-manual pages for more detailed information about **procmail**.

OPTIONS

-d *recipient*	Turns on explicit delivery mode, where delivery will be to the local user *recipient*. Cannot be used with **-p**.
-f	Regenerates a leading *From* line with *fromwhom* as the sender (instead of **-f** one could use the alternate and obsolete **-r**). If *fromwhom* consists of a single -, then **procmail** will only update the timestamp on the *From* line.
-m	Turns **procmail** into a general-purpose mail filter.
-o	Overrides fake *From* lines.
-p	Preserves the old environment.
-t	Makes **procmail** fail softly; if procmail cannot deliver to any a destination, the mail will not bounce, instead returning to the mail queue with another delivery attempt made in the future.
-Y	Works with Berkeley mailbox format, ignoring *Content-Length:* fields.
-a *argument*	Sets $1 to *argument*.

Continued

SIGNALS

TERMINATE	Terminates prematurely and requeues the mail.
HANGUP	Terminates prematurely and bounces the mail.
INTERRUPT	Terminates prematurely and bounces the mail.
QUIT	Terminates prematurely and silently loses the mail.
ALARM	Forces a timeout.
USR1	Equivalent to VERBOSE=off.
USR2	Equivalent to VERBOSE=on.

RELATED COMMANDS

biff

mail

sendmail

readmsg *option(s) selection folder*

PURPOSE

The **readmsg** command extracts messages from a mail folder. You'll usually do this when you're preparing mail in a text editor and want to quote a specific, existing message from your mail folder.

You use the *selection* argument to specify which message to grab from your mail folder. A wildcard (*) means to pull all messages, while a number refers to a specific message (with **0** or **$** referring to the last message in the mailbox). In addition, you can pull messages that contain a specific string; these strings don't need to be enclosed in quotes. In this instance, the first message that contains the string will be returned. (This method, by the way, is case sensitive).

You can also use **readmsg** from within the **elm** newsreader instead of an external editor, but it works a little differently in that situation. The mailbox used for retrieving messages is the current mailbox, not your inbox; the current **elm** message will be pulled; and the numbering scheme is a little different.

OPTIONS

-f *folder*   Uses *folder* instead of the incoming mailbox. This is useful when you want to search through mail you've already sent.

-h   Includes all header information, not just the default **From:**, **Date:**, and **Subject:** fields.

-n   Excludes all headers from retrieved messages.

-p   Places form feeds (**Ctrl-L**) between messages headers.

-a   Returns all messages that returns the *string* on the command line, not just the first.

RELATED COMMANDS

elm

newmail

richtext *option(s) filename*

PURPOSE

The **richtext** displays "rich text" documents—usually mail messages—on an ASCII terminal, using termcap settings to highlight and underline text. Rich text is part of the Multipurpose Internet Mail Extension (MIME) for multimedia Internet mail not Microsoft's Rich Text Format (RTF).

OPTIONS

-c	Displays text with no formatting.
-f	Specifies termcap escape codes for bold and italic text.
-m	Interprets < in multibyte Japanese and Korean sequences as a true less-than symbol and not the start of a rich text command.
-n	Tells the command to perform no corrections on the raw rich text.
-o	Uses overstriking for underlining when appropriate.
-p	Summons system PAGER from environment variables.
-s *charset*	Uses specified *charset* when processing text. *Charset* can be one of *us-ascii* (the default), *iso-2022-jp*, and *iso-2022-kr*.
-t	Overrides termcap escape codes.

RELATED COMMANDS

mailto

metamail

termcap

Linux Commands, Organized by Group

rmail *username*

PURPOSE

The **rmail** command interprets incoming mail received via uucp. With the advent of the Internet, this command has lessened in usage.

RELATED COMMAND

sendmail

Rnmail

Rnmail *destination_list*

PURPOSE

The **Rnmail** command responds to news articles via electronic mail, instead of posting the message to newsgroups. It's an interactive program, which means that it guides you through the process of sending mail, prompting you for information about the recipient of the message and more.

Rnmail includes a signature file, if the file is **.news_sig** and stored in your home directory. The **inews** program adds a signature via the **.signature** file stored in your home directory. (If both files exist, then they both will be added to a news item.)

Rnmail will use the default system editor to compose messages, which is defined with the EDITOR variable. This program also interacts with the **trn** nwsreader; you'll want to look through the online-manual pages for more information.

EXAMPLE

```
$ Rnmail
To:
Title/Subject:
Prepared file to include [none]:
Editor [usr/bin/vi]:
Check spelling, Send, Abort, Edit, or List?
```

OPTION

-h   When used with **trn**, **Rnmail** will insert a previous
                  article that is the subject of the current article.

RELATED COMMANDS

inews

Pnews

trn

showaudio *filename(s)*

PURPOSE

The **showaudio** command plays an audio e-mail message created with **audiocompose**. It is routinely summoned by a mailcap file, generally with the **metamail** program. Usually it will play the audio on your low-fi computer speaker.

RELATED COMMANDS

audiocompose

audiosend

metamail

showexternal *body-file access-type name*

PURPOSE

The **showexternal** command fetches and displays the body of a mail message that is included by reference, using the MIME type *message/external-body*. It's not usually used on its own, but rather called by **metamail** via a mailcap entry.

RELATED COMMAND

metamail

X Window System Command

X WINDOW

shownonascii *option charset-font-name filename(s)*

PURPOSE

The **shownonascii** command displays all or part of a mail message in a non-ASCII font. By default, it will open up an **xterm** using the font named in the first argument, running the **more** command to view all of the files named on the command line.

OPTION

-e *command*   Uses *command* instead of **more** to display the file.

RELATED COMMANDS

mailto

metamail

showpartial *file ID partnum totalnum*

PURPOSE

The **showpartial** command is used to display the body of a MIME-formatted message that is of the type *message/partial*. When it is called on the last piece, it will put together the pieces and call **metamail** to display the full message. It is intended to be called by **metamail** via a mailcap entry.

RELATED COMMAND

metamail

X Window System Command

showpicture *option filename(s)*

PURPOSE

The **showpicture** command displays an image that has been attached to a mail message via MIME. It loads the X Window System **xloadimage** command to do so. It is meant to be summoned by **metamail** from a mailcap file.

OPTION

-viewer   Specifies a new image viewer.

RELATED COMMAND

metamail

splitmail *option(s) filename*

PURPOSE

The **splitmail** command takes a large mail message (stored in *filename*) and splits it into MIME-compliant partial messages, using the *message/partial* MIME type.

OPTIONS

-d	Delivers the mail.
-v	Works in verbose mode.
-i	Applies similar message-ID fields.
-s	Changes default chunk size for message (default is 250,000).

RELATED COMMANDS

mailto

metamail

tftp *hostname*

PURPOSE

The **tftp** command launches the Trivial File Transfer Protocol.

COMMANDS

ascii	Changes to ASCII mode.
binary	Changes to binary mode.
connect *hostname*	Sets the *hostname* to connect to.
get *filename*	Gets *filename* from host.
mode ascii	Changes to ASCII mode.
mode binary	Changes to binary mode.
put *filename*	Puts *filename* on remote host.
quit	Quits **tftp**.
status	Shows the current status.
timeout *timeout*	Sets the total transmission timeout, in seconds.
verbose	Toggles verbosity.

trn *option(s) newsgroup(s)*

PURPOSE

The **trn** command launches a newsreader that allows you to read through threaded Usenet newsgroup articles. Threading means that articles are interconnected in reply order.

This is a complex but useful command. It is worth your time to read through the voluminous online-manual pages for more information.

Linux Commands, Organized by Group

uudecode *filename*

PURPOSE

The **uudecode** command decodes a file, converting it from a format suitable for sending via electronic mail.

RELATED COMMAND

uuencode

uuencode *filename*

PURPOSE

The **uuencode** command encodes a file, converting it into a format suitable for sending via electronic mail.

RELATED COMMAND

uudecode

uustat *option(s)*

PURPOSE

The **uustat** command returns information about the UUCP status. See the online-manual pages for a list of the available options.

uux *option(s) command*

PURPOSE

The **uux** command executes a command on a remote system, or executes a command on the local system using files from remote systems. See the online-manual pages for a list of the available options.

vrfy *option(s) address hostname*

PURPOSE

The **vrfy** command verifies the existence and accuracy of an e-mail address. If the host is known, that information can be added to the command line, increasing the chances that the existence and accuracy can be verified. If the hostname is not specified, the information may have to go through other mail systems, which can decrease the accuracy.

See the online-manual pages for a list of the available options.

wnewmail *filename*

PURPOSE

The **wnewmail** daemon checks every 10 seconds to see if there is any
new mail. It's similar to **biff** and **xbiff**, except with less flexibility.

RELATED COMMANDS

biff

newmail

xbiff

Linux Commands,
Organized by Group

417

X WINDOW

X Window System Command

xbiff *option(s)*

PURPOSE

The **xbiff** command is an X Window System version of the **biff** command, which notifies you when incoming mail is received.

OPTIONS

-file *filename*	Specifies the name of the mail file to be monitored. The default is **/usr/spool/mail/***username*
-update *seconds*	Specifies how often **xbiff** should check for mail, in *seconds*. The default is every 30 seconds.
-volume *percentage*	Specifies the loudness of the bell (system sound), as a *percentage* of the full audio.
-shape	Specifies if the mailbox window should be shaped.

RELATED COMMAND

biff

Continued

X Window System Command

xmh *option(s)*

PURPOSE

The **xmh** command is an X-based front end to the **mh** mail handler.
On its own, it calls the **mh** package.

OPTIONS

-flag	Flags you when new mail arrives.
-initial *folder*	Specifies another *folder* for new mail.
-path *directory*	Specifies another *directory* for mail folders.

RELATED COMMAND

mail

metamail

mh

PROGRAMMING COMMANDS

These are some of the basic programming commands that ship with most Linux implementations. The Linux operating system is actually a programmer's dream environment; these commands will get you going, but there are additional programming tools covered in the online-manual pages.

ansi2knr — Converts ANSI C to K&R C

ansi2knr *input_file output_file*

PURPOSE

This command converts a standard ANSI C file to a file that meets Kernighan & Ritchie C specifications. Be warned that there are no error messages, so if the translation failed, you won't know.

EXAMPLE

```
$ ansi2knr oldfile.c newfile.c
```

GNU Command

ar *arguments membername file(s)*

PURPOSE

The **ar** command is used to create, modify, and extract from archive files. Archive files are a collection of files stored in a single file, which makes them easier to store and manage in filesystem and device usage. All the important elements of files, including permissions, owners, timestamp, and group, are saved in the archive.

This command is used most in programming situations, as it is used to create libraries that contain frequently used subroutines.

A *membername* is a file that already exists within the archive. Some of the options, particularly those that specify the order of files within the archive, rely on a *membername*.

Two arguments to the **ar** command are required: an option of some sort that specifies the operation, and the name of the file. This command can be confusing, since the option usually must begin with **p**.

OPTIONS

-a	Adds new files after a membername.
-b	Adds new files before a membername. This is the same as the **i** argument.
-c	Creates a new archive.
-d	Deletes specified files. If you run this option and don't specify files, nothing will be deleted.
-f	Truncates the names of a file to a specific length.
-i	Inserts new files before a membername. This is the same as the **b** argument.
-m	Moves files within an archive. At times the specific order of files is important in an archive, especially when programming libraries are involved. The named files will be moved to the end of the archive.

Linux Commands, Organized by Group

Continued

-o	Uses original dates when extracting files. This is essential if you want to maintain the original time-stamps, because **ar** will apply the timestamp at the time of extraction to the files.
-p	Prints the names of the file within the archive.
-q	Quick append, which means that specified files are added to the end of the archive. This option is not countered by any other options (such as **a**, **b**, and **i**), since all new files are automatically placed at the end of the archive. However, the archive's symbol-table index is not updated, which means that the **s** argument or the **ars** or **ranlib** command must be used to update it.
-r	Replaces files within the archive. An existing file within the archive with the same name is automatically deleted.
-s	Updates the symbol-table index. This is the equivalent of the **ranlib** command.
-t	Lists a table with the names of files within the archive, or it can match a list of files with the names of the files within the archive.
-u	Inserts only newer files when replacing files with the **r** argument.
-v	Tells **ar** to work in verbose mode, listing the files within the archive that are acted upon.
-x	Extracts files from the archive.

RELATED COMMANDS

ars

ranlib

as *option(s) files*

PURPOSE

The GNU **assembler** command creates object files from assembly files. Basically, it's used to assemble files created with the gcc C compiler before they are linked with **ld**.

You can either assemble from an existing C file or from standard input (your keyboard). If you're inputting a file via keyboard, you'll need to use **Ctrl-D** to tell **as** that input has ended.

OPTIONS

-a	Turns on assembly listings, which is output as files are assembled. However, there are a number of other options that can be combined with:

	-ad	Omits debugging directives.
	-ah	Includes high-level source code if the source file can be found and the code was compiled with **-g**.
	-al	Includes assembly listing.
	-an	Omits form processing.
	-as	Includes symbol listing.
	-afile	Specifies listing filename.

--defsym	Defines the symbol SUM to equal *VALUE* (an integer
ger **SYM=VALUE**	constant) before a file is assembled.
-f	Assembles in fast mode, which skips preprocessing in those cases where the source is compiler output.
-Ipath	Adds *path* to the list of .include directives.
-K	Warns when difference tables are altered for long displacements.
-L	Keeps local symbols in symbol tables, starting with
L.	
-M	Assembles in MRI compatibility mode.
-o *objfile*	Specifies the object-file output as *objfile.*
-R	Folds data section into text section.

Linux Commands, Organized by Group

425

Continued

-v	Returns as version.
-W	Suppresses warnings.
--| *files*	Source files to assemble (| **files**) or assemble from standard input (--).

RELATED COMMANDS

gcc

ld

GNU Command

bison *option(s)*

PURPOSE

The **bison** takes command the grammar specification in the file *filename.y* and generates an LR parser for it. The parsers consist of a set of LALR parsing tables and a driver routine written in C. Parse tables and the driver routine are usually written to the file **y.tab.c**.

It's a GNU replacement for the **yacc** command. There are a few differences between **bison** and **yacc**: for instance, generated files do not have fixed names, but instead use the prefix of the input file. You'll want to check the online-manual pages for more details.

OPTIONS

-b prefix	Changes the prefix prepended to output filenames to prefix. The default is y.
-d	Writes a header file containing macro definitions for the token type names defined in the grammar and the semantic value type YYSTYPE, as well as extern variable declarations.
-l	Doesn't insert code into existing files.
-o outfile	Uses outfile as the parser file.
-p *prefix*	Renames the external symbols used in the parser so that they start with *prefix* instead of *yy*.
-t	Changes the preprocessor directives to include debugging information.
-v	Writes a human-readable description of the generated parser to **y.output**.

RELATED COMMANDS

yacc

cc *option filename*

PURPOSE

The **cc** command is the standard C-compiler command. Linux features **gcc**, the GNU C Compiler, as its C-language tool of choice. Check the listings for **gcc** for more information.

GNU Command

cpp *option(s) inputfile outputfile*

PURPOSE

The C preprocessor is a macro processor that is used by the C compiler to transform your program before actual compilation. For a more detailed explanation, see the **info** entry for **cpp.info** and the online-manual pages.

RELATED COMMANDS

gcc

imake

GNU Commands

GNU COMMAND

ctags *option(s)*

PURPOSE

The **ctags** command creates a tag-table file in a format usable by **vi.** Supported syntaxes are C, C++, Fortran, Pascal, LaTeX, Scheme, Emacs Lisp/Common Lisp, Erlang, Prolog, and most assembler-like syntaxes.

See the online-manual pages for more information.

GNU Commands

etags *option(s)*

PURPOSE

The **etags** command creates a tag-table file in a format usable by **emacs.** Supported syntaxes are C, C++, Fortran, Pascal, LaTeX, Scheme, Emacs Lisp/Common Lisp, Erlang, Prolog, and most assembler-like syntaxes.

See the online-manual pages for more information.

flex *option(s) filename*

PURPOSE

The **flex** command generates scanner programs that recognize lexical patterns in text. This command reads the given input files, or its standard input if no filenames are given, for a description of a scanner to generate. The description is in the form of pairs of regular expressions and C code, called *rules*. The output is a C source file. This file is compiled and linked with the **-lfl** library to produce an executable.

See the online-manual pages for more information.

GNU Command

GNU COMMAND

***g77** option(s) filename*

PURPOSE

The **g77** command compiles Fortran programs. See the **info** listing
for **g77** for information on Fortran and this command.

433

GNU Command

GNU COMMAND

gawk *option(s) filename*

PURPOSE

The **gawk** command is the GNU version of the AWK programming language—not necessarily a complex language, but an involved one. You'll want to check the online-manual pages or perhaps even an AWK programming book for more information.

GNU Commands

GNU COMMAND

gcc *option filename*

g++ option filename

PURPOSE

The **gcc** and **g++** commands are the C-language and C++-language compilers used in Linux. (Also supported is Objective-C.) Both process input files through one or more of four stages: preprocessing, compilation, assembly, and linking. The **gcc** command assumes that preprocessed (**.i**) files are C and assumes C-style linking, while **g++** assumes that preprocessed (**.i**) files are C++ and assumes C++ style linking. Commands work with the following filename extensions:

.c	C source; preprocess, compile, assemble
.C	C++ source; preprocess, compile, assemble
.cc	C++ source; preprocess, compile, assemble
.cxx	C++ source; preprocess, compile, assemble
.m	Objective-C source; preprocess, compile, assemble
.i	Preprocessed C; compile, assemble
.ii	Preprocessed C++; compile, assemble
.s	Assembler source; assemble
.S	Assembler source; preprocess, assemble
.h	Preprocessor file; not usually named on command line

Files with other suffixes are passed to the linker. Common cases include:

.o	Object file
.a	Archive file

A primer on programming and the use of the C language is not presented here; entire libraries cover C programming much better than we can in this limited forum. In addition, there are hundreds of options available for this command; you'll want to check the **info** pages for more information.

Linux Commands,
Organized by Group

gprof *option(s)*

PURPOSE

The **gprof** command produces an execution profile of C, Pascal, or Fortran77 programs. The effect of called routines is incorporated in the profile of each caller. The profile data is taken from the call graph profile file (**gmon.out**, by default), which is created by programs that are compiled with the **-pg** option of **cc**, **pc**, and **f77**. The **-pg** option also links in versions of the library routines that are compiled for profiling.

   Gprof reads the given object file (the default is **a.out**) and establishes the relation between its symbol table and the call graph profile file from **gmon.out**. If more than one profile file is specified, the **gprof** output shows the sum of the profile information in the given profile files.

OPTIONS

-a	Suppresses printing of statically declared functions.
-b	Suppresses printing of descriptions of each field in the profile.
-c	Determines the static call graph of the program with a heuristic that examines the text space of the object file.
-e *name*	Suppresses the printing of the graph profile entry for routine *name* and all its descendants (unless they have other ancestors that aren't suppressed).
-E *name*	Suppresses the printing of the graph profile entry for routine *name* (and its descendants), like **-e**, and also excludes the time spent in *name* (and its descendants) from the total and percentage time computations.
-f *name*	Prints the graph profile entry of only the specified routine *name* and its descendants.

Continued

-F *name*	Prints the graph profile entry of only the routine *name* and its descendants, like **-f**, and also uses only the times of the printed routines in total time and percentage computations.
-k *fromname toname*	Deletes arcs from routine *fromname* to routine *toname*.
-s	Produced a profile file **gmon.sum** that represents the sum of the profile information in all the specified profile files.
-z	Displays routines that have zero usage (as shown by call counts and accumulated time).

RELATED COMMANDS

cc

monitor

profile

prof

X Window System Command

imake *option(s)*

PURPOSE

The **imake** command generates **makefiles** from a template, a set of **cpp** macro functions, and a per-directory input file called an **Imakefile**. This allows machine dependencies (such as compiler options, alternate command names, and special **make** rules) to be kept separate.from the descriptions of the various items to be built.

OPTIONS

-D*define*	Sets directory-specific variables; sent to **cpp**.
-I*directory*	Sets the directory containing the **imake** template and configuration files.
-T*template*	Specifies the master template file.
-f *filename*	Sets name of the per-directory input file.
-C *filename*	Specifies the name of the .**c** file being constructed in the current directory.
-s *filename*	Specifies the name of the **make** description file to be generated, but does not invoke **make**.
-e	Executes the final **Makefile**.
-v	Prints the **cpp** command line used to generate the **Makefile**.

RELATED COMMANDS

make

xmkmf

GNU Command

make *option(s) target*

PURPOSE

The **make** command manages a group of files that make up a program. When there are changes to a program, such as a change in the source code, the **make** command can create a new program, keeping existing portions of the program while incorporating the changes. The **make** command determines which pieces of a program need to be recompiled and issues the commands to recompile them.

The **make** command is used most often with the C programming language (as well as X Window System software), but it can be used with any programming language whose compiler is run with a shell command.

The **make** command uses a **Makefile** to determine what changes are necessary and issues the commands needed to update the files. Typically, the executable file is updated from object files, which are derived from source files.

You typically need only run **make** on a command line to perform all the recompilations automatically. A README file included with the distribution will typically provide more detailed instructions.

OPTIONS

-b	Ignored; included for compatibility with non-GNU versions of **make**.
-m	Ignored; included for compatibility with non-GNU versions of **make**.
-C *dir*	Changes to *dir* directory before doing anything.
-d	Returns debugging information in addition to the normal information.
-e	Uses environment variables over variables specified in **makefiles**.
-f *file*	Uses *file* as a **makefile**.
-i	Ignores errors arising from compilation problems.

Continued

-I *dir*	Specifies *dir* as a location to search for included makefiles.
-j *jobs*	Sets the number of *jobs* (commands) to run simultaneously.
-k	Continues as much as possible after an error.
-l *load*	Specifies that no new jobs (commands) should be started if there are other jobs running and the load average is at least *load* (a floating-point number).
-n	Prints the commands as though they were executed, but does not execute them.
-o *file*	Skips remaking *file*, even if the **makefile** indicates that it should be remade.
-p	Prints the database generated from the **makefile**, then runs the command.
-q	Works in question mode, returning an exit status that is zero if the specified targets are already up to date, nonzero otherwise.
-r	Eliminates built-in implicit rules.
-s	Doesn't print the commands as they are executed.
-S	Cancels the effect of the **-k** option; useful in a recursive **make**.
-t	Touches files instead of running their commands.
-w	Returns the working directory before and after other processing.
-W *file*	Pretends that the target *file* has been modified. Use this with the **-n** option to see what would happen if you actually did modify the file.

RELATED COMMANDS

gcc

makedepend

X Window System Command

makedepend *option(s) sourcefile(s)*

PURPOSE

The **makedepend** command reads a *sourcefile* and parses it like a C-preprocessor, processing all **#include**, **#define**, **#undef**, **#ifdef**, **#ifndef**, **#endif**, **#if**, and **#else** directives so that it can correctly tell which **#include** directives would be used in a compilation.

Every file that a *sourcefile* includes, directly or indirectly, is a dependency. These dependencies are then written to a **makefile** in such a way that **make** will know what to recompile when a dependency has changed.

By default, **makedepend** sends output to **makefile** (if it exists) or **Makefile**.

OPTIONS

-a	Appends dependencies to the end of the file instead of replacing them.
-Dname=def	Defines *name* in the **makedepend** symbol table.
-fmakefile	Defines an alternate filename for the **makefile**.
-Iincludedir	Specifies an include directory by prepending *includedir* directories listed in an **#include** directive.
-m	Issues a warning when a file is to be included more than once.
-oobjsuffix	Specifies a suffix for an object file, instead of the default **.o**.
-pobjprefix	Specifies a prefix for an object file (usually a new directory).
-sstring	Sets a new starting string delimiter for the **makefile.**
-wwidth	Sets the line width. The default is 78 characters.
-v	Runs in verbose mode, where the names of files included is sent to the screen.
-Yincludedir	Replaces the standard include directories with *includedir*.

Continued

RELATED COMMAND

cc

make

X Window System Command

makestrs *option(s)*

PURPOSE

The **makestrs** command makes string table C source files and header. The C source file is written to **stdout**.

OPTIONS

-arrayperabi	Generates a separate array for each string.
-defaultab	Generates a normal string table even if **makestrs** was compiled with -DARRAYPERSTR.
-earlyR6abi	Maintains binary compatibility between X11R6 public-patch 11 (and earlier) and X11R6 public-patch 12 (and later).
-functionabi	Generates a functional abi to the string table.
-intelabi	Works with Intel platforms conforming to the System V Application Binary Interface (SVR4).

msgfmt   Create Message Option

msgfmt *option filename.po*

PURPOSE

The **msgfmt** command creates a message object *filename.mo* from a portable message file *filename.po*, which remains unchanged.

OPTIONS

-**v**   Works in verbose mode.

RELATED COMMANDS

gettext

xgettext

GNU Command

objcopy *option(s) infile outfile*

PURPOSE

The **objcopy** command copies the contents of an object file to another, using the GNU BFD Library to read and write the object files. It can write the destination object file in a format different from that of the source object file.

A long list of command-line options is available with this command; check the **info** pages on **objcopy** for more information.

PURPOSE

Perl is the Practical Extraction and Report Language. It's an interpreted language optimized for scanning arbitrary text files, extracting information from those text files, and printing reports based on that information. It was made popular by the rise of UNIX and Linux servers on the Internet.

That is the short definition. It's also an amazingly complex and useful language, one too complex to summarize here. You'll want to check out the lengthy online manual pages for **perl**; they cover all aspects of **perl** for both the beginner and the advanced user. In addition, you might want to invest in a good **perl** text.

ref *option(s) filename tag*

PURPOSE

The **ref** command displays the header of a function, checking in the **tags** file and then scanning the source file for the function. The information then returned is an introductory comment (if there is one), the function's declaration, and the declarations of all arguments.

OPTIONS

-c *class*	Specifies a *class* for the tag.
-f *file*	Looks for a tag (as a static function) in *file*.
-t	Outputs tag information, instead of the function header.

RELATED COMMANDS

ctags

rpcgen *infile option(s)*

PURPOSE

The **rpcgen** command generates C code to implement an RPC protocol. The input to **rpcgen** is a language similar to C known as RPC Language (Remote Procedure Call Language). See the online-manual pages for a more detailed description.

OPTIONS

-5	Generates code for the SVR4-style of RPC.
-a	Generates all files, including the sample code for client and server side.
-b	Generates code for the SunOS4.1-style of RPC (the default).
-c	Compiles into XDR routines.
-C	Generates code in ANSI C. This option also generates code that could be compiled with the C++ compiler. (Default.)
-D *name*	Defines a symbol *name*.
-h	Compiles into C data-definitions (a header file).
-I	Generates a service that can be started from **inetd**, instead of the default static service that handles transports selected with **-s**.
-k	Generates code in K&R C.
-K *secs*	Sets the default *secs* after servicing a request before exiting. To create a server that exits immediately upon servicing a request, **-K 0** can be used. To create a server that never exits, the appropriate argument is -**K -1**.
-l	Compiles into client-side stubs.
-m	Compiles into server-side stubs, but does not generate a *main* routine.
-n *netid*	Compiles into server-side stubs for the transport specified by netid. There should be an entry for *netid* in the **netconfig** database.
-N	Uses the newstyle of **rpcgen**, allowing procedures to have multiple arguments.

Continued

-o *outfile*	Specifies the name of the output file.
-s *nettype*	Compiles into server-side stubs for all the transports belonging to the class ***nettype***.
-Sc	Generates sample code to show the use of remote procedure and how to bind to the server before calling the client side stubs generated by **rpcgen**.
-Ss	Generates skeleton code for the remote procedures on the server side. You need to fill in the actual code for the remote procedures.
-t	Compiles into RPC dispatch table.
-T	Generates the code to support RPC dispatch tables.

Linux Commands,
Organized by Group

GNU Command

strip *filename*

PURPOSE

The **strip** command strips symbols from object files. The list of object files may include archives, but at least one object file must be given. WARNING: The GNU version modifies the files named in its argument, rather than writing modified copies under different names, so be careful in your naming schemes.

OPTIONS

-F *bfdname*	Treats the original *objfile* as a file with the object-code format *bfdname*, and rewrites it in the same format.
-g	Removes debugging symbols only.
-I *bfdname*	Treats the original *objfile* as a file with the object-code format *bfdname*.
-K *symbolname*	Copies *symbolname* from the source file.
-N *symbolname*	Strips *symbolname* from the source file.
-O *bfdname*	Replaces *objfile* with a file in the output format *bfdname*.
-R *sectionname*	Removes *sectionname* from the file. Be careful—incorrectly removing a section may make the object file unusable.
-s	Removes all symbols.
-S	Removes debugging symbols only.
--strip-unneeded	Strips all symbols that are not needed for relocation processing.
-v	Works in verbose mode, listing all the object files modified.
-x	Removes nonglobal symbols.
-X	Removes compiler-generated local symbols (usually beginning with *L* or .).

xgettext *option(s)* *filename*

PURPOSE

The **xgettext** command extracts strings (text) from C programs. It's used to create portable message files, which contain copies of C strings from the source code in a specified *filename*. The portable message file can be used as input to the **msgfmt** utility, which will produce a binary form of the message file used at application run-time.

OPTIONS

-a	Extract ALL strings, not just those found in
-c_flag_	Adds comments beginning with *flag* are added to *filename* as # delimited comments.
-d	Produce duplicates, not sorting output when writing the file and not overwriting existing output files.
-m_string_	Fills in the *msgstr* line with output from the **xgettext** command.
-n	Adds # delimited line-number comments to the output file, indicating the line number in the source file where each extracted string is encountered.
-o_filename_	Uses *filename* as the default output file.
-p_pathname_	Sets the directory for the output files.
-x_filename_	Excludes the strings found in *filename* from the extraction process.
-P	Includes the strings in preprocessor statements.

RELATED COMMANDS

msgfmt

X Window System Command

X WINDOW

xmkmf *option(s) topdirectory currentdirectory*

PURPOSE

The **xmkmf** command creates a **Makefile** from an **Imakefile**. If your Linux system is not configured to process an **Imakefile**, you'll want to use a **Makefile** instead.

RELATED COMMAND

imake

X Window System Command

xxgdb *option(s)*

PURPOSE

The **xxgdb** command is an X Window System front end to the **gdb** debugger. See the **gdb** command for further information.

OPTIONS

This command accepts all the **gdb** options, as well as the following.

-bigicon	Uses a larger icon.
-db_name	Specifies a debugger to use instead of **gdb**.
-db_prompt	Sets a new debugger prompt.
-i *filename*	Sets the initial **gdb** command file.
-nx	Does not execute **gdb** command file.

RELATED COMMAND

gdb

Linux Commands, Organized by Group

yacc *option(s) filename*

PURPOSE

The **yacc** command reads the grammar specification in the file *filename* and generates an LR parser for it. The parsers consist of a set of LALR parsing tables and a driver routine written in C. Parse tables and the driver routine are usually written to the file **y.tab.c**.

OPTIONS

-b *prefix*	Changes the prefix prepended to output filenames to *prefix*. The default is *y*.
-d	Write the header file **y.tab.h**.
-l	Doesn't insert code into existing files.
-r	Produce separate files for code (**y.code.c**) and tables (**y.tab.c**).
-t	Changes the preprocessor directives to include debugging information.
-v	Writes a human-readable description of the generated parser to **y.output**.

RELATED COMMANDS

bison

NETWORKING COMMANDS

These are commands that will connect you to a remote machine (either on your own network or on the Internet), and—once connected—help you through a session.

Linux Commands,
Organized by Group

dnshostname — Show Domain Name

dnshostname *option hostname*

PURPOSE

The **dnshostname** command returns information about the current hostname, while a privileged user can use the command to set a new hostname.

OPTIONS

-f	Prints the full domain name.
-s	Prints the short domain name.
-F *file*	Checks *file* for the hostname.

dnsquery *option(s)*

PURPOSE

The **dnsquery** command queries nameservers via BIND resolver library calls.

OPTIONS

-n *nameserver*	Specifies the nameserver, either by IP addresses or domain name.
-t *type*	Sets the type of resource record of interest, one of the following:

A	address
NS	nameserver
CNAME	canonical name
PTR	domain-name pointer
SOA	start of authority
WKS	well-known service
HINFO	host information
MINFO	mailbox information
MX	mail exchange
RP	responsible person
MG	mail group member
AFSDB	DCE or AFS server
ANY	wildcard

-c *class*	Sets the class of resource records of interest, one of the following:

IN	Internet
HS	Hesiod
CHAOS	Chaos
ANY	wildcard

-p *num*	Specifies the period to wait before timing out.
-r *num*	Sets the number of times to retry if the nameserver doesn't respond.
-s	Uses a stream rather than a packet.

Linux Commands, Organized by Group

faucet *option(s) port*

PURPOSE

The **faucet** command is a fixture for a BSD network pipe, providing the functionality of pipes over the network. It behaves as the server end of a server-client connection and works well with **hose**, especially when you don't have easy access to the destination account (such as a root account where **.rhosts** are a bad idea). Basically, **faucet** creates a BSD socket, binds it to the *port* specified on the command line, and listens for connections. Every time **faucet** gets a connection, it runs *command* and its *args*.

 The **faucet** command is not considered to be a very secure method of networking. Use with caution.

OPTIONS

There are many more options with this command; these are the most frequently used. Check the online-manual page for a full listing.

-localhost	Specifies that the listening socket should be bound to a specific Internet address on the local host.
-daemon	Specifies that **faucet** should disassociate from the controlling terminal once it has started listening on the socket, using the **setsid()** system call.
-shutdown	Turns the bidirectional socket into a unidirectional socket.
-serial	Tells **faucet** to wait for one child to finish before accepting any more connections.
-pidfile *filename*	Write its process ID into *filename*.

fuser *option(s) filename(s)*

PURPOSE

The **fuser** filename lists the process IDs of those, using a particular file or filesystem. Information returned includes the following:

c	Current directory
e	Executable file
f	Open file
m	Mapped file or shared library
r	Root directory

OPTIONS

-	Resets options to defaults.
-signal	Sends a *signal* to a process. Use **-l** to see a list of the signal names.
-a	Shows all files, not just the ones being accessed.
-k	Kills all the processes accessing the file.
-l	Returns a list of the signal names.
-m	Returns information about a mounted filesystem.
-s	Runs in silent mode.
-u	Returns names of the users of the processes.
-v	Works in verbose mode, returning process ID, user-name, command name, and access fields.

getpeername *option(s)*

PURPOSE

The **getpeername** returns information about a socket connection.

OPTIONS

fd	Specifies file descriptors.
-verbose	Returns more detailed information.

hose *option(s)*

PURPOSE

The **hose** command is a fixture for a BSD network pipe, providing the functionality of pipes over the network. It behaves as the client end of a server-client connection and works well with **faucet**, especially when you don't have easy access to the destination account (such as a root account, where **.rhosts** are a bad idea). Basically, **hose** creates a BSD socket, binds it to the *port* specified on the command line, and listens for connections. Every time **hose** gets a connection, it runs *command* and its *args*.

The **faucet** command is not considered to be a very secure method of networking. Use with caution.

WARNING

OPTIONS

There are many more options with this command; these are the most frequently used. Check the online-manual page for a full listing.

-delay *n*	Specifies how many *n* seconds to wait between tries.
-retry *n*	Specifies that connections should be retried *n* times.
-shutdown r	Makes it a read-only socket.
-shutdown w	Makes it a write-only socket.
-unix	Specifies that *port* is not an Internet port number or service name, but rather a filename for a UNIX domain socket.

Linux Commands,
Organized by Group

host *option(s) hostname server*

PURPOSE

The **host** command prints information about a specified *hostname* or *server* using DNS. You can also specify IP addresses, which will then be converted to hostnames through DNS.

OPTIONS

-a	Looks for ANY type of resource record class.
-A	Looks up the IP address for a hostname, then does a reverse lookup to see if they match. Also looks up the hostname of an address, then does a reverse lookup to see if they match. Also checks IP addresses for all hostnames in a given zone. Returns no information if everything matches.
-c *class*	Looks for a specified resource record *class* (ANY, CH, CHAOS, CS, CSNET, HS, HESIOD, IN, INTERNET, or *). The default is IN.
-C	Lists all machines in a zone, determining of the zone's servers are authoritative.
-d	Works in debugging mode.
-dd	Works in debugging mode, but with more detail than **-d**.
-D	Returns the number of unique hosts in a zone, as well as the names of hosts with more than one address per name.
-e	Suppresses information about hosts outside of a specific zone.
-E	Returns the number of unique hosts in a zone, as well as the names of extra-zone hosts.
-f *file*	Sends output to *file* as well as standard output.
-F *file*	Sends output to *file*, with extra resource data sent to standard output.
-G *zone*	Returns the number of unique hosts in a zone and the names of gateway hosts.
-H *zone*	Returns the number of unique hosts in a zone.
-i	Returns information about an IP address: hostname and class (always PTR).

Continued

-I *chars*	Ignores warnings about hostnames with illegal characters (specified by *chars*) in their names.
-l *zone*	Returns information about all the hosts in *zone*.
-L *level*	Specifies the *level* to search to when using the **-l** option.
-m	Prints MB, MG, and MR records; expands MR and MG records to MB records.
-o	Suppresses sending data to standard output.
-p *server*	Returns information about a primary *server* in a specific zone. Designed for use with the **-l** option.
-P *servers*	Returns information about preferred hosts; *servers* is a comma-delimited list. Used with the **-l** option.
-q	Suppresses warnings in silent mode, but not error messages.
-r	Requests cached information from server, not new queried information.
-R	Searches components of the local command when non-fully-qualified names are found.
-S	Returns all hosts, but not subzones, to standard output, including the host class and IP addresses. Used with the **-l** option.
-t *type*	Requests information about *type* entries in the resource record; *type* is A, ANY, NS, PTR, or *.
-T	Prints time-to-live information for cached data.
-u	Uses TCP instead of UDP.
-v	Works in verbose mode.
-vv	Works in verbose mode, including the defaults on *host*.
-w	Works persistently until host returns information.
-x	Queries multiple hosts and zones; can also be used to query multiple servers with **-X**.
-X	Queries multiple servers as well as multiple hosts and zones.
-Z	Includes trailing dots in resource records, as well as time-to-live data and the class name.

RELATED COMMAND

hostname

hostname *option hostname*

PURPOSE

The **hostname** command returns information about the current hostname, while a privileged user can use the command to set a new hostname.

OPTIONS

-d	Prints Domain Name Server (DNS) domain name.
-f	Prints the full domain name.
-s	Prints the short domain name.
-F *file*	Checks *file* for the hostname.

ping

PURPOSE

The **ping** command send ICMP ECHO_REQUEST packets to network hosts, to determine network performance.

OPTIONS

-c *count*	Stops after sending (and receiving) *count* ECHO_RESPONSE packets.
-d	Sets the SO_DEBUG option on the socket being used.
-f	Outputs packets as fast as they come back or one hundred times per second, whichever is more.
-i *wait*	Waits *wait* seconds between sending packets.
-l *preload*	Sends *preload* many packets as fast as possible before falling into its normal mode of behavior.
-n	Works in numeric mode.
-p *pattern* send.	Specifies "pad'" bytes to fill out the packet you
-q	Works in quiet mode; nothing is displayed except the summary lines at startup time and when finished.
-r	Bypasses the normal routing tables and send directly to a host on an attached network.
-R	Includes the RECORD_ROUTE option in the ECHO_REQUEST packet and displays the route buffer on returned packets.
-s *packetsize*	Specifies the number of data bytes to be sent. The default is 56.
-v	Prints verbose output.

rcp *option(s) file1 file2*

PURPOSE

The **rcp** command copies files between machines. These can be machines on your local network or on the Internet.

OPTIONS

-k *realm*	Obtains tickets for the remote host in *realm* instead of the remote host's realm.
-p	Preserves modification times.
-r	Copies directories recursively.
-x	Encrypts files with DES encryption.

RELATED COMMANDS

rlogin

rsh

rlogin *option(s) hostname*

PURPOSE

The **rlogin** command opens a remote session on a specified *hostname*. It uses Kerberos authorization initially, but if the remote host doesn't support Kerberos, then the standard Berkeley **rhosts** authorization mechanism is used. (See the online manual page for more detailed information on Kerberos authentication.)

OPTIONS

-8	Allows an eight-bit input data path at all times; otherwise, parity bits are stripped except when the remote side's stop-and-start characters are other than ^S/^Q.
-d	Turns on socket debugging on the TCP sockets used for communication with the remote host.
-e	Defines the escape character, replacing the default tilde (~) character.
-E	Prevents any character from being recognized as an escape character.
-K	Turns off Kerberos authentication.
-k	Obtains tickets for the remote host in realm *realm* instead of the remote host's realm as determined by **krb_realmofhost**
-L	Runs session in **litout** mode.
-x	Turns on DES encryption.

RELATED COMMANDS

rsh

kerberos

krb_sendauth

krb_realmofhost

rsh *option(s) hostname command*

PURPOSE

The **rsh** runs a *command* on a remote *hostname*. It copies its standard input to the remote command, the standard output of the remote command to its standard output, and the standard error of the remote command to its standard error. Interrupt, quit, and terminate signals are propagated to the remote command; **rsh** normally terminates when the remote command does.

OPTIONS

-K	Turns off Kerberos authentication.
-d	Turns on socket debugging.
-k *realm*	Obtains tickets for the remote host in *realm* instead of the remote host's realm as determined by **krb_realmofhost**.
-l user*name*	Specifies a remote *username*.
-n	Redirects input from the special device **/dev/null**.
-x	Turns on DES encryption.

X Window System Command

rstart *option(s) hostname command args*

PURPOSE

The **rstart** command is actually a sample implementation of a Remote Start client. It uses **rsh** as its underlying remote execution mechanism.

OPTIONS

-c_context_	Specifies *context* for the command, which is a general environment. The default is X.
-g	Interprets *command* on the command line as a generic command, as defined in the protocol document.
-l *username*	Tells **rsh** that the command be run as the specified *username*.
-v	Runs in verbose mode, discarding output from the remote hostname's **rstart** helper and disconnecting from the **rsh** connection.

RELATED COMMANDS

rsh

rstartd

Linux Commands, Organized by Group

rusers *option(s) hostname*

PURPOSE

The **rusers** command produces information about the users logged in on a specific host (or hosts) or all machines on the local network.

OPTIONS

-a	Lists all machines, even if no one is currently logged on them.
-l	Returns listings in long format: username, host-name, tty that the user is logged in to, the date and time the user logged in, the amount of time since the user typed on the keyboard, and the remote host they logged in from (if applicable).

RELATED COMMANDS

rwho

users

who

rwall *hostname filename*

PURPOSE

The **rwall** command sends a message to all the users logged on a specified *hostname*. The message can be sent via a specified *filename*, or else it can be typed directly and terminated with EOF (**Ctrl-D**).

471

rwho *option*

PURPOSE

The **rwho** command shows who is logged in on local machines.
The output is similar to **who**, except that the information covers
everyone on the local network. If a machine does not report back
to **rwho** in 11 minutes, then the machine is assumed to be down.
Idle time for users under one hour is also reported.

OPTION

-a   Report all users, even those who have not typed at
                      their machines in the last hour.

RELATED COMMANDS

rusers

sliplogin *loginname*

PURPOSE

The **sliplogin** command allows you to login an Internet system using a SLIP connection. It takes information from the **/etc/slip.hosts** file (matching the *loginname*) and then initiates a connection. The **/etc/slip.hosts** file must be configured by a root user.

GNU Command

sockdown *option(s)*

PURPOSE

The **sockdown** command performs a **shutdown** system call on one of its file descriptors specified by *fd*. The possible values for *how* are:

0	convert to write-only file descriptor
writeonly	symbolic for same as above
1	convert to read-only file descriptor
readonly	symbolic for same as above
2	complete shutdown—no reads or writes allowed in the future
totally	symbolic for same as above

talk *username [tty]*

PURPOSE

The **talk** commands allows you to chat interactively with another user currently logged on the system. When both sides are running the **talk** command, the screen splits, with one user's typing appearing in one half of the screen, and the other user's typing appearing in the other half of the screen.

The *username* can be someone on your own system. If you want to chat with a user on another system, then you must specify the username as *user@host*. If a user has more than one terminal going, you can specify a terminal with *tty*.

To quit **talk**, type **Ctrl-D**.

RELATED COMMAND

write

Linux Commands, Organized by Group

telnet *option(s) hostname*

PURPOSE

The **telnet** command launches a connection to a remote host using the Telnet protocol. From there, you can use the remote host as if it were your own machine.

OPTIONS

-a	Attempts automatic login.
-d	Turns on debugging mode.
-e *escapechar*	Sets the *escapechar*.
-l *user*	Sends *user* as the variable USER to the remote system; used with **-a**.
-n *tracefile*	Recording trace information in *tracefile*.

uucp *option(s) sourcefile destinationfile*

uucp *option(s) sourcefile destinationdirectory*

PURPOSE

The **uucp** command copies files between systems. See the online-manual pages for a list of the available options.

write *user*

PURPOSE

The **write** command sends a message to another user, who can choose whether or not to carry on a conversation.

ytalk *option(s) username*

PURPOSE

The **ytalk** command is a multiuser chat program. It can also be used to chat with **talk** users.

OPTIONS

-x	Disables the X Window System interface.
-s	Starts the **ytalk** window in a shell.

RELATED COMMAND

talk

SYSTEM-ADMINISTRATION COMMANDS

These are the commands that make your Linux system run more smoothly, ranging from scheduling system chores to dealing directly with PC hardware.

Linux Commands, Organized by Group

481

at *option(s) time date*

at -c *job-ID*

PURPOSE

The **at** command runs a command or a set of commands at a specific *time* and/or on a specific *date*. These must be self-sufficient commands that require no input from you or another user. Normally, these commands are system-administration commands, relating to system backups, electronic-mail delivery, and so on.

Commands and times for the **at** command are entered directly at the command line. You first enter the **at** command and then the time the command is to be run, followed by the command to be run. When you've finished, press **Ctrl-D**. At the specified time, **at** runs the command; if there is any output from the command, it's sent to you as electronic mail.

You have many options when it comes to setting a job. You can specify a time using **HHMM** notation or **HH:MM** notation (in military time), with the assumption that the command will be run starting with the first upcoming instance. You can also indicate **AM** or **PM**. You can also use words like midnight, noon, or teatime (4 p.m.) to specify a time. Commands can also be set up to be run on specific days, using the forms **MMDDYY**, **MM/DD/YY**, or **DD,MM,YY**. (Note the use of slashes and commas.)

Intervals can also be set at specific times from the present. For instance, you could tell **at** to run a command in two weeks using **today + 2 weeks** as the specifier. Other intervals include **minutes**, **hours**, and **days**. You can combine times and dates in the following manner: **at 4pm + 3 days**. Finally, you can combine a time with tomorrow: **at 1pm tomorrow**.

Not all users have access to this command. The **root** user always has access to the **at** command. In addition, the superuser can specify which users have access to the **at** command, as well as explicitly deny access to specific users, through usernames in the **/etc/at.allow** and **/etc/at.deny** files. If **/etc/at.allow** exists, only those usernames in the file can run the **at** command; if it doesn't exist, then **/etc/at.deny** is checked, with the result that anyone *not* mentioned in **/etc/at.deny** can use the **at** command.

Continued

EXAMPLE

```
$ at 1am
ls
Ctrl-D
```

OPTIONS

-b	The same as the **batch** command.
-d	The same as the **atrm** command.
-f *file*	Takes input (that is, the names of commands) from *file* instead of standard input.
-l	The same as the **atq** command
-m	Sends electronic mail when the job is completed.
-q *queue*	Sets the niceness level for the **at** command, using a queue designation. This designation is a single letter, ranging from **a** to **z**. The higher the letter, the "nicer" the command will run (see **nice** for a description of niceness and the Linux operating system). The default for **at** is **c**, so if you want a command to be run when the system has less stress, you'd choose a letter like **m** as the queue designation. Conversely, if you want a command to be run no matter what, you'd use a queue designation of **a**.
-V	Prints the version number.

RELATED COMMANDS

atq

artm

batch

atq *option user job-ID*

PURPOSE

The **atq** command lists all jobs that are already scheduled with the **at** command (for the superuser) or the jobs of a specific user, as well as a specific job ID. This is the same as **at -l**.

OPTIONS

-q *queue*   Sets the niceness level for the **at** command, using a queue designation. This designation is a single letter, ranging from **a** to **z**. The higher the letter, the "nicer" the command will run (see **nice** for a description of niceness and the Linux operating system). The default for **at** is **c**, so if you want a command to be run when the system has less stress, you'd choose a letter like **m** as the queue designation. Conversely, if you want a command to be run no matter what, you'd use a queue designation of **a**.

-v   Shows jobs that have been completed but not yet deleted from the queue.

RELATED COMMANDS

at

atrm

batch

atrm *option user job-ID*

PURPOSE

The **atrm** command removed jobs scheduled with the **at** command. Superusers can delete all jobs, while other users can remove only their own jobs. This is the same as **at -d**.

RELATED COMMANDS

at

atq

batch

485

batch *option(s) time*

PURPOSE

The **batch** command runs a series of commands one at a time, which are entered from a command line as standard input. The difference between **batch** and **at** is that **batch** automatically runs the commands when the system load is light; in these cases, you don't specify when the command is to be run. However, you can specify an execution time with the **batch** command.

When you have finished entering the commands from the command line, use **Ctrl-D** to end input.

OPTIONS

-f *file*   Runs commands from *file*, not from standard input on the command line.

-m   Sends electronic mail when the job is completed.

EXAMPLE

```
$ batch
pr -a kevin.memo
lp kevin.memo
Ctrl-D
```

RELATED COMMAND

at

cpio *flags option(s)*

PURPOSE

The **cpio** command is used to create archives, either on a local filesystem or on a tape backup. The default is to copy to a tape archive.

FLAGS

The **cpio** command must be combined with one or more of the following flags:

-i *option patterns*	Copies all files that match *patterns*, which can incorporate wildcards. (If you use wildcards, you must quote them so that the shell doesn't interpret them.) If you don't specify a *pattern*, then all files are copied.
-o *options*	Copies all files specified by name.
-p *options directory*	Copies files to a local directory, instead of to a tape archive.

The options available to each flag is part of the explanations of each option.

OPTIONS

-0	Listing of files end with a null, not a newline; files that contain a newline in their names can then be included. (Used with **-i** and **-p** flags.)
-a	Sets the access times of files to now. (Used with **-i** and **-p** flags.)
-A	Appends new files to an existing archive on a disk. This must be used with the **-O** or **-F** options. (Used with **-i** and **-p** flags.)
-b	Swaps half-words and bytes. (Used with **-o** flag.)
-B	Sets block size as 5120 bytes per record, as opposed to the default 512 bytes per record. (Used with **-i** and **-o** flags.)
-c	Reads and writes header information as ASCII text. (Used with **-i** and **-o** flags.)

Continued

-C *num*	Sets block size as *num*, as opposed to the default 512 bytes per record. (Used with **-i** and **-o** flags.)
-d	Creates directories as needed. (Used with **-o** and **-p** flags.)
-E *file*	Extracts files found in archive *file*. (Used with **-o** flag.)
-F *file*	Uses *file* as an archive. (Used with **-i** and **-o** flags.)
-H *type*	Specifies the format *type*, which is useful when moving archives to non-Linux machines. The default is *bin*, for binary. Other *types* are *crc* (SVR4 with checksum), *hpodc* (Hewlett-Packard portable format), *newc* (SVR4 portable format), *odc* (POSIX.1 portable format), *tar*, or *ustar* (POSIX.1 tar). (Used with **-i** and **-o** flags.)
-I *file*	Reads input archive as *file*. (Used with **-o** flag.)
-l	Sets up links instead of copying files. (Used with **-p** flag.)
-L	Follows any symbolic links. (Used with **-i** and **-p** flags.)
-m	Modification times are maintained. (Used with **-o** and **-p** flags.)
-M *mesg*	Prints *mesg* when switching between media. Must be used with **-I** or **-O**. (Used with **-i** and **-o** flags.)
-n	Shows user and group IDs; must be used with **-v**. (Used with **-o** flag.)
-O *file*	Directs the output to *file* on another machine. (Used with **-i** flag.)
-r	Renames files; prompts you for new filenames. (Used with **-o** flag.)
-s	Swaps bytes. (Used with **-o** flag.)
-S	Swaps half-words. (Used with **-o** flag.)
-t	Prints table of contents of a proposed archive; doesn't actually create archive. (Used with **-o** flag.)
-u	New files can overwrite old files unconditionally. (Used with **-o** and **-p** flags.)
-v	Turns on verbose mode, where all files are listed. (Used with all flags.)

Continued

-V   Turns on a modified verbose mode, where dots are
printed instead of filenames. (Used with all flags.)

RELATED COMMAND

tar

Linux Commands,
Organized by Group

crond *option(s)*

PURPOSE

The **crond** command launches the **cron** daemon, which scans **crontab** files and runs their commands at the appropriate times. The **cron** system is a way to set up tasks so that they regularly occur.

OPTIONS

-b	Runs **crond** in the background; default unless **-d** is specified.
-c *directory*	Specifies the directory containing **crontab** files.
-d[*debuglevel*]	Sets the debugging level; the default is zero.
-f	Runs **crond** in the foreground.
-l*loglevel*	Sets the logging level; the default is 8.

ctlinnd *option(s)*

PURPOSE

The **ctlinnd** command sends a message to the control channel of **innd**, the InterNetNews server. In the normal mode of behavior, the message is sent to the server, which then performs the requested action and sends back a reply with a text message and the exit code for **ctlinnd**.

There is a long list of options and commands associated with this command; check the online-manual pages for more information.

RELATED COMMAND

innd

df *option(s) disk_device*

PURPOSE

The **df** command returns the amount of free disk space on your Linux system, either across all mounted hard-disk systems or on a specific *disk_device*. The *disk_device* must be a device name (like **/dev/hd1**, **/dev/hd2**, et al) or a specific directory (like **/bin**). The space is shown in 1K blocks.

OPTIONS

-a	Reports on all filesystems, even those with 0 blocks (empty filesystems).
-i	Reports in inode format: used, free, and percent-used inodes.
-P	Reports in POSIX format: one line per filesystem.
-t *type*	Reports on a *type* of device.
-T	Returns the *type* of each filesystem.
-x *type*	Excludes *type* of device.

RELATED COMMAND

du

diskd *option(s)*

PURPOSE

The **diskd** daemon waits for a disk to be inserted into a specified drive, and then either runs a command or exits. This is useful when you want to automatically mount a disk as soon as it is inserted.

 Using this command repeatedly over a long period of time is known to cause hardware damage in the long run.

WARNING

OPTIONS

-d *drive*	Specifies the drive to be observed. The default is drive 0 (**/dev/fd0**).
-i *interval*	Sets the polling interval, in tenths of a second. The default is 10 (one second).
-e *command*	Specifies the *command* to be executed after the disk is inserted.

Linux Commands, Organized by Group

diskseek *option(s)*

diskseekd *option(s)*

PURPOSE

The **diskseek** command accesses the floppy drive to clear the dust out. (Really!) There are two ways to call this command. You can use **diskseek** to access the drive once, or you can use **diskseekd** to access the drive every 16 minutes.

OPTIONS

-d *drive*   Sets the drive to access; the default is drive 0 (**/dev/fd0**).

-i *interval*   Sets the *interval* (in seconds) to access the drive, if you're running **diskseekd**. The default is 1000 seconds. You can combine **diskseekd** with an interval of 0, which is useful when using **diskseek** from a **crontab**.

-p *pidfile*   Stores the process ID of the **diskseekd** daemon in *pidfile* instead of the default **/var/run/diskseekd.pid**.

du *option(s) file(s) directory*

PURPOSE

The **du** command lists how much disk space is used by a file or a directory (as well as all of its subdirectories) in 1K blocks. If no file or directory is named, the default is the current directory.

OPTIONS

-a	Returns information about all files, not just directories.
-b	Returns information in bytes, not blocks.
-c	Totals all files and directories listed.
-D	Includes symbolic links that are command lines.
-k	Returns information in kilobytes (default).
-l	Totals all files, including links that may already be counted.
-L	Includes symbolic links.
-r	Reports if **du** cannot access a file or directory.
-s	Works in silent mode, reporting only totals.
-S	Excludes subdirectories from totals.

RELATED COMMANDS

df

fdisk *option(s) device*

PURPOSE

The **fdisk** command creates and deletes partitions on a hard disk. A hard disk device is usually one of the following:

/dev/hda

/dev/hdb

/dev/sda

/dev/sdb

The partition is specified with a partition number following the device name. For example, the first partition on the first hard drive is /dev/hda1.

OPTIONS

-l	Lists partition tables for all known hard drives and then exits.
-s*partition*	Prints the size of a non-DOS *partition*.

fdmount *option(s)*

PURPOSE

The **fdmount** mounts a floppy disk. This can be either a Linux-formatted floppy or an MS-DOS floppy. It also checks whether the disk is write-protected, in which case it is mounted read-only.

OPTIONS

-d	Runs in daemon mode.
--detach	Runs daemon in background, and detaches it from its tty.
-f	Attempts a mount or unmount operation even when **/etc/mtab** says that the drive is already mounted or not mounted, respectively.
-h	Shows short parameter description.
-i *interval*	Sets the polling interval for daemon mode.
-l	Lists all known drives with their symbolic name, type, and mount status.
-p *file*	Dumps the process ID of the daemon to *file*.
--nodev	Mounts with the NODEV option.
--noexec	Mounts with the NOEXEC option.
--nosuid	Mounts with the NOSUID option. Ignored for MS-DOS filesystems.
--nosync	Mounts without the SYNC option, even when not running as daemon.
-o *option*	Sets filesystem-specific options for MS-DOS: *check, conv, dotsOK, debug, fat, quiet, blocksize.*
-r	Mounts the disk read-only.
-s	Mounts with the SYNC option.

RELATED COMMANDS

mount

mmount

superformat

floppycontrol

setfdprm

Linux Commands, Organized by Group

497

fdrawcmd *option(s)*

PURPOSE

The **fdrawcmd** sends raw commands to the floppy-disk controller. You must have write permission to the selected drive.

There are a number of commands associated with this command. See the online-manual pages for more information.

OPTIONS

All numbers may be given in octal (0209), decimal (137), or hexa-decimal (0x89).

command	Sends *command* directly.
drive=*drive*	Specifies the drive; the default is 0 (**/dev/fd0**).
length=*length*	Sets the length of the transferred data for commands reading from and writing to the disk.
mode	Specifies various flags or'ed together describing the properties of the *command*.
parameter	Sets a parameter for the *command*.
rate=*rate*	Specifies the data-transfer rate: 0 for high density, 1 for double-density 5.25-inch disks, and 2 for double-density 3.5-inch disks.
repeat=*count*	Repeats a command *count* times.

fdformat *option device*

PURPOSE

The **fdformat** is used to format a floppy drive. This is formatted in the Linux format, not in the normal DOS format. Floppy device names are usually **/dev/fd0** or **/dev/fd1**.

OPTION

-n   Skips formatting verification.

free *option(s)*

PURPOSE

The **free** command returns information about memory usage: total free memory, used memory, shared memory, and buffers.

OPTIONS

-b	Returns information in bytes.
-k	Returns information in kilobytes (the default).
-m	Returns information in megabytes.
-o	Suppresses the *buffer adjusted* line.
-s *time*	Regularly return information every *time* seconds.
-t	Prints information on one line.

RELATED COMMAND

du

ftpd *option(s)*

PURPOSE

The **ftpd** command launches the DARPA FTP daemon, which handles incoming FTP requests. It uses the TCP protocol and listens at the port specified in the ftp service in the **services** file.

OPTIONS

-a	Uses the **ftpaccess** file to control access.
-A	Disables the **ftpaccess** access control.
-d	Turns on debugging mode.
-l	Logs sessions in the syslog.
-L	Logs all sessions in the syslog.
-t *timeout*	Sets inactivity timeout period *timeout* seconds.
-i	Logs uploaded file transfers to the **xferlog** file.
-o	Logs downloaded file transfers to the syslog.

RELATED COMMANDS

ftp

inetd

ftpwho

PURPOSE

The **ftpwho** command shows the current process information for each **ftp** user.

RELATED COMMAND

ftpcount

httpd *option(s)*

PURPOSE

The **httpd** command launches the Apache Web server. It can be launched as a daemon and run in the background at all times (the most efficient configuration), or it can invoked by the Internet daemon **inetd** each time a request to a HTTP service is made.

OPTIONS

-d *serverroot*   Sets the initial value for the *ServerRoot* variable to *serverroot*. This variable specifies where the Web-server program is actually located. The default is **/usr/local/etc/httpd**.

-f *config*   Runs the commands in the file *config* on startup. If *config* does not begin with **/**, then it is taken to be a path relative to the *ServerRoot*. The default is **conf/httpd.conf**.

-X   Runs in single-process mode. This is useful when debugging your Web setup, but to be avoided when offering Web services to the world.

RELATED COMMAND

inetd

imapd

PURPOSE

The **imapd** command launches a mail server that supports the IMAP remote-mail access protocol. It is rarely launched by itself on a command line, but is rather launched with other Internet server tools in the **inetd** daemon configuration.

RELATED COMMAND

inetd

inetd *option*

PURPOSE

The **inetd** command launches a series of Internet services. It's here that incoming requests are routed—this daemon listens for connections on specified Internet sockets, and when a connection is made on a socket, **inetd** decides which service should handle the socket connection. It's usually run at boot time by **/etc/rc.local**.

See the online-manual pages for more information on configuring this file.

OPTION

-d   Turns on debugging.

RELATED COMMANDS

ftpd

telnetd

Linux Commands,
Organized by Group

inews *option(s)*

PURPOSE

The **inews** command reads a Usenet news article (perhaps with headers) from a file or standard input if no file is given, checks to make sure that the format meets Usenet standards, and then passes along the article to a Usenet news server specified in the **inn.conf** file. The input consists of the article headers, a blank line, and the message body.

Check the online-manual pages for configuration options and command-line options.

RELATED COMMANDS

injnews

innd

injnews *option(s)*

PURPOSE

The **inews** command reads a Usenet news article (perhaps with headers) from a file or standard input if no file is given, checks to make sure that the format meets Usenet standards, and then passes along the article to a Usenet news server specified in the **inn.conf** file. The input consists of the article headers, a blank line, and the message body.

Check the online-manual pages for configuration options and command-line options.

RELATED COMMANDS

inews

innd

Linux Commands,
Organized by Group

inews *option(s) filename*

PURPOSE

The **inews** command reads a Usenet news article from a file, adding some headers, and performs some consistency checks. If the news article passes the checks, it's then passed along to the Usenet news server specified in the **inn.conf** file.

OPTIONS

-D	Works in debugging mode.
-o *organization*	Specifies a new *organization*.
-O	Doesn't fill in *Organization* field.
-R	Rejects control messages.

RELATED COMMAND

innd

innd *option(s)*

PURPOSE

The **innd** command launches the InterNetNews daemon, which handles all incoming NNTP feeds. It reads the **active**, **newsfeeds**, and **hosts.nntp** files into memory. It then opens the NNTP port to receive articles from remote sites and a named pipe for use by **ctlinnd** to direct the server to perform certain actions. It also opens the **history** database and two log files to replace its standard output and standard error.

Once the files and sockets are opened, **innd** waits for connections and data to be ready on its ports by using **select** and non-blocking I/O. If no data is available, then it will flush its in-core data structures.

Configuring this command can be a complicated affair; check the online-manual pages for more information.

lilo *option(s)*

PURPOSE

The **lilo** command installs the Linux boot loader, which controls how Linux boots. Formerly, when you wanted to use Linux on a system in conjunction with other operating systems, you'd install **lilo** to make sure that the preferred operating system—or a preferred kernel, for that matter—was loaded. Today, there are other boot tools that work better than **lilo**. WARNING: If you're a new user, don't use **lilo** as a boot manager.

OPTIONS

-v	Runs in verbose mode, providing more information about its activity.
-q	Lists the currently map files from **/boot/map**.
-m *map-file*b	Uses *map-file* instead of the default map file.
-C *config-file*	Specifies a configuration other than the default.
-d *delay*	Waits *delay* deciseconds before loading the first kernel on the list.
-D *label*	Uses the kernel with *label*, instead of the first one on the list, as the default kernel to boot.
-r *root-directory*	Performs a **chroot** to *root-directory*; used when repairing a setup from a boot floppy.
-t	Tests without writing a new boot sector or map file.
-c	Turns on map compaction, which merges read requests from adjacent sectors.
-f *disk-tab*	Sets the disk-geometry parameter file; the default is **/etc/disktab**.)
-i boot-sector	Sets a new boot-sector file; the default is **/boot/boot.b**.)
-l	Generates linear sector addresses instead of sector/head/cylinder addresses.
-P {fix|ignore}	Fixes or ignores corrupt partition tables.
-s *save-file*	Saves old boot-sector information in *save-file*.
-S *save-file*	Saves old boot-sector information in *save-file*, overwriting if it already exists.

Continued

-u *device-name*   Uninstalls LILO by copying *device-name* (a saved
boot record) back, and checks the time-stamp.

-U *device-name*   Uninstalls LILO by copying *device-name* (a
saved boot record) back, but does not check the
time-stamp.

-R *command line*   Sets a default *command line* for the boot loader
the next time it executes.

-I *label*   Specifies the pathname of the running kernel, as
specified with *label*.

makefloppies *option(s)*

PURPOSE

The **makefloppies** shell script creates a new floppy block device files. It uses the **floppycontrol** program to translate the minor device numbers into meaningful names. It also uses these names to decide whether to create a given block device file or not, depending on the type of the physical drive.

OPTIONS

-l	Works with a local directory, not **/dev**.
-n	Reports on what would have been done, but not do it.
-t	Names the devices for drive type, not floppy type.

RELATED COMMANDS

floppycontrol

mtools

rawcmd

setfdprm

superformat

md5sum   Checks MD5 Message Digest

 GNU Command

md5sum *option(s) filename*

PURPOSE

The **md5sum** command computes and checks the MD5 message digest. It produces a 128-bit fingerprint or message digest. It also checks whether the message digests are the same where they exist in other files.

OPTIONS

-b	Assumes that all files are binary files.
-c *file*	Checks that the *file* (the MD5 sum, a binary/text flag, and a filename) is as it should be.
-s *string*	Computes a message digest for *string*.
-t *text*	Assumes that all files are text files.

Linux Commands, Organized by Group

513

mount

PURPOSE

The **mount** command mounts filesystems. This is an involved command meant for use by system administrators; check the online-manual pages for more information.

GNU Command

mt *option operation count*

PURPOSE

The **mt** command controls a magnetic tape drive. The name of the default tape drive is **/usr/include/sys/mtio.h**, but this can be overridden with the environment variable TAPE or a command-line option to **mt**. Every command line with this command must end with an operation.

OPERATIONS

asf *count*	Sets the absolute space to file number *count*. Equivalent to rewind followed by **fsf** *count*.
bsf *count*	Backward spaces *count* files. The tape is positioned on the first block of the next file.
bsfm	Backward spaces *count* file marks. The tape is positioned on the beginning-of-the-tape side of the file mark.
bsr *count*	Backward spaces *count* records.
eof, weof *count*	Writes *count* EOF marks at current position.
eom	Spaces to the end of the recorded media on the tape (for appending files onto tapes).
erase	Erases the tape.
fsf *count*	Forward spaces *count* files. The tape is positioned on the first block of the next file.
fsr *count*	Forward spaces *count* records.
offline, rewoffl	Rewinds the tape and unloads the tape.
retension	Rewinds the tape, then winds it to the end of the reel, then rewinds it again.
rewind	Rewinds the tape.
status	Prints the status information about the tape unit.

OPTION

-f *device*	Uses *device* instead of the default tape drive.

Linux Commands, Organized by Group

pkgtool *option(s)*

PURPOSE

The **pkgtool** command is the standard package maintenance tool provided with the Slackware Linux distribution. It is called by the **setup** utility to perform system installation. It can also be called without any arguments, and will then allow the user to install, remove (or view, in the case of the color version) software packages through an interactive menu system. There are two versions of the **pkgtool** utility: **/sbin/pkgtool.tty** and **/usr/lib/setup/cpkgtool**. These function in a similar fashion, but the first one uses standard tty text output, while the second uses full screen (and possibly color) ncurses output. The color version depends on the presence of the **/usr/lib/terminfo** terminal library.

OPTIONS

Most users will not want to use any options when running **pkgtool**. These are generally used only when **pkgtool** is run by **setup**. Feel free to try them, but be careful.

-sets #A#B#C#	Installs the disk sets A, B, C. Separate the disk-set names with # symbols.
-source_mounted	Does not attempt to unmount and remount the source device with each disk.
-ignore_tagfiles	Installs every ***.tgz** package encountered regardless of what the tagfiles say.
-tagfile *tagfile*	Specifies tagfile.
-source_dir *directory*	Specifies the directory in which the subdirectories for each disk are found.
-target_dir *directory*	Specifies the location of the target root directory.
-source_device *device*	Specifies the source device to install from. This is not used if you've provided the **-source_mounted** option. It's usually used when installing from floppy, as in **-source_device/dev/fd0u1440** or **-source_device /dev/fd1h1200**.

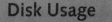
quota *option(s)*

quota *option(s) user*

quota *option(s) group*

PURPOSE

The **quota** command displays disk usage and limits for specific users, all users, or groups.

OPTIONS

-g	Prints group quotas for the group of which the user is a member.
-q	Returns information on filesystems where usage is over quota.
-v	Display quotas on filesystems where no storage allocated.

readprofile *option(s)*

PURPOSE

The **readprofile** command passes along **/proc/profile** information to print the following data in three columns: clock ticks, the C function in the kernel where those many ticks occurred, and the normalized load of the procedure, calculated as a ratio between the number of ticks and the length of the procedure.

OPTIONS

-a	Prints all symbols in the mapfile.
-i	Provides profiling step information used by the kernel.
-m *mapfile*	Specifies a *mapfile*, which by default is **/usr/src/linux/System.map**. This is useful when the mapfile isn't the last one you compiled.
-p *profile*	Specifies a different profiling buffer, which by default is **/proc/profile**.
-r	Resets the profiling buffer.
-t	Provides output in terse output (unfilled).
-v	Provides output in verbose format: in four columns and filled with blanks. It adds the RAM address of a kernel function.

relaynews *option(s)*

PURPOSE

The **relaynews** command broadcasts (network) news articles read from its standard input.

OPTIONS

-a	Doesn't carry duplicate articles.
-d	Turns on debugging.
-g	Automatically generates an *Xref:* header in each article.
-i	Redirects standard output to **/var/lib/news/log**.
-n	Enables NNTP mode, in which history entries generated as articles are rejected.
-o *days*	Drops articles more than *days* days old.
-r	Redirects standard output and error messages to **/var/lib/news/log** and **/var/lib/news/errlog**, respectively.
-s	Warns before discarding an article.
-u	Unlinks (removes) any filename arguments after successful processing.
-x *excluded-site*	Excludes *excluded-site* from the list of netnews neighbors.

rexecd

PURPOSE

The **rexecd** launches the remote execution server, which allows remote users to open **rexec** sessions.

rmmod *option module*

PURPOSE

The **rmmod** command unloads a loaded module from the kernel, as long as they are not in use by the kernel or other modules. You can specify multiple modules, and they will be removed in the order they are referenced on the command line.

OPTION

-r   Removes modules recursively; if a top module is named, then the modules used by the top module will be removed as well.

RELATED COMMANDS

insmod

lsmod

ksyms

modules

X Window System Command

rstartd *option*

PURPOSE

The **rstartd** command is a sample implementation of a Remote Start **rsh** helper, working in conjunction with the **rstart** command.

The **rstartd** command is actually a shell script that invokes **rstartd.real** with the **-c** option.

OPTION

-c *configfilename*   Specifies configuration file.

RELATED COMMANDS

rsh

rstart

sendmail *option(s)*

PURPOSE

The **sendmail** command sends and receives electronic mail via the Internet. Users don't actually access it directly; instead, friendlier front ends (like **mail**) are employed by users, and the messages are then sent to **sendmail**, which handles the actual mail transport.

Configuring **sendmail** can be a tricky business and is far too involved for this format. Check the online-manual pages or a **sendmail** text for further guidance.

X Window System Command

sessreg *option(s) username*

PURPOSE

The **sessreg** command managed utmp/wtmp entries for **xdm** sessions. See the online-manual pages for a more detailed description.

OPTIONS

-a	Adds this session to utmp/wtmp. One of **-a** or **-d** must be set.
-d	Deletes this session from utmp/wtmp. One of **-a** or **-d** must be set.
-l *line-name*	Sets the line name of the entry. For terminal sessions, this is the final pathname segment of the terminal device filename (like *ttyd0*). For X sessions, it should be the local display name given to the user's session (usually *:0*).
-u *utmp-file*	Sets an alternate utmp file.
-w *wtmp-file*	Sets an alternate wtmp file.
-x *Xservers-file*	Sets the *slot-number* to be the number of lines in the *ttys-file* plus the index into this file where the *line-name* is found.
-t *ttys-file*	Sets an alternate file for the **-x** to use to count the number of terminal sessions on a host.

RELATED COMMAND

xdm

setfdprm *option(s) device*

PURPOSE

The **setfdprm** command sets floppy-disk parameters. It can be used to clear old parameter sets or to enable diagnostic messages. With no options, **setfdprm** loads the device file with a new parameter set found in the **/etc/fdprm** file.

OPTIONS

-c *devicename*   Clears the parameter set of the *devicename*.

-n *devicename*   Disables format detection for the autoconfiguring *devicename*.

-p *devicename*   Permanently loads a new parameter set for the *devicename*.

-y *devicename*   Enables format detection for the autoconfiguring *devicename*.

setterm   Set Terminal

setterm *option(s)*

PURPOSE

The **setterm** command sets terminal attributes through a long list
of options. You can find these options in the online-manual pages.

superformat *option(s)*

PURPOSE

The **superformat** command formats floppy disks. It works with Linux formatting, but it also calls **mformat** to place an MS-DOS filesystem on a formatted floppy. (Installing an MS-DOS filesystem is optional.)

OPTIONS

The basic options are listed below. In addition, there are a number of advanced options that you may never use; see the online-manual pages for more information.

-2	Formats a high-capacity disk readable by the **2mf** program.
-B	Verifies the disk with the **mbadblocks** program.
-d *drive*	Specifies the drive to format; the default is the first floppy drive (**/dev/fd0**).
--dd	Formats a double-density disk.
-D *drive*	Specifies the DOS drive letter for **mformat** to use, either **a:** or **b:**.
-f	Skips verification.
-H *heads*	Describes the number of heads (the default is 2).
--hd	Formats a high-density disk.
-1	Doesn't use 2m format.
--no2m	Doesn't use 2m format.
-s *sectors*	Sets the number of sectors. A "sector" is not the number of physical sectors, but the number of equivalent 512-byte sectors.
-t tracks	Sets the number of tracks. The default is 40 or 80, depending on the drive type or the density.
-v *verbosity-level*	Sets a numerical verbosity level: *1* prints a dot for each formatted track, *2* prints a changing sign for each formatted track, *3* prints a complete line listing the head and track, while *6* and *9* prints debugging information.
-V	Verifies the formatting at the end of the process, not after each track is formatted.

Continued

RELATED COMMAND

fdrawcmd

floppycontrol

getfdprm

mtools

xdfcopy

X Window System Command

X WINDOW

SuperProbe *option(s)*

PURPOSE

The **SuperProbe** command probes your PC's video system to determine what kind of hardware is used and how much memory is present.

WARNING: Note that SuperProbe can cause your system to hang, so don't use it in the middle of an important computing session. However, newer versions of SuperProbe are more reliable than the online manual pages would indicate, and it can be used safely with all PCI-bus PCs.

At this time SuperProbe 2.5 can detect a wide range of MDA, Hercules, CGA, MCGA, EGA, and VGA chipsets, including those from Western Digital, Cirrus Logic, ATI, Tseng, Weitek, and more. Use the **-info** option to SuperProbe to see which chipsets can be detected.

EXAMPLE

```
$ SuperProbe
...
WARNING - THIS SOFTWARE COULD HANG YOUR MACHINE.
        READ THE SuperProbe.1 MANUAL PAGE BEFORE
        RUNNING THIS PROGRAM.
        INTERRUPT WITHIN FIVE SECONDS TO ABORT!
First video: Super-VGA
        Chipset: S3 Trio64
        Memory:  2048 Kbytes
        RAMDAC:  Generic 8-bit pseudo-color DAC
                (with 6-bit wide lookup tables (or in 6-bit mode))
$ SuperProbe -verbose -no16
...
WARNING - THIS SOFTWARE COULD HANG YOUR MACHINE.
        READ THE SuperProbe.1 MANUAL PAGE BEFORE
        RUNNING THIS PROGRAM.
        INTERRUPT WITHIN FIVE SECONDS TO ABORT!
BIOS Base address = 0xC000
Doing Super-VGA Probes...
        Probing WD...
        Probing Video7...
        Probing MX...
```

Continued

```
        Probing Genoa...
        Probing UMC...
        Probing Trident...
        Skipping ATI (16-bit registers)...
        Probing Ahed...
        Probing NCR...
        Probing S3...
First video: Super-VGA
        Chipset: S3 Trio64
        Memory:  2048 Kbytes
        RAMDAC:  Generic 8-bit pseudo-color DAC
                 (with 6-bit wide lookup tables (or in 6-bit mode))
```

OPTIONS

-bios base	Specifies the base address for the BIOS. The default is 0xC000.
-excl port	Excludes the specified port from the probe.
-info	Lists chipsets that **SuperProbe** can identify.
-mask10	Masks the card to 10 bits; useful when probing older and cheaper 16-bit cards. Used in conjunction with -excl, but performs basically the same function as **-no16**.
-no16	Avoids probing for 16-bit addresses; original ISA standards called only for 10 bits.
-no_bios	Skips reading of the video BIOS.
-no_dac	Skips probing of the RAMDAC type when a VGA or SVGA card is detected.
-no_mem	Skips detection of amount of video memory.
-noprobe list	Specifies which chipsets the SuperProbe command should avoid. List must be a comma-delimited set of chipsets; use the -info option to see which chipsets can be detected by SuperProbe.
-order list	Uses a specific list of chipsets (in order) for testing. List must be a comma-delimited set of chipsets, and you can use the **-info** option to see which chipsets can be detected by SuperProbe.
-verbose	Provides full information as the probe is performed.

telnetd *option(s)*

PURPOSE

The **telnetd** command launches a **telnet** daemon, which will listen for **telnet** requests. It's launched and managed by the Internet server daemon **inetd**.

OPTION

-D   Turns on debugging mode.

RELATED COMMANDS

inetd

telnet

umount *filesystem*

PURPOSE

The **umount** command unmounts filesystems. For more information about mounting filesystems, see the **mount** command.

RELATED COMMAND

mount

xdfcopy *option(s) source target*

PURPOSE

The **xdfcopy** command copies and formats Xdf floppy disks, a format used by the OS/2 operating system.

OPTIONS

-D*dosdrive*   Specifies the DOS drive letter to format. There are a slew of conditions with this option; check the online-manual pages for more information.

-n   Does not format the disk before copying an image to the disk.

RELATED COMMANDS

mtools

floppycontrol

performat

Linux Commands, Organized by Group

MTOOLS

The Mtools series of commands work with MS-DOS files and directories on floppy disks. This allows you to use Linux with MS-DOS-formatted diskettes.

mattrib *option(s) msdosfile(s)*

PURPOSE

The **mattrib** command changes the file attributes to an MS-DOS file stored on a floppy drive. Adding attribute flags is done with +, and removing attribute flags is done with -.

ATTRIBUTES

a	Archive bit.
h	Hidden bit.
r	Read-only bit.
s	System bit.

mbadblocks *drive*

PURPOSE

The **mbadblocks** scans a specified *drive* (an MS-DOS floppy) for
bad blocks. It marks the bad blocks as being unread.

mcd *directory*

PURPOSE

The **mcd** command changes the current directory on an MS-DOS floppy. With no directory specified, it returns the current device and directory.

RELATED COMMAND

mdir

mcopy *option(s) sourcefile targetfile*

mcopy *option(s) sourcefile(s) targetdirectory*

PURPOSE

The **mcopy** command copies MS-DOS files to and from a Linux system, usually using a floppy drive. It can be used to copy a file to a target file, or it can be used to copy multiple files to a specified directory.

When using a MS-DOS floppy, you'll need to add **A:** to the file or directory names.

OPTIONS

t	Performs a text file transfer, translating carriage returns/line feeds to just line feeds.
m	Preserves the file modification time.
n	Works with no warning if you are overwriting an existing file.
v	Works in verbose mode.

RELATED COMMANDS

mread

mwrite

Linux Commands, Organized by Group

mdel *option msdosfile*

PURPOSE

The **mdel** command deletes an MS-DOS file, usually on a floppy drive.

OPTION

-v   Works in verbose mode, where the names of files are printed to the screen as they are being deleted.

mformat *option(s) drive*

PURPOSE

The **mformat** adds an MS-DOS filesystem to a low-level Linux-formatted diskette. This formatting includes a boot sector, FAT, and root directory.

OPTIONS

1	Overrides the use of a 2m format, even if the current geometry of the disk is a 2m geometry.
2	Works in 2m format—the number of sectors on track 0, head 0.
h	Specifies the number of heads (sides).
H	Specifies the number of hidden sectors.
l	Sets an optional volume label.
M	Sets the software sector size.
n	Sets the serial number.
t	Specifies the number of tracks (not cylinders).
s	Specifies the number of sectors per track.
S	Specifies the sizecode.
X	Formats the disk as an Xdf disk, used by OS/2.

RELATED COMMAND

mlabel

mrd *option msdosdirectory*

PURPOSE

The **mrd** command removes an MS-DOS directory tree, as well as any files and subdirectories within. This occurs on an MS-DOS filesystem on a floppy drive.

OPTION

-v   Works in verbose mode, listing every file and directory as it is deleted.

mdir *option(s) msdosdirectory*

PURPOSE

The **mdir** command displays the contents of an MS-DOS directory,
usually on a floppy drive.

OPTIONS

a	Lists hidden files.
w	Prints in wide output, without displaying the file size or creation date.

mlabel *option(s) drive new_label*

PURPOSE

The **mlabel** command creates an MS-DOS volume label on a floppy drive. With no options, it displays the current label. If the **c** or **s** option is not set, you are prompted for a new label; at this time, if you don't enter a new label and press **Return**, the existing label is deleted.

OPTIONS

c	Clears an existing label, without prompting the user.
s	Shows the existing label, without prompting the user.

RELATED COMMAND

mformat

mmd *option directory*

PURPOSE

The **mmd** command creates an MS-DOS subdirectory on a floppy drive. An error occurs if the directory already exists.

OPTION

v   Works in verbose mode, returning the names of the directories as they are created.

RELATED COMMANDS

mrd

mmount *drive mountargs*

PURPOSE

The **mmount** command mounts an MS-DOS disk. It reads the boot sector of an MS-DOS disk, configures the drive geometry, and mounts it, passing *mount-args* to **mount**.

RELATED COMMANDS

mount

mmove *option sourcefile targetfile*

mmove *option sourcefile(s) targetdirectory*

PURPOSE

The **mmove** command moves or renames an existing MS-DOS file or subdirectory.

OPTION

v   Works in verbose mode, displaying the new file-
                name if the new name is invalid.

RELATED COMMANDS

mren

mren *option sourcefile targetfile*

PURPOSE

The **mren** command renames an MS-DOS file on a floppy drive.

OPTION

v   Works in verbose mode, displaying the new file-
                    name if the new name is invalid.

RELATED COMMANDS

mmove

mrd *option msdosdirectory*

PURPOSE

The **mrd** command removes an MS-DOS directory from a floppy disk.

OPTION

v   Works in verbose mode, displaying the directory
                     name as it is removed.

RELATED COMMANDS

mdeltree

mmd

mread *option(s) msdosfile unixfile*

PURPOSE

The **mread** command copies an MS-DOS file to a Linux system. This is an obsolete command, but some older scripts may support it. The preferred command is **mcopy**.

RELATED COMMANDS

mcopy

mtype

mtest

PURPOSE

The **mtest** command reads the mtools configuration files and prints the cumulative configuration to standard output, which can then be used as configuration files. You can use this to convert old configuration files to new configuration files.

mtype *option(s) msdosfile*

PURPOSE

The **mtype** command displays an MS-DOS file.

OPTIONS

s   Strips the high bit from the displayed file.
t   Assumes that the file is a text file.

RELATED COMMANDS

mcd

mread

mwrite *unixfile* **dosfile**

PURPOSE

The **mwrite** command copies a Linux file to an MS-DOS filesystem on a floppy disk. This file is considered to be obsolete and exists only to provide backward compatibility with older shell scripts; use **mcopy** instead.

RELATED COMMANDS

mcopy

Linux Commands,
Organized by Group

6

Linux Shells

You can't run Linux without running a **shell**, a tool that interacts with you and provides a way to directly communicate with the core of the operating system. What you assume is being done by the operating system is most often being done by the shell: It accepts your commands, interprets them, and passes them along to the core operating system; it provides its own set of commands (some of which were covered in Chapter 5 as operating-system commands; it's really a distinction without difference); and it provides its own scripting mechanisms.

Most Linux distributions include at least six or seven shells, but people usually stick with the default Bourne Again Shell (bash) from the Free Software Foundation, a clone of the popular Bourne shell found on most UNIX systems. In addition, many users switch to the C shell (csh) or a scaled-down version of the C shell, tcsh. (When you install your Linux distribution, you're typically asked which shells you want installed on your system. A slew of Linux shellsare available, including ash and zsh.) To see which shells are installed on your system, use the following command line:

```
$ chsh -l
/bin/sh
/bin/bash
/bin/csh
/bin/tcsh
...
```

To change your login shell, use one of the following command lines:

```
$ chsh -s /bin/csh
```

or

```
$ exec /bin/csh
```

We're not going to spend a lot of time on shells; there's more than enough online documentation for them, and there are more than enough books on the market about shells and their usage. Instead, we'll spend some time covering shell variables.

Shell Variables

These variables are set by the shell. They are used in a wide variety of circumstances, but typically they're involved in shell scripts.

VARIABLE	EXPLANATION
IFS	The Internal Field Separator that is used for word splitting after expansion and to split lines into words with the read built-in command. The default value is **space-tab-newline**'.
PATH	The search path for commands. It is a colon-separated list of directories in which the shell looks for commands. The default path is system-dependent and is set by the administrator who installs bash.
HOME	The home directory of the current user; the default argument for the **cd** command.
CDPATH	The search path for the **cd** command. This is a colon-separated list of directories in which the shell looks for destination directories specified by the **cd** command.
ENV	If this parameter is set when bash is executing a shell script, its value is interpreted as a filename containing commands to initialize the shell, as in **.bashrc**. The value of ENV is subjected to parameter expansion, command substitution, and arithmetic expansion before being interpreted as a pathname. PATH is not used to search for the resultant pathname.

Shell Variables (Continued)

MAIL
If this parameter is set to a filename and the MAIL-PATH variable is not set, **bash** informs the user of the arrival of mail in the specified file.

MAILCHECK
Specifies how often (in seconds) **bash** checks for mail. The default is 60 seconds. When it is time to check for mail, the shell does so before prompting. If this variable is not set, the shell disables mail checking.

MAILPATH
A colon-separated list of pathnames to be checked for mail. The message to be printed may be specified by separating the pathname from the message with **?**.

MAIL_WARNING
If set, and a file that **bash** is checking for mail has been accessed

since the last time it was checked, the message *The mail in mailfile has been read* is printed.

PS1
Sets the primary prompt. The default value is **bash\$.**

PS2
Sets the secondary prompt, used by many applications to provide input. The default value is **>.**

PS3
Set the prompt for the **select** command.

PS4
Sets the value of the character used before commands in an execution trace. The default is +.

HISTSIZE
Sets the number of commands to remember in the command history. The default is 500.

HISTFILE
Sets the name of the file where command history is saved. The default is ~/.bash_history.

HISTFILESIZE
Sets the maximum number of lines in the history file. The default value is 500.

IGNOREEOF
Controls the action of the shell on receipt of an EOF character as the sole input. If set, the value is the number of consecutive EOF characters typed as the first characters on an input line before **bash** exits. If the variable exists but does not have a numeric value, or has no value, the default value is 10. If it does not exist, EOF signifies the end of input to the shell. This is only in effect for interactive shells.

Shell Variables (Continued)

TMOUT

If set to a value greater than zero, the value is inter-preted as the number of seconds to wait for input after issuing the primary prompt. **bash** terminates after waiting for that number of seconds if input does not arrive.

FIGNORE

A colon-separated list of suffixes to ignore when performing filename completion. A filename whose suffix matches one of the entries in FIGNORE is excluded from the list of matched filenames. A sample value is ``.o:~''.

7

Window Managers

A *window manager* controls the interface when you launch the X Window System in the form of XFree86. It controls the shape of the windows and the form of the scrollbars, allocates memory, and oversees applications.

The default window manager for most distributions of Linux, including Slackware Linux, is **fvwm**. (No, **fvwm** doesn't stand for anything.) Basically, **fvwm** has some things in common with the Motif Window Manager (which we'll cover a little later), but there are enough differences to deter any interest from copyright attorneys. Other window managers found with Slackware Linux are the Open Look Window Manager (**olwm**), based on the OpenWindows interface from Sun Microsystems; the Tab Window Manager (**twm**), and the **fvwm-95** window manager, which mimics the Windows 95 interface. The **fvwm**, **olwm**, and **twm** window managers are shown in Figures 7.1, 7.2, and 7.3, respectively.

Figure 7.1 The fvwm window manager.

Figure 7.2 The olwm window manager.

Figure 7.3 The twm window manager.

As you can tell from the figures, each window manager presents windows on the screen differently. All have menus at the top left of the screen, all have titlebars that present a description of the application, all have scrollbars, and all have handles at the corners that resize the window. Beyond that, however, there are some look-and-feel differences that don't necessarily affect the applications but might affect how you interact with the application.

In addition to the aforementioned window managers, most Linux distributions—including Slackware Linux—have *virtual window managers* that present a desktop larger than the average screen size. These virtual screens tend to eat up a lot of RAM because the unseen portions of the screen are still drawn to video memory. (This doesn't apply to **fvwm**, which uses a different method for storing unseen portions of the desktop.)

These no-cost window managers differ from the commercial arena, where the Motif Window Manager (**mwm**) reigns, either directly or through its implementation in the Common Desktop Environment (CDE). Because **mwm** is commercial software, it is not available via Linux or XFree86, although many third-party vendors, such as Metro Link, offer the Motif libraries and **mwm** for a fee.

There's a drawback to using a window manager: They tend to suck up a lot of memory. The X Window System was designed for RAM-jammed workstations and isn't as efficient as it could be. You should plan to devote at least 4MB of RAM just for using the X Window System. This situation improves somewhat with XFree86, which uses shared libraries to cut down on memory usage. In addition, **fvwm** is the most memory-efficient window manager available, using about half the memory of **twm**.

We're not going to spend a lot of time explaining window managers; the best way to learn about a window manager is to play around with it. If you need more information, check out the Bibliography for a list of other Linux texts.

Working with a Window

When you look at Figure 7.1, you can see that a window can be broken down into a few basic elements. There's a three-dimensional shading to the window. On the sides of the window are bars, with corner elements called *frames* used to resize the window. In addition, there's a titlebar on the top of the window that displays the title of the window.

To move the window, place the cursor over the titlebar or the side bars, press the first mouse button, and drag the window to its new location.

There are two buttons beside the titlebar. The left button calls a menu that can be used to move, resize, minimize, maximize, or close the window. The button on the right turns the window into an icon.

Command-Line Options

Here are the command-line options supported by **fvwm**:

OPTION	RESULT
-d *displayname*	Works with *displayname* instead of the default displayname, stored in the environment variable $DISPLAY.
-debug	Works in debugging (synchronous) mode, useful for generating accurate error messages.
-f *config_file*	Uses *config_file* instead of the default **.fvwmrc** configuration file.
-s	Limits **fvwm** to one screen in a multiscreen display, as set with the **-d** option.
-no-m4FP	Overrides m4 from preprocessing the **.fvwmrc** configuration file.
-m4-prefix	Prefixes all built-in commands with *m4_*.
-m4opt *option*	Passes *option* to m4.

Configuration Files

When you launch **fvwm**, it looks for an initialization file named **.fvwmrc** in your home directory. This file contains information on key and button bindings, as well as color schemes and start-up applications and options.

When you look at a file, you'll see a long list of options. Some of them begin with #, which comments out the line and neutralizes it.

The following options can be set in the **.fvwmrc** file:

OPTION	PURPOSE
StdForeColor *colorname*	Sets the foreground color for menus and nonselected windows to *colorname*. A monochrome display defaults this color to black.
StdBackColor *colorname*	Sets the background color for menus and nonselected windows to *colorname*. A monochrome display defaults this color to white.
StickyForeColor *colorname*	Sets the foreground color for nonselected window sticky titles to *colorname*. A monochrome display defaults this color to black.
StickyBackColor *colorname*	Sets the background color for nonselected window sticky windows to *colorname*. A monochrome display defaults this to white.
HiForeColor *colorname*	Sets the title color for a selected window. A monochrome display defaults this color to black.
HiBackColor *colorname*	Sets the background color for a selected window. A monochrome display defaults this color to white.
MenuForeColor *colorname*	Sets the color for the menu foreground.
MenuBackColor *colorname*	Sets the color for the menu background.
MenuStippleColor *colorname*	Sets the color for unavailable (shaded-out) options on a menu.
PagerBackColor *colorname*	Sets the pager background color.
PagerForeColor *colorname*	Sets the pager foreground color.
Font *fontname*	Sets the font for menus, resize indicators, and icon labels.
WindowFont *fontname*	Sets the font for the window title bar.
PagerFont *fontname*	Sets the font for window icon names.
IconFont *fontname*	Sets the font for icon name labels.

Configuration Files (Continued)

OPTION	PURPOSE
NoTitle *windowname*	Suppresses a title for a specified *windowname*.
NoBorder *windowname*	Suppresses decorative borders for a specified *windowname*.
Sticky *windowname*	Sets a *windowname* as "sticky," not moving the viewport into the virtual desktop changes.
StaysOnTop *windowname*	Tells *windowname* never to be obscured by other windows.
StartsOnDesk *windowname* *desk-number*	Tells *windowname* to be placed on a specific *desk-number*, if you're using multiple desks.
CirculateSkip *windowname*	Skips *windowname* when circulate-up or circulate-down functions are invoked.
CirculateSkipIcons	Skips icons when running circulate and warp operations.
WindowListSkip *windowname*	Omits *windowname* from the window list.
Style *windowname options*	Can be used with the previous commands to place all the settings with one comprehensive command.
CenterOnCirculate	Centers the target window when circulating.
DeskTopSize *Horizontal*x*Vertical*	Sets the virtual desktop size in units of the physical screen size.
DeskTopScale Scale	Sets the virtual desktop scale with respect to the screen.
BoundaryWidth *Width*	Sets the boundary width on decorated windows; the default is 6.
NoBoundaryWidth *Width*	Sets the decoration width for windows with no boundaries. The default is 1.
XORvalue *number*	Sets the value with which bits are XORed when doing rubber-band window moving or resizing.
EdgeScroll *horizontal vertical*	Sets the percentage of a page to scroll when the cursor hits the edge of a page.

Configuration Files (Continued)

OPTION	PURPOSE
PagingDefault *value*	Determines whether paging is enabled (where *value* is 1) or disabled (where *value* is 0).
EdgeResistance *scrolling moving*	Sets the parameters for moving a mouse over the edge of the screen (set with the *scrolling* value) and moving a window over the edge of a screen (set with the *moving* value).
OpaqueMove *percent*	Sets the maximum size window with which opaque window movement should be used.
ClickToFocus	Sets keyboard input with an active window until another window is explicitly selected.
SloppyFocus	Sets focus with the mouse.
MWMBorders	Uses **mwm**-style window borders.
MWMButtons	Uses **mwm**-style button configurations.
MWMMenus	Uses **mwm**-style menus.
MWMDecorHints	Uses **mwm**-style window hints.
MWMFunctionHints	Uses **mwm**-style window functions.
MWMHintOverride	Uses **mwm**-style hint overrides for iconifying.
Lenience	Tells **fvwm** to ignore an ICCCM convention.
OpaqueResize	Resizes window with its borders, not with an outline.
DontMoveOff	Doesn't allow windows to be moved off the desktop.
AutoRaise *delay*	Sets the autoraising of windows and specifies the delay (in milliseconds) between when a window acquires the input focus and when it is automatically raised.
Pager *X Y*	Sets the paging style of a window moving across the desktop, as a window appears at *X* and *Y*.

Configuration Files (Continued)

Mouse *Button Context Modifiers Functions*	Sets several mouse parameters: *button* the button number, *context* is the binding context (R for root window, W for application window, T for titlebar, S for window bar, F for window frame, I for icon window, or 0 through 9 for titlebar buttons), *modifier* is a key modifier (N for no modifiers, C for **Ctrl** key, S for **Shift** key, M for **Meta** key, or A for any), and *function* for a built-in function.
Key *keyname Context Modifiers Function*	Binds a key to a function: *key* is the key, *context* is the binding context (R for root window, W for application window, T for titlebar, S for window bar, F for window frame, I for icon window, or 0 through 9 for titlebar buttons), *modifier* is a key modifier (N for no modifiers, C for **Ctrl** key, S for **Shift** key, M for **Meta** key, or A for any), and *function* for a built-in function.
IconBox *left top right bottom*	Sets the regions of the screen to place icons.
StubbornIconPlacement	Tells IconBoxes not to be covered by windows.
StubbornIcons	Tells the window to expand icons into their original position.
SuppressIcons	Suppresses icons.
StickyIcons	Places icons in the same place, no matter where you move the virtual screen.
IconPath *path*	Sets the pathname for the location of black-and-white icons.
PixmapPath *path*	Sets the pathname for the location of color icons.
Icon *windowname bitmap-file*	Sets the bitmap for a specific *windowname*.

565

Configuration Files (Continued)

OPTION	PURPOSE
DecorateTransients	Decorates transient windows.
RandomPlacement	Places windows randomly, instead of waiting for users to place them.
SmartPlacement	Places windows in an open area, instead of waiting for users to place them.
StubbornPlacement	Places windows anywhere but over an icon, instead of waiting for users to place them.
NoPPosition	Ignores the *PPosition* field when adding new windows.
ClickTime *delay*	Sets the delay (in milliseconds) between a button press and a button release.
ModulePath	Sets the path for modules.
Module *ModuleName*	Sets a module to load when launching. The choices are: GoodStuff (recommended), FvwmPager, FvwmBanner, FvwmWinList, FvwmClean, FvwnIdent, FvwmSave, FvwmScroll, FvwmDebug, and FvwmSound. These modules have their own man pages.
Cursor *cursor_num cursor_type*	Changes cursor style.
ButtonStyle *button# WidthxHeight*	Sets the shape in a titlebar button.
AppsBackingStore	Sets backing store for applications, which fails ICCCM guidelines.
SaveUnders	Sets save-unders.
BackingStore	Sets backing store for the window manager, which fails ICCCM guidelines.
Popup *Popup_Name*	Sets a pop-up menu, to be later bound to a mouse button or key.
Function *Function_Name*	Sets a function, to be later bound to a mouse button or key.

Fvwm Variables

The **fvwm** window manager supports the following variables:

Variable	Purpose
SERVERHOST	Sets the name of the machine running the X server.
CLIENTHOST	Sets the machine running the clients.
HOSTNAME	Sets the canonical hostname running the clients.
USER	Sets the name of the user running the program.
HOME	Specifies the user's home directory.
VERSION	Returns the X major protocol version. This can be important to some X applications.
REVISION	Returns the X minor protocol revision. This can be important to some X applications.
VENDOR	Returns the vendor of your X server. Usually very unimportant.
RELEASE	Returns the X-server release number, such as 6 for X11R6.
WIDTH	Sets the width of your display in pixels.
HEIGHT	Sets the height of your display in pixels.
X_RESOLUTION	Returns the X resolution of your display in pixels per meter.
Y_RESOLUTION	Returns the Y resolution of your display in pixels per meter.
PLANES	Returns the number of bit planes supported in the default root window.
BITS_PER_RGB	Returns the number of significant bits in an RGB color.
TWM_TYPE	Returns the **twm** type; it's always **fvwm**.
CLASS	Returns the visual class (one of StaticGray, GrayScale, StaticColor, PseudoColor, TrueColor, DirectColor, or NonStandard).
COLOR	Returns *yes* for a color, *no* for a gray.
FVWM_VERSION	Returns the **fvwm** version.
OPTIONS	Lists the options compiled in the window manager.
FVWMDIR	Sets the path for modules.

Bibliography

This book is part of a series of books covering Slackware Linux from MIS:Press. The Slackware series covers Slackware Linux in a variety of situations. Here's a listing:

Linux Configuration and Installation, second edition, Patrick Volkerding, Kevin Reichard, and Eric F. Johnson, $39.95. Two CD-ROMs. 523 pages. ISBN 1-55828-492-3. A third edition (ISBN 1-55828-566-0) is planned for 1997.

Linux Programming, Patrick Volkerding, Eric Foster-Johnson, and Kevin Reichard, $39.95. CD-ROM. 374 pages. ISBN 1-55828-507-5.

The Linux Database, Fred Butzen and Dorothy Forbes, $39.95. CD-ROM. 456 pages. ISBN 1-55828-491-5.

The Linux Internet Server, Kevin Reichard, $39.95. CD-ROM. 512 pages. ISBN 1-55828-545-8.

You can get more information about each title at *http://www.mispress.com/linux/booklist.htm.*

Index

571